Right
Before
Your Eyes

# Right
# Before
# Your Eyes

---

## *Penetrating the*
## *Urban Environment*

---

GRADY CLAY

**PLANNERS PRESS**

AMERICAN PLANNING ASSOCIATION
WASHINGTON, D.C.   CHICAGO, ILLINOIS

Grateful acknowledgement is given for permission to reprint the following:

"Midway at the Brink," copyright by Southern Living, Inc., July 1976.

"What Makes a Good Square Good? (Square One)," copyright by *Fortune,* April 1958.

"The Street as Teacher," excerpted from *Public Streets for Public Use,* edited by Anne Moudon, copyright 1987 by Van Nostrand Reinhold Co., Inc. All rights reserved.

"Remembered Landscapes," copyright 1957 by *Landscape* magazine.

The following chapters were reprinted with permission from *Landscape Architecture:*

"Micro-Appalachia," "Sense and Nonsense of Place," "Prairie Preservation," "Trekking on Down to Kodachrome Town," "Poland: Tunnel Vision Along the Vistula," "The Copper Basin of Tennessee," "Square Two: Action Revisited," "Superblockbusting," "Harboring Afterthoughts on Baltimore," "Vantage Pointing: The View from on High," "Zero Runoff: All Rain That Falls on Me Is Mine, Right?", "War Monsters," "Territorial Defense," "Industrial Archeology," "Turning Left: Taking It to the Street," "Ultimate Flood Weapon: Indian Bend Wash," "The Olmsted Code," "Making It in the Scruburbs," "Marketing Arousal: The Arena Effect," "Cruising the Urban Fronts."

Copyright 1987 by the American Planning Association
1313 E. 60th St., Chicago, IL 60637
ISBN 0-918286-47-6
Library of Congress Catalog Number 87-70550

# Contents

# Foreword

# The Grammatical Landscape

Ready and waiting to be found out there in our visible landscape, there exists an observable and universal order that speaks eloquently to us, that will tell us far more of ourselves and our future than we can see at any one moment. Furthermore, we can discover those hidden orders, those concealed possibilities, by watching the way our environments arrange themselves in response to the basic forces of gravity, wind and sun and rain—and by observing the patterns in which they are rearranged by human acts for human purposes.

This turns out to be a remarkably orderly universe. There is no chaos. Once we have observed and sorted out its elements, linking them to what we already know, it offers us a form of universal and useful grammar. This basic grammar helps us to understand what we see, it helps us describe the world as we see it and as we describe it—both for ourselves and for others. And it prepares us to deal with what comes next.

I am assured that this way of viewing the world is a form of naturalism. It emphasizes the reality of that world. It requires of us observers that we stick close to nature. It demands that we begin our ideas, conceptions, our constructions, our generalizations—our every act and thought—with evidence from the real world rather than from invisible abstractions within our selves, our psyche, or our prealigned consciousness. The environment is our Supreme Court. To it we must ultimately take our appeal.

Such a way of collecting and of organizing observations is not so much one man's subjective interpretation but, rather, it relies on a general observed agreement about what constitutes a "grammatical" landscape—that is, a landscape readily recognized by ordinary viewers and users as being orderly, understandable, coherent, and

1

responding perceptibly to natural and/or human pressures and influences. No buzzing, booming confusion. It all can make sense.

If any landscape confronts all observers, all travelers, with similar combinations, similar sequences, with recognizable arrangements—even though such an observer may apply a personal discount or filter to what he or she sees—then that landscape can itself be recognized as evidence of a general, observed agreement.

Stated another way, each man-made landscape, whether it be city or countryside, local or foreign, stable or changing, natural or artificial, is a kind of treaty. It records those agreements we have made—together with the loose ends left dangling—between us and our physical environment.

Furthermore, the grammar we choose, and the language that we use to write those treaties, and to deal with that environment, have a powerful effect on what we see, on how we perceive it and organize it and otherwise deal with it. We see what we are able to describe.

The key word is "describe." Not prescribe. Any description that starts off by recommending a course-of-action is in trouble at the outset. What you have already determined to do will interfere with what you are able to observe along the way.

The thing not to begin with is "a problem." When we say "I have this problem" (with my house, my commuting trips, my neighbor), we have already shifted our attention away from solutions that may lie within our surroundings, within the situation, or within us. We have already subconsciously let "the problem" take root in the back of our mind, lurking back there to alter and often to warp or twist what we see. Problem-solving is not our first best step, and we should put behind us advisors who insist on it. Rather, we should attend to activities and to places that are able to speak to us, and to start that interchange that is the beginning of all learning.

In exploring many of the places described in this book, I have learned to move modestly, to start small, and to avoid predeterminations and preconceived solutions. Toting around a preconceived solution is a sure way to stumble. One can look no further than one's own back yard for an example. In these days of packaged gardens, plans, and solutions, it is far too easy to start out to design one's own place by clipping out house plans, ideal gardens, Stately Examples, and saying, "This is the Solution I like." Far better, I think, to move from within one's own person and house to the out-of-doors in small steps. Perhaps we want to enjoy the sun on a bright, cool day, to sit out of the wind, to enjoy a little table under a tree, with a glass and book upon it, and a comfortable seat nearby. Here we shuffle about and finally conclude, "It feels just right." But notice that the first creative step is not that just-right feeling but rather the first move we have made into the out-of-doors, choosing a chair, table, and place in which that just-right feeling can take shape.

Our next step is to look and feel within ourselves and around this place so as to learn what's going on between us. There's bound to be something stirring, some change in the wind, some change in us. It's up to each of us to explore and possibly to record our feelings within this place, our responses to it, as well as the emanations and currents from the place itself.

Once we are open to the place, then we can recognize its promises, excitements, repose, inspiration, or even that indefinable something called "challenge" or magic that comes from some places and not others. If we have moved well and chosen well, we are suddenly piqued, we are aroused. And of all the states of heightened inspiration, arousal is one of the most generative of emotions, ideas, insights, and even "solutions."

Such a commitment to a place enables us to analyze what it has done to us, or forces us to go back into memory and our records to explore other places that aroused us in the past. If we are list-makers, we think back to the details, back to the nuts-and-bolts that combine to generate feelings, knowing all the while that there is an ineffable, indefinable spirit to a situation that can never be fully recaptured by listing its ingredients. The more we are willing to explore these first-hand experiences and memories, the more we can get in touch with what we expect out of our surroundings.

# Introduction

# Megalopolis in Passing

Back in 1969, when student unrest was rampant around the United States and abroad, when schools and colleges were traumatized by the Vietnam war and by the passions it had set loose, back when an international fervor for change was sweeping through the universities, I was given a curious assignment.

Would I spread myself around the country, journalistically speaking, and sum up what I discovered about the state of American city planning and design in a memorial lecture to be given in honor of a distinguished American planner, the late Dennis O'Harrow? This I was more than happy to do. The request came from the American Society of Planning Officials,[1] and I was eager to respond, having admired O'Harrow as both an eloquent planner and a superb writer. His wit, his playfulness with language, and his mastery of metaphor I had long enjoyed. Furthermore, I was curious about what was happening under that oft-tainted label of "planning" in a nation dedicated, at least in most public pronouncements, to being against planning as a governmental activity.

And so I ventured around mid-America in my first four-cylinder car, sitting in on a dozen or so public hearings and meetings at various levels of acrimony and conspiracy. I talked to scores of politicians, citizen activists, planners, architects, landscape architects, and others.

And everywhere I found the same story: school yards crowding, sewers and septic tanks overflowing, parking lots jamming, shopping centers opening, and commuters clogging the new expressways and interchanges. The public-hearing dockets were packing up, the landing zones stacking up. And on every horizon loomed new and fast-accumulating surpluses.

The spectre that loomed over those public hearings and private

5

wrangles in 1969 was the national surplus of agricultural products and agricultural land. Years of unusually favorable weather had produced a glut of corn, wheat, soybeans, and other products. Nobody in his right mind was defending the zoning of land for exclusive agricultural use because the country was plagued with surplus crops. Everybody I met assumed that agricultural land use was a stepping stone to what was called "a higher and better land use," if not to the Promised Land. People at those public hearings looked at the multicolored land-use maps on the wall and saw as the Number One crop not soybeans or corn but capital gains for the owner of a well-located parcel of land. The emotion let loose at these non-alcoholic symposia was the lust for speculative gain.

Years before that, when I was a green public-affairs reporter bumbling through the first textual thickets of a local comprehensive plan, I had been instructed by a kindly elder that planning was merely "the rational application of due process and forethought to the allocation of scarce commodities such as urban space."

But no! By the year 1969, planning looked very much like a manipulative process for the expert handling of surpluses. All these evidences of the Sixties' boom were the by-products of slack-to-nonexistent population control after some 10 million troops, civilians at heart, had been let loose after World War II, and at last united in a search for carnal knowledge. This was the beginning of the great splurge when the United States stomped on the throttle of expansion-and-exploitation, determined to grab the goodies while they were still there.

After some 25 years of this exuberant accumulation, I discovered, planning had turned into a method of surplus disposal. No longer did city planners think of themselves as reformers, as part of the great American tradition of land reform that stemmed from the Populist and other distributist movements. Now they were hooked, though some of them reluctantly, to the surplus disposal business.

That was my thesis in 1969. And to test it further, I then inquired as to where the new allied professions— planners, architects, and landscape architects—were most likely to be found. Beating the bushes in the backwaters of scarcity and poverty? Doing missionary work in the underdeveloped regions, moving to the Sicilies and Nigerias of their vastly different but somehow United States? Finding clients in the clapped-out countryside and fees in the fallen forests?

Of course not. Planners and designers and the land developers with whom they were aligned were consumed by bonanza fever; they were concentrated, of course, where the forces of urbanization and speculation were strongest, where the new and enriched middle class foregathered to follow the advice of advertisers even unto the outer limits of inner bankruptcy. And where money flowed like wine, where there was a surplus to buy longer automobiles, wider suburban lots, bigger houses, to pollute air and waters—and to hire planners and designers of every description.

In the Twin Cities, I discovered, Alan Altshuler had already done a study of Minneapolis and St. Paul, concluding that "planners owe their very existence to the problem of by-product control." Was it any accident, then, that 75 percent of the American Institute of Planners' members were located in the nation's 20 largest metropolitan areas? I recall seeing, on the bulletin board at that same 1969 conference of the American Society of Planning Officials, a recruiting poster asking, "Where have all the planners gone?" And its answer was, "To Cleveland," a city still coasting from earlier boom times.

The closer I examined it, the more that "planning" began to look like an export commodity that cities produced and the countryside and small towns were forced to consume. The planning process, and most planners themselves, had been enlisted to become weapons of city against hinterland, of rich communities and regions against poor ones. And because planning agencies were increasingly controlled or influenced by large private and public corporations (who had money and motives for hiring planners), they came to be viewed by nonmetropolitan people as the enemy. For these people were afflicted by scarcities rather than by surpluses, and the idea of planning for the distribution of poverty made no sense at all. How else could one explain the almost universal opposition to city planners that erupted from rural townships, country commissioners, and farmers? Such opposition could be blamed only in small part on the assumption that non-metropolitan people were backward, suspicious, clannish, close-minded bumpkins. Rather, it appeared, planning had become a technique for distributing surpluses that city folks controlled, and something noncity folks hadn't yet gotten hold of.

In the course of all this reportorial trekking-about, I had been forced to look beyond the neat labels that architects had fastened on the visible world: stylistic tags such as Classic, Neo-Classic, Contemporary, Modern, New Brutalist, and other variations (though it was not yet time for Neo-Modern to make its appearance). What were the forces that lurked under the surface of the Modern Movement? What energies had made possible these vast new suburban explosions called shopping centers and industrial parks?

My journals remind me that on a visit to the huge public docks along the Willamette River at Portland, Oregon, I made this rather pontifical entry:

> The dynamism that concerns me is the changing aspect of cities that reflects changing sources, supplies, and values attached to energy. I have lived in dynamic places. Their differences are endless and fascinating. It does no good merely to count up vehicles, foot-pounds, ergs, or kilowatt hours to express "energy." But it does make sense to take account of the way these energies work their way into the landscape and into our lives. To describe these energies with language based on objects and stage-sets is foolish. (Author's *Journal*, Vol. 31, page 86 ff., June 14, 1971)

By the fall of 1971, after further travels, I had begun to see that the control of energy was beginning to replace the familiar control of geographic places as a means of exercising power, and I even went so far as to assert, at a symposium in London, that "place is dead as the central focus for future struggles over rare resources—even though men will continue to fight for, and to pay exorbitant prices for, particular places which they highly value . . . Access to the energies necessary to survive in urban life is becoming the most important access of all. In urbanized nations, you can get to most places easily today, if not by highway, then by helicopter or other cheap travel, via television and rapidly cheapening information channels. Once you are there—anyplace—you are still helpless without imported energy or imported information, and the modern ability to handle multichannel messages." (Needless to say, I failed to anticipate the rising flood of emotion that, within a few years, was to rise up around home turf and local neighborhoods, a trend I catch up with later in this book.)

Consequently, I predicted the continued explosion of urban regions, the shift of footloose industry and offices outward into rural, small-town, or outer suburban locations and, further, what I called the continuing death of centrality. Newer and cheaper forms of electronic information would, I concluded, make it easier to do business anyplace. Anyplace. And the moment anyplace is as good as any other place for essential purposes, the public begins to choose those places that are most comfortable and pleasant to live in. What I saw then was a long-term population drive to the coastal peripheries of the nation, and a continuing boom in property values, especially on rivers, harbors, and along beautiful lakefronts. This has continued, although in another context many observers now construe this as a "shift to the Sunbelt" and its golden coasts.

I recall, on a flight into Phoenix in 1971, peering down into a desert valley west of that city, flat and barren except for one isolated array of green, irrigated fields. Standing guard over this vast greenery, like a sentry box, was a tiny rectangular cluster of brown houses at the lower end of the green fields. Here was where the farmers collected all that stored energy off their fields—tons of hay and grain—and stacked it in bales of latent energy ready for shipment into town. It was a simplistic vision, yet it stuck with me as an efficient way of looking at invisible flows of energy that were transforming North America. By this time I had adopted a name—Stacks—to attach to all these accumulations of surplus energy. And immediately I began to envision every scene with its surpluses as taking part in a grand cadence, its pulses and rhythms changing the scenes as I watched. This was one of those transforming moments. Never again could I see haystacks and crops or raw materials as static objects. All were part of dynamic processes, and it might take me a lifetime to trace their flows.

Then in 1980, thanks to a lively encounter with a brilliant television photographer-producer, Clay Nixon, I was able to try out these ideas and images in a television documentary called "Unknown Places: Exploring the Obvious." Together we set out in a series of cross-section trips through Los Angeles; Manhattan, Kansas; Louisville, Kentucky; Columbia, Maryland; and Boston to "do some footage," as I learned to say.

Here was a chance to explore on videotape the transformations that I had been reporting in other media and in university lectures. Building on my earlier conclusion that planning had been corrupted to become a process for distributing city surpluses, I concluded that "a city is a device for distributing surplus energy. Without surpluses there can be no city. Without food from someplace else, cities starve. Without gasoline, traffic stops. With no gas, no oil, no firewood, no sunshine, cities freeze in the dark."

Now as the merest observation will tell you, surpluses do not spread themselves around according to the Bill of Rights. Some

places, some neighborhoods, get more than others—more customers, more newcomers, more investments. Or favors from city hall.
They all depend on energy, often achieved at the cost of someone or
someplace else.

But to pick out and detect these particular, uniquely local
places—largely unknown to the majority, and never to be found on
the usual city maps—we need to develop our own X-ray vision,
together with our own language. For language, I had come to
believe, was a universal lubricant for smoothing out the connections
between the eye and brain; it is a translation medium by which
understanding can be speeded up, so long as we are careful to
perfect our own powers to describe what we see.

But mere observation and pure description are never enough, for
the forces and energies in the landscape are constantly rearranging
themselves, often in patterns not readily visible to the casual
observer. Once I had begun to take some pains at looking about me, I
began to organize the visible world in terms of its energy systems, in
a pecking order that began with the places my Southern upbringing
had forced upon me—places that I will describe in this book as
backwaters. These are the depressed regions, underdeveloped or
backward zones, towns, and neighborhoods bypassed by the great
forces of urban innovation, expansion, and development.

Along the way I began encountering other places that deliberately
or accidentally had become holdout zones against the forces of
change. Tightly held in the grip of poverty were some of them—
such as Savannah when, as a teenager, I first encountered it. This
aged town was still enduring a pervasive poverty in which there was
no money or other form of energy to repaint, fix up or tear down
those lovely eighteenth- and nineteenth-century buildings. They
simply sat there in a state of genteel decay, until preservation-
minded outsiders arrived with jobs, money, and a determination to
"save historic Savannah." The results are plainly visible today in this
extraordinarily preserved city of squares and town houses and
boulevards and new paint.

These holdout zones, almost all of them, had been preserved
more or less unchanged into the present, by three forces: by poverty
as in Savannah and its neighbor Charleston, South Carolina; by
plutocracy, as at the famous resorts and enclaves of the wealthy at
Newport, Rhode Island; Tuxedo Park, New York; or Jekyll Island,
Georgia; and by privacy—the isolation of remote locations that kept

them off the tourists' beaten path, and out of sight of prospective buyers. One of the more spectacular examples is in Brazil: The sixteenth century gold port town of Parati, isolated down at the foot of the coastal mountain range, remote from the modern world until a new highway built during the 1970s brought it within three and a half hours' driving time of Sao Paulo, the world's third largest city.

But beyond these backwaters and holdout zones lie the great energy centers of modern cities, boomtown resorts, oil and mining towns suddenly grown large, and smaller towns caught up in a favorable influx of energy. These energetic places take many forms, from that object of almost universal upperclass scorn, the suburban highway strip, to old fishing dock districts such as Baltimore's Harborplace, which became the darling of city boosters in the 1980s and inspired scores of developers to "do a Harborplace" in their own hometowns.

Whatever may lie ahead for city-regions in the coming years, it will depend in great part on their ability to tap national markets, to expand their own exporting abilities. It will depend on their capacity, as Jane Jacobs suggests in her book, *Cities and the Wealth of Nations*, to replace imports with their own products and services for export. Some of the changes will come from sudden injections of foreign or national investments—a new military base or contracts, as for the Boeing Company in Seattle; the influx of a bonanza crop of tourists or fair-goers; or the tides of fashion and publicity that make a San Francisco or an Atlanta, or a once-isolated Knoxville, or a Scottsdale, Arizona, a suddenly busy scene of innovations, investments, and newcomers.

This is not the place to predict all that is yet to come, but there is no doubt in my mind that the seeds of future changes are already visible around us. There should be no shocks in store for the wary, no surprises for the creatively watchful. While it is true that cataclysms may come to upset all such evidence—a massive earthquake, meteorite impact, or a nuclear disaster—short of such incalculable generators of extinction, we can and should stay aggressively in touch with the visible evidence all around us. To see is to believe in what is certain to come.

### NOTE

1. In 1978, the American Society of Planning Officials merged with the American Institute of Planners to create the American Planning Association.

# 1

# Backwaters

---

## Objectivity and Place

Objectivity has been in some dispute in the 1980s, with Third World propagandists claiming that no North American journalist could possibly be objective about non-American subjects; with black urban slum dwellers insisting that no college-trained Whitey could possibly write objectively about black culture and its neighborhoods; and with businessmen insisting that only a trained-in-business journalist should be allowed to interpret the American corporation.

Long before Third World arguments of this sort intruded themselves into meetings of professional journalists, I had embarked on my own course of looking-for-myself so as to get beyond the limits of my own background. I had begun to explore for myself places that already had been squeezed much too neatly into my own stereotypes or those being peddled by others. Was my hometown of Atlanta truly the ideal boomtown of the Sixties? Was Haight-Ashbury truly a cesspool crawling with degenerate hippies? At every opportunity I took what might have appeared to be the radical—and time-consuming—course of withholding judgment until I had been to That Place, had walked and looked and talked my way through and around it—only then being willing to write either learnedly, objectively, or even superficially about it.

One advantage in having Louisville, Kentucky, as my base during those contentious years was that it was easier there not to get swept up among Manhattanized tricksters practicing the New Journalism— "making the trade safe for bullshit," as someone observed[1], or spinning my wheels trying to do warmed-over Watergate investigations on my own daily rounds. For all the faults wonderfully visible to its denizens, Louisville provided a somewhat receptive backwater from which to view and to judge the solar flares sweeping outwards from the Watts rioters of Los Angeles, the Mafia invasion of Atlantic City, or the drug ringsters of Miami.

During that era of the 1960s, I was called on to deliver an obituary in the great vaulted space of the National Cathedral in Washington, D.C. The man we honored was the late Dennis O'Harrow, whom I mentioned earlier in this book. He was, I observed with some admiration, determined to do his thing "out there in Chicago"— maintaining there the office of the American Society of Planning Officials—while all the world of professional planners was high-tailing it to Washington, D.C., thereby pushing up the skyline and rent levels of that one-industry town. I hammered away, as one tends to do in emotional moments, at O'Harrow's love affair with Out There, his determination to keep himself rooted in the Midwest. And I was certainly reflecting my own belief in maintaining a close contact with what I saw as the heartland of America. In my own case it was a location partly central, somewhat Midwestern, with a southern exposure—two hours flight from New York, Dallas, or Toronto, and three from Denver. The ambiguities of being "from Louisville"—a city millions of Americans can barely locate on the map much less in their own psyche—forced me constantly to ask questions about place and placelessness. For Louisville, as I came to learn on reporting trips around the continent, barely existed on the new mental maps of urbanologists, upwardly mobile young professionals, and others playing the game of What's Your Favorite City?

I recall being accosted at a Washington, D.C., reception by a rather grandiose public relations man whose Washington clients included the American Institute of Architects. He had just read, and professed to have been impressed by, an article of mine published in *Horizon* magazine, then in its early and lavishly oversized full-color format.

"What," demanded my new acquaintance with a look hovering between concern and disdain, "What is this Louisville bit?" At once I sensed his real meaning: What was somebody who could write that well doing way the hell out there in a noplace called Kentucky? Why go through such an act? Why wasn't I in Washington? I do not recall my exact answer except that it was extremely rude and challenging but apparently acceptable to my accoster. And I did succeed in convincing him—or so it appeared after subsequent drinks—that a journalist can find both a reasonable stance and a world worth writing about while maintaining home and office Out There, "beyond the Beltway," far from the shores of the Potomac River and the taint of Potomac Fever.

What I was doing Out There came to be titled, especially in Manhattan, as a form of The New Journalism. But I was and remain a nonpractitioner of what Seymour Krim has called "journalit," meaning a form of writing that blurs the distinction between fiction and nonfiction. Rather than plumbing the depths of my own psyche to invent dialogues that might have taken place among public figures, I turned to the evidence of my own eyes as the firm anchor for observation, conclusions, and speculation. To those who were puzzled by my insistent focus on things seen I would explain that I had been "converted from 'that's what-the-man-said' journalism to 'this is what I've seen' journalism."

But hardly a schoolboy or girl achieves puberty these days without knowing from television that what we "see" is socially, psychically, and economically predetermined by childhood training, by class position, or by propagandists. Yet such half-truths hardly begin to explore the complexities of learning about the world by observing it carefully, technically, and over long periods of time. If we make our world by constructing it as a series of mental images, we can make sense of that world by looking at it cautiously, dispassionately, and with the full range of our critical faculties. I recall a lucid statement from Prof. Lillian B. Allen at a conference we attended at the University of Manitoba in Winnipeg: "You have to stand and stop and stare and store." And, I would add, compare, compare, compare. One of the best yardsticks I know is Oliver Cromwell's great and thundering dictum, "Think ye, by the bowels of Christ, ye may be wrong!"

Being wrong when one writes about places produces quick penalties. Hell hath no fury like a suburbanite whose street name has been misspelled, or a tourist who is certain that the famous cathedral doors open toward, rather than away from, the local sunrise. All writers who put out geographic anchors incur geographic risks. That particular place may have gone through changes since your last visit! This I had been forced to learn quickly enough in the mid-Sixties when city councils and their traffic engineers from

Aroostock to Acapulco were caught up in the fervor to convert downtown into a network of one-way streets—only to tinker and rejigger the net as pressures changed. Yesterday's Broadway-going-South can quickly change to north, no matter what the city maps may tell you. All maps gather untruths from their moment of printing.

Risk is inherent in the open marketplace. Each person is his own expert, claiming to possess not only his neighborhood and his home town, but the right to correct all others who venture near. The very nature of the place makes it possible for everyone to double-check on what a writer has just asserted. A reporter's account, otherwise bursting with insight and ultimate truth, falls flat on its face when any child can plainly see—regardless of the written word to the contrary—that you go upstream from Kennedy Center to Georgetown-on-the-Potomac, or downstream from the United Nations to Brooklyn Bridge. Or that the Haymarket in Louisville no longer sells hay, the fishmarkets at Baltimore's Harborplace have gone indoors, and that there is no dock on Dock Street in Philadelphia. Unlike television, where you must be the owner of a $500 videorecorder before you can run down yesterday's big lie or small gaffe, one reporter's observations in print about the visible marketplace can be checked quickly by map or by visit.

Regardless of such risks, it seemed compelling to me to focus my travels and writings on discernible, describable places and to be challenged by those most difficult to describe. I was and expect to be drawn to the ever-shifting tension between places and people, between the plaza and its passing throng, between public places and public favor—between assertions about places and the realities they offer.

And I found myself continually attracted to places where, it was asserted, there was "nothing going on." For inevitably, it turned out that the slower pace and lessened intensity of events in small towns, dead ends, quiet hamlets and placid backwaters offered endless occasions to see the bigger picture writ small, the larger problem in its bare-minimum version. I found that the most useful places to begin an exploration of large matters was in such dead ends and places left-behind, where Progress never penetrated, or else has been long gone. Just as there can be no silence without the sounds which distinguish it, there can be no understanding of city life without understanding country, of booms without knowing depression, of the best without experiencing the worst. Compare, compare, compare! turned out to be the best advice for all such journeys.

---

# Alleys

To skulk and prowl, as I often find myself doing, through an American alley is to step backward in time, downward on the social ladder, and quickly to confront the world of trash collectors, garbage-pickers, weekend car mechanics, and children. Refugees, all of them, from the wide-open world of the big street and the Out Front.

Backstaged, the alley is the outback world of unmentionable, if not the unwanted, the displaced persons, places, things of modern society. A few glaring exceptions—unpaved greenways through old bucolic suburbs, or posh little stashes of elegant townhouses along refurbished alleys in Georgetown, D.C., and other Early American enclaves—silhouette themselves against a dark and vast majority. For most people, the American residential alley has been out of sight, out of mind, becoming the academic, geographic, and social outcast of the built environment for at least a half-century.

As one observer has noted, "The written history of architecture and town planning has a visual fix on frontality, a permanent obsession 'en face'." When, at the Library of Congress, I examined the literature on alleys, I found it to be rudimentary, to say the least; so that now seems to be the time to consider what the alley is, and what it might become—a hidden resource waiting to be recognized.

Alleys penetrate and reinforce the structure of most nineteenth-century cities, but have become near-wastelands, haunts of the unwanted, sinks for the unspeakable. In many downtowns, commercial and industrial alleys are feared for the criminals and prospective muggers-rapists who lurk, especially among the mental images that suburbanites maintain. In Eastern and most colonial cities such as Boston, an alley walk brings you face to face with an almost medieval pattern of wendy-windy alleys, many of which have even survived that most alley-destructive of all forces, urban redevelopment of the sort practiced until the late 1970s.

But the wendy-windy configuration is quite an old one, for the national land survey of 1785 determined the future layout of

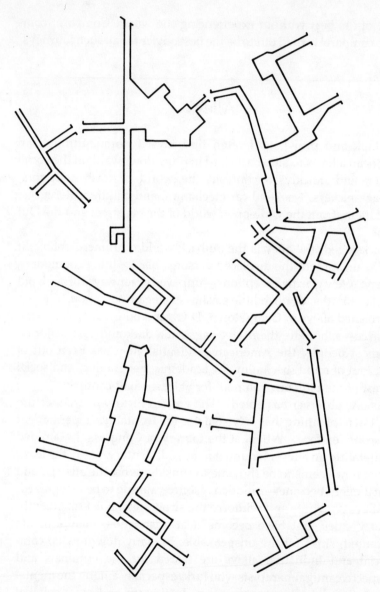

1-1. In Eastern and most Colonial cities such as Boston, an almost medieval mosaic of wendy-windy alleys leaves patterns such as these, pre-dating the north-east-south-west patterns in later all-square cities based on the Jefferson grid.

America's new West, by applying its mile-square gridiron to the countryside, a pattern that also influenced the carving up of cities into rectangular blocks and lots. Thus the grid is thought of as an American invention when, in fact, it occurred along with alleys as early as the fifth century B.C. in Greece.

When the Utopian reformer Frances Wright wrote about New York City in 1821, she observed that it had "no dark alleys, whose confined and noisome atmosphere marks the presence of a dense and suffering population."

In most cities, alley land is under-used and under-built except in portions of the central business district. In cities where new building lots in the suburbs may sell for $12,000 to $50,000, alley lots or land fronting on some alleys can be had for a few hundred dollars or less. Except for a few middle-to-upper-class blocks, most alleys reflect a shrinkage of public investments, when in fact, alley investments by public agencies were always less than money put out front on the main streets.

But the denigration of the alley need not be inevitable. Thousands of alley blocks can be transformed by simple reforms. As energy costs go up, as moving and commuting costs increase, the value of older city blocks is likely to stabilize or even to soar in select locations. And the value of land inside those blocks—which often means land accessible only via alleys—is bound to increase.

The best-documented alley system in the United States lies in the shadow of the national Capitol in Washington, D.C. When more than 30,000 runaway slaves and freedmen inundated Washington, D.C., during and after the Civil War, that city's alleys became a racial and political problem, and later the most heavily researched alleys in the nation. They are a by-product of the famous L'Enfant Plan, which laid out the capital city into large, nonrectangular blocks. As the city grew, property owners in 1852 cut up the first five big blocks, inserting alleys and selling off back lots. Most alleys came to be laid out in hidden or blind-alley fashion: This produced an H-shape alley pattern within the block, but only one or two outlets to big streets. This hidden feature disturbed police and reformers alike, but apparently satisfied the rest of the nonalley public, which was content to have alley dwellers concealed from public view.

In 1858, two-thirds of Washington alley residents were white, but the influx of blacks during and after the Civil War changed everything. Within 10 years after war began in 1861, Washington's population increased by 48,000; more than half were black. Most of these settled in alleys or in shacks on military lands. A few alley houses were built by philanthropists, but most were erected by speculators who could get "about twice what is considered a fair return in street property," according to a later survey.

By 1897 there were 333 alleys in the District of Columbia, and more than three-quarters of their 19,000 inhabitants were black. Alley districts had such names as Goose Level, Froggy or Foggy Bottom, Hell's Bottom, Swampoodle and Bloodfield. In such names, Washington was following a familiar Southern pattern of giving its low-lying districts names reflecting both the wetness of the ground and blackness of the people: Little Africas abounded across the South.

While Theodore Roosevelt was president, Senate investigators found that the Senate's barbershop towels were laundered in notorious Willow Tree Alley. The outraged senators appropriated money to wipe out the alley and install a playground that was said to work badly, in part because it was surrounded by alley houses. The site was later eliminated for the new Social Security Building. In 1870 Congress set up the District of Columbia Board of Health with power to condemn and demolish; 20 years later, District commissioners got the power to convert alleys into "minor streets." In 1892 Congress prohibited the occupancy of houses built in alleys that were less than 30 feet wide and without water or sewers; in 1914 Congress forbade the use of alley dwellings after 1918. During the last days before her death, the first Mrs. Woodrow Wilson told a friend: "I would be happier if I knew the Alley Bill had passed." It did. But later the 1918 deadline was extended to 1923 and the act eventually declared null.

Finally, in 1934, the New Deal Congress gave the power to condemn land to an Alley Dwelling Authority, which by 1944 had been expanded to become the National Capital Housing Authority.

By 1970, after 30-odd years of clearance, at least 20 Washington alleys remained inhabited. I spent a half-day's drive in April, 1977 to find dozens of alley blocks still occupied. But the existing dwellings appeared to me to be in much better shape than when I had visited them in the early 1960s.

One result of urban redevelopment practices in the 1960s was that large areas were superblocked. Thus in Southwest Washington, for example, there are no alleys left in that officially renewed district. A few interior cul-de-sac courtyard streets, however, recaptured something of the secluded intimacy of the old interior alleys—this time for much better-heeled occupants.

In several large neighborhoods, especially since the 1967 riots, regular streets and boulevards have become slum sites, so that there is no longer any need to seek out back-alley and leftover lots for the manufacture of slum housing. As it has turned out, regular streets can be made to serve that purpose admirably.

As for older alleys in Georgetown and on Capital Hill, many have become posh home sites for well-off Washingtonians. In my own city, it has pleased most proper Louisvillians to leave alleys to the general poor, to the domestic poor (i.e., servants), and to others with little choice in housing. In 1909 Janet E. Kemp studied five districts for the Louisville Tenement House Commission and concluded that no study of congestion and unsanitary conditions could be complete if it neglected alleys, which she called "horizontal tenements." By 1977 many alleys she had photographed in central Louisville had been wiped out by expanding businesses, parking lots, and the North-South Expressway. One noxious tenement cluster Miss Kemp photographed in 1909 was also photographed by the *Courier Journal* when I investigated it and found conditions in 1955 almost identical to those of 1909. The buildings were finally razed for a new expressway in the 1960s.

However, the basic pattern of alleys in every city where I have visited them is as clear today as when the alleys were laid out in the nineteenth century. Alleys serve property; they provide access to the rear; they form a sub-network that offers queerly distorted mirror images of the main street systems of the city.

There is a general rule here, applicable to most cities I have visited: Show me an alley and I will show you a block that pre-dates World War I. In some nineteenth century commuting suburbs, alleys were built cheaply and without paving. Along many a steep and rolling hillside, the alleys were never "made" at all, but were left as open easements to puzzle if not plague later generations of title lawyers and property owners, but also to be enjoyed by the residents.

Boston's remnant alleys, especially in its North End, reflect a squiggly pattern now becoming rare in American cities, but most nineteenth century alleys reflect the ubiquitous grid, and echo its monotonous rectangularity. And so, in the great wave of downtown renewals of the 1960s, hundreds of old alleys were wiped away as superblocks, plazas, and vistas took their place.

It is clear from the evidence of the alleys themselves that property owners who developed them, and officials who sanctioned them, conceived of access to land in hierarchical terms: Out front there was the respectable world that paid taxes; out back were servants and riffraff to do the dirty work. Expensive materials went into the front of the houses, cheaper stuff on the sides and back. Earth removed in

1–2. From *Alleys: A Hidden Resource.*

"One may still hunt up by night waifs who make their beds in alleys and cellars and abandoned sheds. This last winter two stable fires that broke out in the middle of the night routed out little colonies of boys, who slept in the hay and probably set it on fire."

The trouble with these big old houses is that they're hard to keep up, and you get all these creeps and winos coming in off the alleys. I tell you it's not an easy proposition.

What kinda democracy is this where they close off your street and never put it to a vote of the residents?

We ought to get some little shops into those carriage houses out in the back. It's just a short way over to those Oak Street stores and this could turn into a nice little shopping district.

They push me any farther and I'm going to sell out and I won't be particular who I sell out to, either.

They keep telling me what color I can paint my house, and they call this a preservation district. It sounds like a confiscation district to me. I want to use any color I choose.

A Cadillac can't make that turn back there into the Mayflower Garage. You got to fix that corner so people can use it and not bang up their fenders. There's no room to turn.

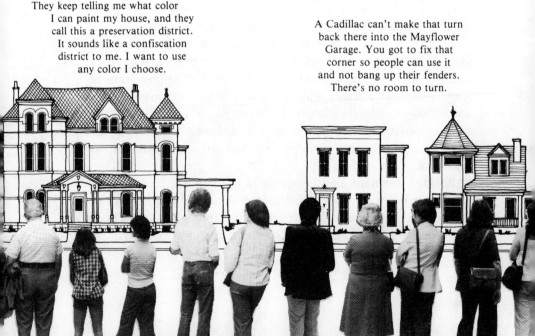

building streets was piled up in front yards to provide a podium or raised platform for the houses of the wealthy.

Most alleys, therefore, became a second city (and second-class city) within the framework of the houses and buildings out front, which presented their united facade to passers-by. Alleys proved to be a handy Siberia into which powerful interests in the community could relegate or shove those persons or activities offensive to proper view and viewers. The alley thus became a Sink (in the sense

How long does it take to get some little red stop signs on that alley? We have been talking about that for six months and all we get out of those bureaucrats is bullshit.

How long is this temporary closing going to be? We never saw no questionnaire out of City Hall. They never asked me a thing.

If you look back in that big brick garage you'll see the owner's Rolls-Royce. Somebody must be doing OK in this neighborhood.

Whatever they write about this neighborhood better be good or else we'll stop that whole publication. We want positive things in print about us.

That little carriage house back there on the corner would take $38,000 to fix it up and you can buy one of these whole houses for that money. Who's going to fix it up with figures like that there?

You wouldn't believe the things people will say at a public hearing but I was there, and that's what they said. Except that thing about the waifs. That's from a history of New York City.

When we moved in here it was just all run down, and now there's a bunch of us owners, fixing up. But it's getting to be a battleground, with all that commerce coming down on us.

I explored more fully in *Closeup: How to Read the American City*).

But alleys do not stand alone; they are parts of a larger system. The generations that produced nineteenth-century alleys looked upon the city as a mechanism that needed mass-produced services, water, police, gas, electricity. It also needed mass-produced access, so that streets, alleys, sidewalks were viewed as elements of a single system, and systems-thinking was an important civic discovery of the nineteenth century. Even though the parts were small-scale in the early 1800s, they nevertheless worked in a systematic way: to get people to and from work, to service homes and businesses, and to provide for easy walking on dry pavements as a bare minimum.

The streets and alleys also show that the landscape, which later was to be viewed romantically for its aesthetic potential, was seen in the early nineteenth century merely as a set of physical conditions needing revision and improvement, by whatever means were handy. Rights-of-way containing clay for brick-making could be dug out down to future street level, which left the houses high and dry. When streets and alleys encountered hills too steep, the street bent and the pattern broke. The idea that alleys could become important to the aesthetic image of the city was still generations away.

## THE END OF THE ROAD

By World War I, the fad for curvilinear suburbs was on the rise, and these new wendy-windy layouts left no room for alleys.

Furthermore, the quick jump in national automobile ownership from 2,490,932 in 1915 to 9,239,161 in 1925 meant that alleys were no longer required as access for horses, barns, and stables, with their manure, smells, and animal noises. The auto speeded up what the trolley lines had begun, spreading out the old walk-in city where people had crowded together to make the tightest use of scarce land.

In the wild boom of the 1920s, thousands of lots were laid out around cities in the cheapest, most easily platted form possible. This was a time when the fastest bucks could be made by platting with minimum utilities and minimum access, which cost land and money. Alleys were out.

The no-alley trend was reinforced by the 1930s depression and its search for cost-cutting layouts, and further by the Federal Housing Administration, which carried the new spartan layouts into the housing boom after World War II.

1–3. A renewed alley (behind trees) now joins a new public parkground (foreground) to the gardenesque backyard of the Natural History Museum. After being photographed, the blank-walled warehouse beyond the park was converted to condominiums. Main Street at Seventh Street, Louisville, Kentucky.

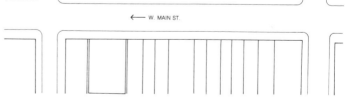

1–4. Close to the Ohio River (top), Louisville's Seventh Street forms the eastern end of a redeveloped alley, which extends westward (to left) along the backs of renewed warehouses. A new overpass connects the museum to parking areas shown at the top of the map.

Another blow to alleys came in the 1940s, when U.S. automakers began exuberantly to lengthen and fatten their new models. Every foot of length, every inch of girth helped squeeze these new monsters out of old garages. Million by million, year by year, garages in backyards, in houses, and along alleys became obsolete and thus available for demolition or reuse. This, in turn, shifted cars out onto front yards and streets and on display. And there they remained, affluential tokens into the late 1970s, when they began to shrink in size again.

For all these reasons, alleys by the late 1940s had become distinctively old-hat. By 1955 the American Society of Planning Officials published—rather jubilantly, it seemed to me at the time— a report that alleys were vanishing.

In 1961 the *Community Builders' Handbook* issued by the Urban Land Institute, which reflected accepted wisdom among real estate men, was saying, "Alleys in present day single-family or two-family residential neighborhoods are no longer desirable nor considered necessary. A rear property line easement is preferred to an alley." The handbook added that "the disappearance of the alley . . . is one of the advances which has been made in land planning during the motor age."

Meanwhile, if one looks back over three great disrupters of urban landscapes since the 1930s—federally aided highways, slum clear-ance-plus-public housing, and large-scale urban redevelopment—it is clear that these programs killed off thousands of existing alleys. In these processes, large-scale replatting and "superblocking" were favorite devices, their justification going back to a well-documented article in the *Architectural Forum* of July, 1940, "Superblock vs. Gridiron." This laid out the economic advantages of the former by reducing the street and alley network of the latter. Look at any major redevelopment project in the U.S. and observe, as we noted earlier, that former alleys have disappeared under redeveloped sites, leaving hardly a trace.

## BEYOND SIBERIA

There is no reason to assume that American society will suddenly become wholly egalitarian and abandon its historic tendencies to shove into the backwoods, backwaters, and backalleys those weak and defenseless or outcast portions of society. But such domestic deportation and municipal exile is now more subtle and more discreet; it is no longer legally possible for whole communities to decree publicly that certain back streets are for blacks, Mexicans, Indians, Orientals, or Hispanics. There was a time when Mormon husbands could set aside alley blocks in Salt Lake City for cottages where dwelt the "other wives," but those blocks are now just another part of the housing fabric of that city.

There is some reason, however, to suspect that a wealth of affection for alleys can be found among many disillusioned suburbanites as well as among confirmed city-dwellers. One account of Parisian alleys observes that they were "laden with mystery and almost erotic meaning." During a recent discussion of urban problems, a prominent Boston politician of Italian descent observed to me that "everybody in the North End (of Boston) has a favorite alley. That's where we all got laid the first time." Some of the old-time mystery and small-scale charm that the nineteenth-century city possessed is today most highly visible in refurbished alleys and courts.

My own "favorite" among my early prowlings turned out to be San Francisco's Maiden Lane, which I first explored in 1959 as a footloose observer for a magazine team that produced *The Exploding Metropolis*. Maiden Lane, I discovered, had come a long way since the days when knife-toting and gold-packing miners made a beeline down from the hills to the cribs, bagnios, and rows of whorehouses that once crowded the narrow little two blocks of Maiden Lane.

By the 1950s, and even more so in the 1980s, Maiden Lane had become one of the plushest, lushest little shopping spots one is likely to find in any major city, a place of high rents and high-fashion goods where some of the West Coast's best-dressed women swing along. If anybody's flesh-peddling in San Francisco, it's someplace besides Maiden Lane.

This little masterpiece shows how a shopping district can be imploded, expanded within itself, how the store and show-window frontage can be doubled by treating the outback as upfront, thus increasing the display space per city block by 50 percent at little cost. Maiden Lane is only two blocks long, 21 feet wide, with six-foot sidewalks. Its intimacy becomes rarer still as surrounding blocks are further packed with skyscrapers.

And so, many an alley can be turned around as was Maiden Lane, cleaned up and improved to become once again a special world, not so much a place for the discards and helpless, but for a wider range of city dwellers. The alley offers one of the few urban rather than suburban or rural "retreats," an enclave just off the busy street, a step away from the hurly-burly. It is precisely these "just-off" locations that American tourists seek when they go to Europe. It is just this sort of intimacy that, when well-designed, can be offered by the interior of thousands of city blocks. For when such sites are redesigned and especially when they are controlled by their residents, they provide land that is serviced by utilities and is close to jobs, schools, churches—all such reinforcements that city families need.

It is time to revise rules that make difficult the re-subdivision of urban lands into more effective layouts and to look at hidden alleys for their potentials as good places to live. Just take that next turn to your left off Main Street.

---

# In Defense of
# the Dangerous City

Everybody wants things safe: safety belts in cars (even though we may not use them), safety barriers along roads, safe investments, a pocketful of safety matches, and a list of well-balanced industries and jobs to keep your home town from depressions.

Kids know better. They know that if you always play it safe, you'll get noplace fast. Like the kids in Decatur, Illinois. They know better. The Decatur parks director went out recently and chopped down all those "dangerous" trees at the end of the Nelson Park coasting run. The kids deserted the place. Looking around, the parks director found all the kids had moved to another hill—one where there were scads of dangerous trees at the bottom of the sled run.

Kids know things about cities their parents have forgotten. Part of the excitement in cities is danger. Not necessarily danger from muggers, child molesters, or hoodlums. "Never speak to strangers," all the advisors say. But how queer can you get? I'm speaking of constructive dangers.

What the city does offer—and might offer in bigger doses and variations—is the exciting danger of natural sport found in the landscape. This is the danger of creeks, steep banks, tall trees, cliffs, caves, and walls to climb; monkey vines to swing on. This is the

1-5. Leftover dirt piles or
construction wastes offer places
where kids can learn to deal with
danger on their own, away from
over-solicitous playground
supervisors—or Mom. Photo by
Jacques Simon.

healthy danger you run into sliding down a snowy hillside with
trees at the bottom; climbing up a cliff with uncertainty at the top;
scaling a cliff on a hot day, aware that a copperhead snake might be
sunning on the next ledge; wading in unknown waters (if you can't
swim you're a dope and deserve to drown). Where and how else do
you learn to measure risk against dare, safety against exposure?

There are still, in the midst of a few built-up neighborhoods,
occasional wildernesses of natural danger, beloved by small boys,
animals, and a few adults. These are feared like plague by mud-
ridden Mommas.

For Momma, with mud on her floor and blood in her eye, can see nothing educational in a creek, nothing of adventure in the mud. It all constitutes a threat to her freshly scrubbed kitchen floor. But to most youngsters, even the tiniest wilderness with honeysuckle thickets to hide in, and steep banks and brush piles to swarm over, are places of challenge and adventure.

This is why I've got a fondness for cliffs and crummy places in cities. (They're not crummy to me; that's a Momma's word.) They represent backwaters away from the rigid regularity of just-so streets and sidewalks and fenced property lines, which offer no places for adventures that can't happen on flat asphalt playgrounds.

The all-safe city is the all-dead city. It has been made flat and predictable and insurable, like that damned playground. It is full of barriers and safety belts; gone from the sledding slopes are those dangerous trees, disappeared from view are those mucky ditchbanks. Piped away underground are all the natural streams and all the natural rainfall and quiet springs. All the juices, all the excitements are bottled. Danger is for television; excitement is for somebody else.

So far I have been describing, and not prescribing. But it so happens that I brought along a dose or two that might help out. Just for instance: setting aside all creek valleys and steep hills in or near every growing city, and resurrecting the remnants that still survive in older cities; stopping the dumping and the pollution; adding more all-weather walkways to and through the wild places so you can walk the wilderness without getting mucky—a slight concession to Momma.

Such valleys with cliffs, caves, and swamps, such steep hills with their long views and challenging drops should be treasured beyond price, valued beyond subdivision. You cannot buy the kind of adventure they offer. Once they're gone, buried under a rigid overlay of bulldozed dirt, streets, lots, and Mommas, not all the money in the world can bring them back.

---

## Lassithi and
## the Plastic Pipe

On the coast road eastward from Knossus the sea gleams bright and the flat fields stretch back from the beach road to the sharp, gray, rough mountains. Soon the windmills of Crete appear. Some are

1-6. What makes this placid scene work in Crete's "Breadbasket," the irrigated Lassithi Valley, is wind, gravity, and a network of cheap plastic pipe—while the energy-rich U.S. concentrates on pumps, heavy pipe, and pressures of 75 pounds per square inch.

what one would see in the American Great Plains, metal-bladed on metal scaffolding. Occasionally, the more romantic canvas-bladed types turn like white scimitars in the sunlight. This is our first exposure to the irrigated farmsteads that spread along the Mediterranean coast, depending on water pumped up by windmills. Whole fleets of them begin to appear, 22 miles east of Knossus.

From the coast we wiggle and wind our way for 40 kilometers in a rented car up a series of valleys toward the interior, and the Plains of Lassithi. At Knossus, a guide less skilled than those we'd met in Greece had given us a quick but halting history: how the Lassithi Plateau, an ancient volcanic crater, had become the breadbasket of Crete, its rich farmland protected over the centuries from raiders, invaders, Saracens and Turks by a rim of sharp mountains and easily defended passes. Ancient history clustered around in deep caves.

Giant ruins of sixteenth-century windmills could still be seen on the great pass.

So upward we climb to the pass and there, like megaliths across the V-shaped horizon, stood the great squared and stony bases of the old mills. From the pass one looks down to the Plains, a fairyland of modern dancing, whirring canvas windmills. Our guide, perhaps with more than the whole truth, had told us that "4,000 windmills" were on the valley floor.

We can hardly wait to careen down the zigzag road, to wander in a happy daze along summery shady lanes, past tiny fields, orchards heavy with apple and other fruit, vines loaded with squash, melons, and what seemed to be an odd-shaped local cucumber. At one moment we counted 13 threshing scenes—black-coated women around hard-packed threshing floors, plodding oxen going round and round a central yoke. Behind each pair of oxen, an old woman was seated in a wooden chair anchored on a heavy sled, the sled's runners crushing out the grain. Children and women guided the animals, and forked more wheat onto the threshing floor. Except for a far-off corner of the great valley, all the fields were small, perhaps 10 to 15 acres at the most, and all separated by stone walls and fruit-laden hedgerows.

Gleaming and interrupting the muted background, pink, yellow, and blue plastic piping caught our eyes in every direction. Thin stuff, cheaply made, and easily rolled into coils, the plastic tubing stretched across the fields, to pipe water to distant crops.

It all came together as a marvelously integrated landscape charged with life: windmills pumping water from deep underground (a natural aquifer far below stored the water from last winter's melting snows) and into cottage-sized concrete tanks. From the tanks, in ditches and through pipes, the water reached every field. Here and there were the newcomers: gasoline pumps, perched at the lip of a deep well, to supplement the windmills' flow. We could see some fields, quite new, and somewhat higher than the wells, now being supplied altogether by the pumps, this new technology reaching hitherto inaccessible bits and pieces of old land.

As an amateur vegetable grower back in the States, I was dazzled by this fruitful yield from irrigation and was determined to follow the Crete example to my own small valley garden. If the Greeks had taken 4,000 years to perfect this system, surely it should work in an old Kentucky suburban landscape formed since the 1880s.

Once I was back in the U.S., I was determined to get for my own garden some of that cheap though gaudy plastic pipe the Cretan irrigators were using. But what did my friendly plumbing supply warehouseman tell me—after digging through all 14 American manufacturers' catalogs? Nobody he could find in the United States was making that kind of cheap stuff. But, if I wanted real pipe, heavy-duty polyvinyl chloride pipe, he could get all I wanted, and in several colors, mostly black. It was 75 pounds-per-square-inch pipe. That's what everybody in the business was demanding, he told me, pipe that would carry liquids under high pressure. Having just come from the cautious, abstemious, traditional, and energy-hungry Island of Crete, I was astounded. No low-pressure pipe to be found in the technological treasurehouse of North America?

I kept looking and months later, rather by accident, I found some of that cheap, thin stuff at an irrigation warehouse in vineyard country near Claremont, California, east of Los Angeles. I have never seen any of it for sale in all the years and places since that moment.

Eventually, the truth dawned on me. Nobody in the American pipe industry was interested in gravity. Everybody in the United States who had anything to do with moving liquids owned a pump. Not just any pump, but a power-driven pump—a 75 pounds-per-square-inch pump. And in a nation of high-pressure pumps, you build heavy pipe to handle high pressures. Or, stated another way, in a nation with energy to burn, "to hell with cheap plastic pipe." And therefore, "to hell with gravity."

This discovery forced me to take a hard look at other wasteful practices, at all those other ways in which we were saying "To Hell with Gravity," which was another way of saying "To Hell with Nature." That was in 1968, and it radicalized me in ways that no amount of Earth Day rhetoric was able to do. The evidence was right in front of my own eyes. We were a nation drunk on cheap energy— in a world where billions of other people were still making do with human muscle-power, the donkey, mule, windmill, water wheel, and small engines doing small jobs, using tiny amounts of fuel.

I was still shocked at the wastefulness I saw everywhere in America in 1971, when I put some of my concerns into a paper for an international building conference in London. It was there I wrote that "control of energy is replacing the control of geographic places as a means of exercising power . . . access to the energies necessary to survive is becoming the most important access of all."

Steadily in these intervening years, we've all watched the growth of high-pressure pipe. Plastic heavy-duty PVC pipe is all around us, carrying gas under pressure, water, sewage, and the effluent from disposal plants. My favorite seed-and-garden store has tripled in size, and stacks its heavy irrigation pipe and gas pipe in bright blue and white, outdoors in the sun. All these years later, and a decade into higher priced gasoline, natural gas, and fuels, I can find none of those thin Cretan gravity-fed plastic pipes. This high-energy world still does its thing under pressure—75 pounds per square inch.

---

# Micro-Appalachia

For some years now I have been wrestling in a modest way with the problems of the underdeveloped world—that vast realm, invisible to most North Americans, in which three-quarters of this globe's human population live, beyond the reach of modern transport, shut away and out, dependent on what they can forage, steal, mine, or otherwise cheaply extract from their immediate surroundings.

It has been a sobering experience. And even though my life did not depend on it—my bit of the Third World was, after all, only a family pond and vegetable garden tucked away in an inaccessible valley in urban middle-America—it nonetheless suggested a way to look at cities and to think about the way they develop around us.

My own tiny underdeveloped world was, in fact, a secluded and formerly tax-delinquent valley lot of three acres in an 1893 suburb, which had been surrounded and engulfed by a sizable city. Its nearest, newest neighbor was an interstate expressway interchange, its heavy traffic only 400 feet from my beets and rutabagas. My Third World was inaccessible except on foot or horse or possibly by Jeep. Our building materials came by muscle power down the steep slopes of up to 35 percent grade. In this secluded little enclave, gravity was my normal enemy and only on special occasions was it a friend.

Here I worked and mused and grew my vegetables in a to-pographic slum where the weight of things often was more important than their value. It was a microcosm of Appalachia that was, in turn, a miniature of Alaska or Ghana or Siberia. Here were compressed the problems of underdeveloped regions everywhere. We had to haul in drinking water in closed containers. If we had drunk from a nearby limestone spring, its contaminated waters would have needed expensive chlorination and purifying. Our every move had to be planned; everything was brought in by hand or was back-packed or wheelbarrowed, usually in packages or bottles. Tools had to be securely stored and locked against thievery, seeds tucked into cans against rodents. It took me some five years to pick the broken glass, plastic shards, and brickbats out of the new soil that I hauled in from a nearby creekbed. This in its turn had been replenished by a large pipe that drained the gutters of a nearby street and was beyond my control.

In this rude ravine I built a rough barn from materials scrounged mostly on the site. One corner post was a handy osage orange tree. Another came from a dead tree trunk. One wall we laid up with stone from a nearby creek and from the blastings for a sewer that penetrated the valley. There was nothing here that could not be carried by two men. The rule of the site was: Use it up, Wear it Out, Make it do. Or do Without.

The little barn of trunks and limbs merged into its background and became nearly invisible, so that marauders and trespassers did not perceive it as a target. As a piece of real estate the entire valley was what experts called "a real dog." It flooded regularly; and in 1937, during the Great Flood of the Ohio River, it had been the scene of a now-legendary runaway Army tank, which plunged its crew to death in the flooded valley. Along my Little Appalachia's southern boundary ran a major street—but it was at the top of a precipitous bank and offered no access whatever. Below the bank was a huge buried pipeline carrying white lime slurry from the municipal waterworks a half-mile away. Cracks in the pipeline regularly erupted small fountains of creamy goo into our creek—a pollution that took years of negotiations to stop. Such was the steepness of that little valley that nothing had been built for more than a mile downstream from my place. It remained part of an urban wasteland, until the arrival of the interstate highway. And all around it were strong boundaries, not the least of which was an abandoned quarry just over the hill.

Gradually I developed what could only be called an umbilical relationship with this place. Should anyone trespass, I was at once alert and often watching with binoculars. I knew every nook and cranny, discussed its history with the survivors of a Fine Old Family that had left this property and its tax delinquency, moving to newer suburbs a generation earlier. Life in this primitive little private world forced me to reflect on what power would be required to dramatically change it. I had once brought a bulldozer onto the property in a momentary fit of prudery to "open up the view" and get rid of a great tangle of old fencing, vines, and downed trees. The resulting scar took years to heal, and remained as vivid evidence of the cataclysmic energies that I had loosed on the place.

In the usual course of progress, this little semi-wilderness would continue to be bypassed by the forces of development until some traumatic day when its increased development value would outweigh the high cost of bringing in streets, sewers, and new occupants.

But by that time it will have performed several classic functions that standard planning doctrine tends to overlook. It will have provided enjoyment for several generations of owners as well as neighbors and their kids. Starting around 1900 my predecessors had planted an orchard, built a barn, kept a cow, added cold frames, laid down outdoor waterlines, and built a rustic swimming pool. From the few of their surviving old orchard trees we preserved apples and pears, and got stone from the ruins of their barn for several small jobs of my own. The steepness of the site forced developers to go around it and build on cheaper and flatter farmland in the newer suburbs. And so it was that my little Appalachia stayed off the market until that moment when price and demand would make it feasible to bring to an end this splendid small isolation with which my story began.

## OBJECT LESSON

That first wilderness I have since left behind, but its recent history is an object lesson for all of Micro-Appalachia. After I gave up possession, its new owners set up the first local Scenic Conservation Easement to cover its two ponds, the spring, and 1.6 acres of the valley bottom. This was the first such easement under a new state law that allows owners to donate to their municipality all rights to develop the land. This guarantees that the easement will stay in its semi-natural state. However, the next owners were developers who set out to build 100-plus condominium apartments on land overlooking the easement. This prompted the neighborhood association to furious opposition. After three years delay, in and out of court, the developers backed off, giving most of the site to a community foundation just before an advantageous tax law expired in 1986.

Subsequent to all this I found myself preoccupied with another small and steep urban valley of some two acres, less wild, less isolated, closer to streets, roads, and access. I now can get truck deliveries of lumber or concrete almost to its very center. Much of it had been accessible to neighboring kids and to trash-dumpers. We removed five truckloads of junk—old bedsprings, auto tires, cow bones, bottles—from the creek. Every square foot of it could now, by stretching the term, be considered ripe for development. But it is a lovely respite from the busy city around it, and in my obstinacy I persist in seeing all such places not so much as potential building sites but as human retreats from traffic, noise, deadlines, pressures, and urban progress as defined by most chambers of commerce. My particular way of looking at leftover bits of the natural landscape— the valleys, cliffs, old quarries, marshes, and tangled woodlands— is part nostalgic but also part hard-headedness. For when I look at such places, I see assets where others may see nothing. My latest Micro-Appalachia once had a trickle of a limestone spring emerging from the roots of giant sycamore trees. The trees are long gone, destroyed by the great 1974 tornado, but the spring itself is still there, cleaned out, uncovered, and now enclosed in a stone springhouse that may save it from future generations of polluters and dumpers.

One fine spring day, just after the springhouse was finished, I sat in the sun watching incoming birds swirl in for landings alongside the tiny stream that trickles down below the springhouse. In three minutes I counted 21 birds washing and drinking in its waters. As I watched, many a bird fluttered up to the wooden edge of the nearby vegetable garden and sat preening, and feather-fluffing in the sun. It became a predictable sequence: birds bathing, fluff-drying, and then bug-hunting in the garden. Fully half the birds I counted in the shallow stream ended up foraging in my garden for bugs, grubs, and grit. Thus this tiny trickle of a stream, flowing barely two gallons a minute in dry weather, was doing me the double favor of supplying both irrigation water and insect-eating foragers for my garden. And thus helping to maintain the neighborhood bird population.

Progress, it was once said, consisted of the ability to look upon a vast and unpopulated landscape and envision it teeming with great new cities. Perhaps the vision more appropriate to today is one in which we examine our packed and teeming cities, and find in them places where nature can be preserved or restored to its rightful and more important place in the world.

# Midway at the Brink

Everything you always wanted to know about the Good American Life, all of it to be found within a five-minute walk. All the virtues but only some of the wretchedness exposed to view or to gossip. A garden of your own making, a feeling of being on your own—of knowing your neighbors, of being at home in a manageable environment.

All such nostalgic peaches-and-creamery cluster around the American small town today, especially in the South, still the home and haunt of small-town life. Hardly a week goes by without yet another statistical discovery of yet another trend Back to the Small Town. Pollsters predictably point (for press release on dull Mondays) to a significant slice of the American population that hankers for small-town life or is making tracks away from a big city and its billion-dollar problems back to some bucolic and as-yet unsullied Four Corners.

Having absorbed more than my share of such puffery, I had grown cynical beyond my years about these trendy reports from the urban fronts. But lately I have forced myself to put aside such doubts and dig back toward the roots of The Movement.

And I must confess that even preliminary excavations reveal that The Movement is real, that it goes beyond a mere statistical blip on U.S. Census computer tapes, and that a significant portion of American citizens are exhibiting, in hundreds of ways, their own versions of escaping the big city to rediscover small-town life and pleasures.

From the Census Bureau we learn that nonmetropolitan counties gained an average of 353,000 persons per year from 1970 to 1973, compared with annual losses of some 300,000 during the 1960s and that a significant proportion of this shift in growth "is occurring in small towns and rural areas far away from any cities."

Between 300,000 and 500,000 persons migrated from urban areas to rural areas from 1972 to 1974, a figure that the Stanford Research Institute estimates could have been higher "if there were more economic opportunities in rural communities."

There is, of course, nothing new in such conclusions. Back in 1933 in his prescient book, *Flight from the City,* Ralph Borsodi wrote that "what we have had for many years are intolerable conditions in the country driving people out of the country, and then intolerable conditions in the city, driving them back again."

This two-way process has been spectacularly Southern, although its by-products have gone national. It was the South—bled white by a Civil War, then bled still whiter by exporting generations of blacks—that persistently clung to small-town economics and thus to small-town ways of life. It has kept a preponderance of smaller towns (under 25,000) rather than the typical Midwestern or Northeast-industrial version of 50,000 and up. Meanwhile, keeping one-foot-in-the-country—tied to the old homestead or to a patch of rough land far out of town—remains today a more distinctly Southern way of life.

Now to generalize: To particularize is Southern, and I will conform to regional courtesies by making my points from a very particular place, a smaller-than-typical small town of distinctively Southern history, located in what once would have been called a Border State.

I come now as a visitor to this town of Midway, Kentucky (pop. 1,300), an 1832 railroad town with one track down Main Street, 30 residential blocks, one block of business, an empty feed mill being converted to boutiques, one pants factory, a small women's college, and a new interchange a half-mile out, all encompassed by an open and well-tended landscape of Bluegrass horse and cattle farms. A mile down the road is Airdrie Stud, a splendiferous thousand-odd acres of white-fenced paddocks and fields, setting the visual tone for all the farms around.

## FRAMED, ORDERED, PREDICTABLE

The town itself has the simplicity of storybook quality. I like it here, the calmness, the slow pace, and pervading sense of communal unity. But it is easy to see that a black face on the main street, a

1–7. A rare scene in a gentrifying town: the sharp edge of Midway, Kentucky, where closely held old family Bluegrass farms come right up to the edge of town, with no sprawling suburbs to mar the contrast.

1–8. New paint and cutesy decor greet customers from far and near who flock to fixed up shops along Main Street (and occasionally step aside for trains right through the middle of town).

Hispanic name on the Amex credit card is not expected around here.

This is a romantic place, in the sense that such a townscape conforms to an ancient image now grown rare and unattainable for most Americans—a town of visible limits, enframed and neatly edged behind its greenbelt of farms. No sloppy extensions, no ticky-tacky suburbs, no highway strips, only white fences zigzagging outward beyond a predictable horizon, which exhibits its own rational, agricultural order.

It is like a Renaissance painting—framed, ordered, predictable. Houses stand back from street and road in neat array—flush with sidewalks like eighteenth-century London, or set back behind clipped lawns, or withdrawn in baronial privacy on low hills and rises.

Look again at the 22 businesses on Main Street. Eleven face outward to the region, selling pricey antiques, fashion goods, and boutiquey gimcracks to roving shoppers from far off. Here one sees an incipient regional magnet somewhat like the little exurban stringtown of Long Grove, Illinois, which between 1972 and 1975 became overrun with Chicago suburbanites looking for country bargains and meals.

Here at Midway the outside world stands ready to intervene if not to pounce. Most Midway workers commute to Lexington (25 minutes), Frankfort (30), Versailles (20), and many shop in Louisville (60) or Cincinnati (90). Recently Midway became a target for young house-hunting families who can't buy the big farms of their elders but settle in here, jostling up the cost of houses. On weekends, Midway teems with shoppers from well away.

As I sit in the old corner bank, now the city hall, and while away an afternoon in talk, the outside world of big corporations, bankruptcy of the big city, of congested freeways, high minority unemployment, all dwindle into faraway television images. Midway has few poor, no congestion, and a sense, expressed casually but often with fervor, that here lies the real future of America. Someday those dreadful cities off beyond the white-fenced horizon will blow sky-high and then . . .

## VULNERABLY TAPROOTED

A sitting duck for either refugees from urban troubles or for the next wave of commuters, Midway is unequipped to absorb or to prevent radical change. Larger towns, with a variety of business firms and complex organizations, may absorb what comes, but Midway stands lovely and vulnerable. From here, the monopolistic world of big business and big cities looks to be one giant scheme to wreak the worst and to blow away the best. Here remains a sense of community, of face-to-faceness, of familiar scenes, and of noncataclysmic scale. The current rush to organize neighborhoods in bigger cities appears to be a rush to recreate what the Midways have never lost.

Still tightly clutched in Midway is a sense of and familiarity with landscape and natural processes. This sense is still especially, although not exclusively, Southern. A high percentage of Southerners still maintain psychic if not functional contact with small towns and farming communities, going "back home" for fishing, hunting, reunions, counselling, negotiating. As this percentage dwindles, the South may become less Southern, its taproot anchor to the land less firm, a process that sociologists insist is well under way.

Meanwhile, the nation's economy and its government policies remain biased toward big cities. A 1974 study of "City Size and the Quality of Life" by the Stanford Research Institute concluded that both the current economics of city size and the costs and benefits of government are "either neutral or slightly favorable" to the large metropolises, adding to their continuing magnetism as places to get jobs. "Economics continues to favor the growth of the large if not the largest . . . "

Standing back from all this, on a platform only history can provide, we see the present "flight from the city" as part of a longer historic process, an oscillation that resembles the inhale-exhale pattern of daily commuting—in and out, expansion and contraction—in long historic waves. In the Middle Ages, small shops and industries coalesced in and around the castles, manors, and villages. Then came the early industrial concentration into new mill towns. By the late 1800s in Europe and the U.S., the rush of people toward big city jobs was in full swing.

The counterflow began in the 1920s, when Henry Ford and Detroit made suburban land cheap by making it auto-accessible—a suburbanizing process already begun by the railroads. From the 1940s into the 70s jobs went suburban, following roads and homes, and today the pendulum pauses while millions wait. Will rising gasoline prices and other costs tell us how far we can afford to commute—how far one dare flee from the city in search of that better life in a small town?

I do believe there exists a prospective Southern Solution. It requires determined support of every institution, law, and regulation that makes possible the good life at low densities, which supports the kind of territorial justice that lies behind road, school, irrigation, and other districts that distribute public services—regardless of distance. It requires continued political antagonism toward global, multinational corporations and the U.S. executives who treat small towns as faceless, voteless fiefdoms from which to extract raw materials and profits.

A while back I used the word "romantic" to describe Midway, Kentucky. Romanticism, as an art movement early in this century, and the modern Romantic person share the sense that transformation of one's own world—by design and for the better—is still possible. I would hope that in another generation, Midway will show that the South can retain the best of that potent tradition.

---

# Gudgel's Cove

There can be no rhyme or reason to my discovery of Gudgel's Cove, for it came about during one of those hurried reportorial trips across mid-America. And it was off the beaten path that I stumbled upon Gudgel's Cove, a somewhat-Midwestern-with-a-Southern-exposure sort of town, and even now, some years post-discovery, I continue to turn to it as my own particular touchstone of historical revelation. Gudgel's Cove did not just happen. And, like so many towns that began as a speculator's dream, this, too, was an invention.

They still talk about the day urbanization ended down in Gudgel's Cove. It was on that morning some 40 years ago that young Ezekiel Gudgel woke up, nudged his sleeping wife Nellie awake, and broke the news, "Honey, we've got to move."

That is how urbanization came to a stop in Gudgel's Cove. The outer world knows about this event only through the writings of Ezekiel Gudgel's nephew, who turned sociologist, went North, and was not heard from again until he emerged with, or as, a Ph.D., and immortalized his family, his hometown, Gudgel's Cove, and the end of its urbanization in an oft-reprinted thesis.

History tells us Gudgel's Cove began in the 1830s on the map of an exuberant speculator in western Pennsylvania, his intentions high, his prose gaudy, but his geography meager.

## LUMBER AND GONORRHEA

He founded Gudgel's Cove under another name and his own misapprehension that the local river was navigable. This was true, but only for keelboats whose pilots were drunk. Gudgel's Cove had its first recorded legal trial over the murder of two drunken Pennsylvania loggers by the proprietor of the local brothel, name of Gudgel. The testimony had it that Gudgel was defending not so much the virtue of his young ladies as he was their rights to extraterritorial fees charged out-of-state visitors, a nineteenth-century version of today's speed trap. It turned out that the cudgel that Gudgel used was good material for mayhem, and also for a limerick, the latter unfortunately lost to history.

Because of the limerick, which caught the local judge's fancy, Gudgel was set free, became a local hero and fastened his name upon the growing town.

One kindly historian tells us that the town's major exports were lumber and gonorrhea. Its future economic base seemed to be secured when the first wagon road was opened up across the mountains—a road that, naturally, had been opposed in Congress by representatives of Eastern states for promoting "premature subdivision" in the West. Any geographic determinist could have told Gudgel·that here, at the classic juncture of two modes of transportation, was the beginning of a future megalopolis.

But this was not to be. For the railroad locators who surveyed into this region well before the Civil War knew a boggy hole when they saw one. And so they bypassed Gudgel's Cove, swinging their route away to the north, which was blessed with flat topography. That land also happened to be owned by a member of the state legislature who, along with all his land and most of his fellow-legislators, was up for sale. And so progress and the new railroad main line bypassed Gudgel's Cove.

But it also happened that the railroaders bought up much of the land around Gudgel's Cove and extended spur tracks down into the remaining virgin forests. For the next century, they hauled away most of the timber and coal, leaving behind a pittance in taxes and a populace trained for jobs that gradually ceased to be. In the 1920s an

1-9. They still talk about the day urbanization ended down at Gudgel's Cove, when young Ezekiel Gudgel, dismayed over farming eroded and worn-out land, said to his wife, "Honey, we've got to move." Abandoned farms such as this are the byproduct.

enterprising grandson of one of the old railroaders, fresh out of the New York School of Forestry at Syracuse, discovered a technique for extracting profitable lumber off the cutover hillsides he had inherited, and managed to make money in absentia killing the last of the forests until 1933, by which time they too were gone; not all the tree-planting schemes of the New Deal could bring them back again. That was also the time when the only professional planner ever came to visit and study Gudgel's Cove. He wrote a detailed report that got him the reputation of being "soft on white Appalachians."

That was the winter when the great rains came, and conveyed the eroding hillsides slowly downward into Gudgel's Cove, making the river—as we have come to say about so many others—"too thin to plow and too thick to drink."

That was the last time Gudgel's Cove tried to pass a bond issue. Ever since the fantastic over-bonding of the 1870s, when the captive legislature manufactured windfalls for bondholders by inflating the so-called assets of these little semi-Southern towns, Gudgel's Cove had been voting against bond issues, and this time Ezekiel said, "Honey, it's time to move." And, since Ezekiel first saw the wheel of fate moving away, most of the others have followed, and they would now be lost to us and unrecorded, had it not been for his sociological thesis-writing nephew. For the Ezekiels of the world, black, white, yellow, and in between, have little interest to planners, economists, or even historians when they pack up and leave town.

On the other hand, had Ezekiel been a newcomer, arriving to take a new job in a booming Gudgel's Cove furniture industry, he would have become a producer of "multiplier effects," and therefore the darling of the chamber of commerce, carefully counted by the State Industrial Development Board. The State Commissioner of Commerce would have issued a press release, asserting that for each new basic job like Ezekiel's added to Gudgel's Cove's economy, a multiplier effect would have taken hold, so that instantly, by the miracle of public relations, a magic percentage of point-five, or one-point-nine other new jobs would also have been created as soon as the money from Chicago and Indianapolis and Cincinnati and Louisville and Chattanooga began flowing into the new furniture factory, and into Ezekiel's paycheck, and into and out of his wife's pocketbook, slithering and cascading its way through the local economy.

But what happens when one tries to discover the "negative multipliers," or the "divisors?" Geographers and planners and economists and city boosters grow silent and morose and their files turn unproductive when they confront nonspectacular nongrowth. There's no money to be made in retrogression, and little political capital in stagnancy. Such places are thought to be un-American, guilty of sloth, lack of enterprise, populated by men whose boots have no straps. These nongrowth cities and nongrowing regions tend to disappear from the records. Their image is weak, their imageability tenuous. They become the "nigger districts" of the nation, invisible to the more prosperous, sunk into that other America of city and country ghettos that only in cataclysmic times gets noticed by the dominant majority.

When Ezekiel and his family take off, that fact has little statistical interest—until that horrid day when Gudgel's Cove joins hundreds of other abandoned or declining towns to become an economic disaster area qualifying for large doses of whatever current subsidies are available, or else sends up political hurricane warnings telling of a new third party or populist movement.

I once took part in a journalistic exploration of the Twin Cities, and in Minneapolis had occasion to look at maps of the Upper Midwest Economic Study by geographer John Borchert. They offered a clue to the way we deal with declining regions. Those maps show the growth rate of communities in four categories: "Very Fast" (32 percent or faster), "Fast" (25 to 31 percent), and "Moderate" (11 to 25 percent). All other towns and cities, whether suffering depopulation, slow growth, or merely stability, are lumped into one category labeled "slow or decline." Thus we are accustomed to being four times as precise in our analysis when the Gudgel's Coves are growing.

What else, then, is so special about Gudgel's Cove? First, one cannot find it on a single map, for it is assembled from bits and pieces of my journalistic encounters with many such places scattered throughout the South, New England, the Midwest, and the Ohio Valley. It represents thousands of towns dying on the vine, many of them based on old geographic advantages turned sour, or on mineral resources now exhausted; or else they are towns being slowly sucked dry by distant cities.

## "DECLINING URBAN CENTERS"

It is not unique and it is not alone. Between 1940 and 1960 there were, in the continental United States, 6,034 "declining urban centers," most of them incorporated, and a few of them quite large cities such as Boston and Buffalo. The great majority, 91 percent, had populations of less than 3,000, and part of their problem is due to the fact that they were small in an age when bigness counts.[2]

These Gudgel's Coves were concentrated in eastern and western Pennsylvania, in southern Illinois, in southwestern Iowa—northern Missouri—eastern Nebraska, and another cluster north of Salt Lake City on the Utah-Idaho border.

Urban centers "in relative decline" had spread across the eastern Great Plains, and in the northern Appalachians, especially east-central West Virginia. Meanwhile, depopulation continued in a great region having few towns in the first place—the woodland plantation belt extending for about 700 miles from South Carolina to Louisiana. There was one 70-mile stretch of land in southwest Georgia where little existed except large private holdings of pinewoods for sawmills, bob-white quail for the absentee owner-huntsman, and barbed wire for what was left of the local population.

This is only one sample of the results of industrialized agriculture, encouraged by years of federal policy and subsidy, which kept food prices low for us city folks and drove labor off the land, "freed" from the land, as the saying goes—"freed" to move to the slums of distant northern or western cities. In 10 years from 1950 to 1960, nearly a half-million Negroes and over one million whites lost jobs in Southern agriculture. Considering their wages, living, and working conditions in the fields, they had little choice but to wake up some morning and say, "Honey, it's time to move out." [Widespread farmers' bankruptcies of the 1980s continued the process.]

Such an uprooting and the migration that follows has, for millions of Americans, taken place across Mason and Dixon's Line. It happens that the Ohio River marks one of those great fault lines in the American economy; on either side of it the differences in income, capital formation, college education, and the generation of electricity have continued to be the sharpest in the nation.

As one of the break-points in the American fabric, such a differential exposes the failure of a national political system to accord equal treatment to all its citizens, to each of its regions. Far from being a quibbling trifle, the Mason-Dixon Line, as it is popularly called, still marks regional disparities that once broke the nation apart.

During the Civil War the Mason-Dixon Line was no joke, for it shut Cincinnati off from the Southern trade on which it had grown. After the Civil War, Cincinnati found it necessary to buy the Kentucky legislature in order to get a right-of-way and franchise for its own railroad to "open up" the Southern territory for its trade. Most Southern legislatures during and after Reconstruction were so desperate for industry, for capital from any source, on any terms, that they were wide-open to bribery and chicanery.

## TAKING A WRITE-OFF

Any time a nation "writes off" a whole region, as the South was written out of the national economic and political system for 16 years of Reconstruction and as other regions have been written off—and as urban slums have been written off—by more subtle forms of oversight and neglect, the after-effects are long-lasting and persistent.

And those after-effects include generations of ill-trained, uneducated, deprived, and often desperate millions of people from the backwaters, the dying towns, the mined-out, eroded, nonindustrialized, or disadvantaged regions. The South, of course, had no monopoly on exporting its surplus people, since the economic failures in any region support the booms of another by siphoning off the surplus. This system of exporting population worked well in the days when receiving regions and their cities needed untrained, uneducated, and unexpectant laborers. But the system works less well when the flow of the poor and untrained clog up the central cities and their welfare rolls.

So why should anyone have been surprised when such families, black and white, facing new miseries in the cities of their choice, should turn in the 1960s to robbing one another and to burning and looting in their desperation? So long as exploitation continued to generate the exodus from Gudgel's Cove, "moving out" will continue to be at least a temporary solution.

Ever since my first encounters with the bits and pieces that make up the Gudgel's Cove story, I have been encouraged to continue my research and to bring matters somewhat up to date.

There's been a sudden change of fortune. One of the state's senators inherited (through the railroad branch of the family) a half-interest in several thousand acres of those cutover hillsides upstream from Gudgel's Cove. And, perhaps by coincidence, the U.S. Bureau of Mines conducted a pilot research program in the region. It turns out that beneath those hillsides lie great treasures of hitherto undetected tityllium, baranium, and other rare minerals at depths formerly thought to be too deep for economic mining. The costs of tunnelling were dropping sharply, and everybody knows that a sharp change in costs anywhere inevitably has cataclysmic effects someplace else.

That someplace else happens to be Gudgel's Cove. The town has been inundated by newcomers, black-suited, attache-cased types with helicopters, photogrammetry, and seismographic records nobody in the state knew existed, plus caseloads of printouts on land transactions, ownerships, and acreages—storehouses of knowledge that have quite overwhelmed the county and local officials of

Gudgel's Cove who literally didn't know what they had. In six months, over 50 percent of the land parcels in the county changed hands.

The town's population soon tripled, the water supply ran out every evening by suppertime, the price of a ham'n'eggs breakfast was up from 65 cents to $5.50. The senator's interest in his extensive landholdings had already been syndicated three times, the first time some weeks before the federal bureau's findings were published, and are now split out among hundreds of hungry speculators, some from as far away as Pennsylvania in a complicated reenactment of the speculative drama that had created Gudgel's Cove in the first place 150 years earlier.

The governor declared the town an emergency area and applied for federal disaster-relief on the grounds that the newly discovered minerals were essential to winning the still ongoing war in Vietnam. This caused the first public protest meetings in Gudgel's Cove since the farmers dumped milk in the main street to keep up the prices in 1934. Since most of the protesters were youthful keepers of Gudgel's Cove's conscience, from a state college in the next county, Gudgel's Covers were able to argue they were being inundated by "outside agitators" and petitioned the governor to send in the National Guard to preserve order and maintain production of essential minerals. Only two people were shot, and the local grand jury exonerated the National Guard.

The State Planning Commission had been busy helping fill out forms for the local communities that couldn't translate federal guidelines. Now the commission has been thrown into the Gudgel's Cove fracas after an angry state legislator from that district demanded an investigation into why people were going thirsty in Gudgel's Cove, while radical, long-haired college students were getting all the water they wanted at that college just over the district line.

In this state, the historic function of planning has been to cope with the after-effects of industrialization, which generally meant covering the body to stop the smell without asking who fired the shot. The last place the battle-weary state planners wanted to investigate was Gudgel's Cove. Besides, the only accurate records on water supply are controlled by the private utility company, which is also under attack by the legislature for failing to predict the demand for water. It isn't about to produce records except under subpoena.

The first chapter of Environmental Action, Inc., formed up to ask, "Where do you intend to put the mine refuse?" It turned out that the dumps would be just downstream from the diggings, where lies one of the few lovely secluded stretches of "white water" in the states. It was designated as a "wild river" three years B.D. (before the minerals discovery) by the state planning office at the insistence of the State Department of Tourism as a come-on for tourists. All the landowners along the white water have joined Environmental Action.

The utility company, which gets its high-quality water from that same white-water stretch, is secretly subsidizing Environmental Action. It does this through three anonymous middlemen, hoping to keep its clean water supply at little cost and without getting labeled "do-goodnik."

Just the other day the state planners managed to publish the first draft of a county land-use plan, and nobody was much surprised to find a "special resources zone" encompassing all the syndicated mineral lands and several thousands of acres around them. The traditional purple or black color, used to indicate "industry" on most land-use maps, was abandoned for a more innocuous green color, so as to pick up some of the Environmental Action vote.

Thus at Gudgel's Cove as elsewhere, the process of planning turns out to be surplus disposal. Its function is to ratify the acts and wishes of the dominant industrial interests. And so the land-use plans go their predictably weary way from one angry and frustrating public hearing to the next—until that long awaited day, many years off in the future, when the mining operations, with their dust and old-fashioned disposal methods, are at last declared illegal by the state Supreme Court. (As a matter of record, this will have occurred shortly after it was discovered that the mineral supply was about to be exhausted anyway.)

We are not yet done with Gudgel's Cove. Just the other day I heard of a local entrepreneur who has schemed up a way to franchise flea markets. Out of the gaunt, unpainted houses in the hills and coves around Gudgel's Cove, old men and women survivors are digging out their last "collectibles" for the new markets. As their household goods decant into the roadside markets, Gudgel's Cove appears about to come into its own again as the home of yet another scene of bust and boom.

## NOTES

1. Stephen Rynkiewicz of Oak Park, Illinois, writing in *The Quill*, April 1984.

2. These trends continued into the 1980s, with exaggerated declines noted in many major cities, especially in the old Northeastern states (a.k.a. Rust Belt). See *Urban Decline and the Future of American Cities*, by Katharine L. Bradbury, Anthony Downs, and Kenneth A. Small (Brookings Institution, Washington, D.C. 1982.) But even this prestigious study focuses more upon well-known big cities and their Standard Metropolitan Statistical Areas than upon the relatively obscure but cumulatively important "declining urban centers" of smaller size and fame.

# 2

# Holdout Zones

## Sense
## and Nonsense
## of Place

A new sensation has been set loose in recent years, a subtle shift that has moved beyond its initial penetrations into a few professions and specialties. It breeds new fads and publications. It generates new pressure groups and college courses. And it gives off some, but in its early stages not all, of the effluvium of a Movement.

The focus of all this coalescence has been a growing interest in Place and Places, with a capital P. It has many implications and it is not likely soon to disappear, for quite early in its career it generated a mindset with political overtones.

Are there deep forces at work to create backward and deprived places, to ensure that for every place that prospers there is an equal and opposite place that declines and loses energy? For each and every action, in the classical language of the Second Law of Thermodynamics, is there not an equal and opposite reaction?

The sense of deprivation among have-not nations, regions, and neighborhoods grew by leaps and bounds after World War II, and by the 1980s had fueled a new and obsessive concern with My Place.

This obsession expresses itself variously. On the upbeat sides—in this era of chronic housing shortages—there is the evident and widespread pressure to make the most of one's present place of residence. Vast populations choose a home far below what they would have preferred, and settle in for the long haul; they double

2–1. Buzzwords for the manufacture of a "Sense of Place," found in contemporary real estate advertisements. This mix-and-match grid will help assemble a suitable array of enticements for merchandising purposes.

| | | | |
|---|---|---|---|
| 0 Luxurious | waterfront | estate | (mint condition) |
| 1 Spacious | prestigious | location | (close to . . .) |
| 2 Exclusive | country | horse farm | (great view) |
| 3 Impressive | waterfront | seat | (unique) |
| 4 Commodious | antique | penthouse | (panoramic vista) |
| 5 Unique | restored | place | (rare find) |
| 6 Elegant | English | landmark | (historic ambience) |
| 7 Ultimate | historic | establishment | (all amenities) |
| 8 Gracious | colonial | retreat | (14-foot ceilings) |
| 9 Stately | classic | enclave | (servants' quarters) |

Examples: 0962 = Luxurious classic landmark (great view)
7111 = Ultimate prestigious location (close to . . .)
6969 = Elegant classic landmark (servants' quarters)

---

up, they fix-up, paint-up, make do, and do over. They join and pay their dues to neighborhood protective associations, set up "Neighborhood Watch" signs and willingly over-invest in house, garden, surroundings, and fences, with an obsessive concern that only occasionally extends beyond their neighborhood to their city and their region.

On the downside there is a populistic and close-minded attitude toward one's own Turf—a growing belief that "nobody but us homefolks" has the right to decide, or even to propose, what should happen to our region, our city, our community, our neighborhood, our block, or My Property. The watchwords, fueled in the United States by the Moral Majority and in other nations by Communist or other entrenched ideologies, have become, "If you're not with us, you've gotta be against us!"

On an international level, Third World nations have begun to assert their right to a "developmental point of view" that should be acquired by, or else forced upon the world press, especially Western-nation journalists. "Unless you write positively about us, you must be against us," they assert, meanwhile developing a sophisticated rationale for "developmental journalism." Their views penetrated UNESCO in the early 1980s, and so vigorous and anti-American did their campaign turn that the Reagan administration sought to pull out of UNESCO.

On a local level, neighborhood associations carry out this new feeling of protectionism by entering local politics, stacking council meetings, fighting city hall, obstructing through-traffic, and asserting profound rights to Their Street, Their Place. How many emotions have been set loose in the defense of hundreds of streets against . . . against . . . against . . . and the list grows longer: new traffic lights, through-traffic, trucks, strangers, odd-colored buildings, new and nonconforming architecture, all-day parkers, outsiders of every description.

## POPULISM DIFFUSION

Some of the expanding literature of such political activists is old-fashioned radical populism; its authors are against official power of any sort, whether held by state highway departments, or by planners and designers working for "Big Government." Some of it comes from student radicals of the 1960s who have undertaken the "long march through the institutions" advocated by the late German radical Rudi Deutschke and others—and have come to rest or pause in the environmental movement, on university faculties, and in various bureaucracies.

As a result of these pressures, any developmental proposal must now get clearance, if not formal agreement, from the neighborhood it affects. One Louisville lawyer, who represents suburban land developers and was hamstrung by turf-tending opponents, accosted me not long ago with the argument that " the Neighborhood Plan now supercedes the City-County Plan; it's the first port-of-call to get clearance from." Such is one manifestation of the rise of Place in the new mental landscape.

One of the more eloquent predecessors to this latest outburst was Lawrence Durrell. In his 1969 collection of essays, called *Spirit of Place*, Durrell set an early, airy tone by asserting that "the important determinant of any culture is after all the spirit of place . . . What is the curious constant factor that we discern behind the word 'Greekness'?" he asks. And he answers: "It is surely the enduring faculty of self-expression inhering in landscape."

In his own charming, unscientific way, Durrell asserted that the reason such a powerful religion as Catholicism is different in Ireland, Italy, Spain, and Argentina is that the religion is "subtly modified to suit the spirit of place." And he went on to say, "People have little to do with the matter except inasmuch as they themselves are reflections of their landscape."

With this flat-out declaration of landscape determinism, we are shaped, we are formed, we are brainwashed by Place, according to Durrell.

The word itself has long had connotations of *specialité*. Speak of "our little place in the country," and the listener at once is given to understand that this is, indeed, no little place. Mrs. Hannelore Hahn, publisher of *Places* directory, says it all when she says, "We consult with places" (i.e., with the owners of mansions and estates-for-hire). Artist Allen Gussow in 1971 did a beautiful picture book, *A Sense of Place*, using the phrase as a vehicle from which to dangle a series of American artists' landscape paintings. And, briefly during the 1970s, there appeared *Places*, a quarterly variously out of Palo Alto and Walnut Grove, California. It was a random, opinionated compendium of what passed for wisdom among the anti- and nonurban writers of those times. It was subtitled *A Workingman's Guide to the Universe*, copyrighted by Natural Wonders, Inc. If you find a copy, grab hold; it is a rare example of the down-to-earth movement that still fuels many a local rally, cause, or riot, usually directed against outsiders. On a much more scholarly plane, beginning in 1974, Donald J. Ballas, a geographer living in Indiana, Pennsylvania, started a geographic journal called *Places* (again), but it failed to find a place in the market and disappeared after three years.

## SPIRIT-SNIFFERS

Durrell and these others were only forerunners of the latest interpreters. Today, the power of place is being seized upon by architects, efficiency experts, psychics, and hustlers of every description as their own opening wedge toward power—toward a better "place in the world."

We pick up the story after Durrell et al. with the phrase, "genius of the place," now being given wide currency. Its history goes back to Pagan and Classical Greece, where local gods were real, spooks inhabited their special haunts, and every inhabited place reeked with personalities, characters, and guardian spirits. Closer to our own times, the phrase appeared in a poem by Alexander Pope, "An Epistle to Lord Burlington."

" . . . To build, to plant, whatever you intend,
to rear the Column or the Arch to bend,
To swell the Terras, or to sink the Grot;
In all, let Nature never be forgot.
Consult the Genius of the Place in all
that Tells the waters or to rise, or fall."

The word got around. In the mid-1700s, a British landscape gardener, as they were called then, would advise a client that "the first and most material to consult is the Genius of the Place. What is, is the real guide as to what ought to be."

The most conservative of all admonitions—"What is, is what ought to be," i.e., "Nothing shall be, that has not been before" still permeates the profession of landscape architecture in the Western world and has penetrated the value system of hard-core preservationists and the wider world of preservationists-at-large. The Old, The Valued, The Traditional—the True and Beautiful! It became a well-worn litany, and was enshrined by the Internal Revenue Service, which gave tax breaks to property developers who find "adaptive reuses" for selected and certified remnants from yesteryear.

The subject has been nudged further into public attention by such scholars as Norway's Christian Norberg-Schulz in his 1979 book, *Genius Loci: Toward a Phenomenology of Architecture,* available since 1980 in paperback from Rizzoli. Norberg-Schulz was fawningly taken up by the *Journal of Architecture Education,* its reviewer all too willing to overlook Norberg-Schulz's European bias and dense style, and to see in this book still another weapon for architects to use in their search for relevance.

Make no mistake about it—and Norberg-Schulz was as clear on this point as he was obscure on most others—expressing "the spirit of the place" is the prime function of the building architect. No matter how many buildings of the Modern Movement appear to be totally removed from their site, divorced from their Places—no matter what the evidence, Norberg-Schulz takes comfort from the writings of Le Corbusier and Louis Kahn to argue that now "we (i.e., the architects) may create places which serve the complexities and contradictions of contemporary life." Buildings, he says, are a "means to concretize the genius loci."

Or, if one may interpret him not too broadly: "If we architects can just take over the place, then our buildings will recover their right-to-be and finally establish their identity."

Of all these recent authors, Norberg-Schulz came closest to the admission that no building is complete unless it is well-sited and suitably rooted in its setting; unless it fully exhibits genius of the place. But he appeared unable to shake loose from the assumption that only his fellow-architects were qualified to sniff out the spirit of the place.

Nor is he alone in this frantic casting-about for relevance, this international search for new heroes suitable for enshrinement by the architectural profession. On all sides, architectural theorists such as Robert Venturi have sought new directions and inspirations for structures that, for so long, were firmly rooted in nonplace concepts such as Classical, Contemporary, Modern, and now, Post-Modern.

Not for nothing did Venturi, Charles Moore, and other spokesmen for architecture as currently practiced in the U.S. talk and write about "context." For they, too, had discovered that the roots of architecture, once nurtured by the soil of Classical and later styles, must extend beyond the demands of the client, beyond the styles of European modernists, and discover and exploit the genius of the place.

There is, in fact, a vast horde of engineers and building-architects whose work has consisted of almost total disregard of "the spirit of the place," and whose depredations have brought on worldwide opposition to typical development. So much so, it is easy to forget that, back in the 1960s, there was a huge segment of traditional opinion that greeted the writings of Ian McHarg, author of *Design With Nature*. I recall that when his first published writings appeared in *Landscape Architecture* magazine under my editorship, they were greeted with scorn by traditionalists as being "not landscape architecture." By now his particular technique for arriving at the genius of the place has been widely accepted, internationally copied, and duly criticized.

It is also worth noting that historic preservationists by the 1970s had embarked on a large expansion of their own profession. They, too, had been first hooked on buildings—on historic houses where George Washington slept, or where their own, largely Anglo-Saxon, ancestors had lived. They, too, have finally "leapt the garden wall" and taken all the manmade landscape within their scope, if not their grasp. And they, too, are properly concerned with interpreting or discovering the genius of the place, although usually on historical terms. The Texas A & M booklet, *Maintaining the Spirit of Place*, is a good example of the drive to preserve through identification and publication.

The rash of new books in the 1980s reached a peak in 1983, when several books were on the "must" list for place-freaks. One of the best efforts to capitalize on this movement was *The Sense of Place*, by Fritz Steele, a management specialist who consults to business and industry "on organizational and environmental change." He coauthored another book called *The Feel of the Work-Place*.

Steele's was probably the most straightforward, nonacademic book available on the subject, and its 91-item bibliography (almost exclusively of books published since the early 1960s) an excellent, although historically shallow, shopping list for beginners. He wrote with none of Norberg-Schulz's turgidity, and emerges as a somewhat withdrawn professional advisor, looking at places for their experience-generating power, urging his readers to wake-up-and-live.

Once past these interpretations, we should look briefly into a new field of place-makers' books, mostly by professional designers and planners. Two of the recent best are *Place Makers*, by Ronald Lee Fleming and his wife Renata von Tscharner, and *Common Ground*, by Fleming and Lauri A. Halderman. The former ran some of the same course as Richard Wurman's book of a decade ago, *Making the City Observable*, but focuses on "public art that tells you where you are." Fleming's work is a well-organized compendium of 47 examples, or "profiles," each with the necessary seed-catalog information (name, project, artist, agency, etc.) and each with a summary of background, description, and design impact. The second Fleming book focuses exclusively on the idealized, New England town greens and commons, as they might be improved upon and adapted to cities elsewhere. (A 1987 book, *New Providence: A Changing Cityscape*—is a superb example of scene-shifting.)

And, as inspirational reading, the Washington clearinghouse called Partners for Livable Places publishes monthly "The Magazine of Livability" entitled, as would be apparent by now, *Place* (subscriptions are $24 per year from Partners for Livable Places, 1428 Twenty-First Street, Washington, D.C. 20036). Full of peptalk and Good

Examples, most issues of *Place* report on Good Places in the U.S. and abroad, and serve as a vehicle for free planning-and-design advice.

## THE NEW NARCISSI

All the foregoing is but a sampling of the vast outpouring of self-conscious and place-conscious writings that permeated the book-stores of North America. The United States had embarked upon the same sort of self-conscious splurge as Canada has endured for the past decade. It is an inundation of narcisisstic books—handbooks, guidebooks, mapbooks, how-to books—that examine, often uncritically and sometimes ineptly, every facet and shade of Us and Our Place. Few memorable places are now unpublished in Canada, and the place-consciousness that infuses the U.S. books mentioned here is far from running out of steam.

Nor is place-interpretation by any means exhausted as an academic hunting-ground. As a sample, I was asked to come to two universities in 1984-85 to present seminars on "How Places Work" and to summarize a conference on historic interpretation for museum directors, and my mail has been loaded with announce-ments of this or that program about The Sense of Place.

More is at hand: two new periodicals, both place-named. The first, *Place*, is a quarterly with editors at the University of California-Berkeley and the Massachusetts Institute of Technology, and spon-sored by M.I.T. Press. Its first two editors are well known: Donald Lyndon, of the architectural faculty at Berkeley, succeeding the late Donald Appleyard, and William L. Porter, who has headed M.I.T.'s Department of Architecture.

They assert the journal to be "a home for designers and others who believe that the ultimate test of a place comes from those who use and live in it. We will look at the production of places, their creation, management, and evolution."

The second periodical, started in 1978, is a biennial called *Places*, its 1982-83 edition having a circulation of 10,000. Out of New York, it has become a compendium of interesting, unusual, and often historic "places" (read mansions, estates) available for rent for parties, conferences, and the like. In order to get your Place listed, it must have a certain "ambience," according to the publisher.

Here we go back to Lawrence Durrell, back to eighteenth-century England, back to the Greeks. "That certain ambience" could well be called Genius Loci, or the Spirit of the Place.

All this commotion around the notion of place may be no more than the death struggle of territoriality—the last-ditch efforts by millions of locally oriented citizens who watch their world "going national" around them. They see mom-and-pop stores replaced by chain drive-ins, and handmade local tools and antiques snapped up by outsiders paying astronomical (i.e. nonlocal) prices. They see their local stores replaced by chains. Their familiar countryside is smeared by television scriptwriters as being Noplace, far out in the boondocks; their local accents are mocked by experts from fields of knowledge that hover in what Melvin Webber called "the Non-Place Realm." The citizens of overlooked and by-passed localities will provide a market for place-oriented books so long as the contrast between This Place and Other Places manages to survive or can be contrived.

### KNOWING ONE'S PLACE

By far the most profound and original contribution to this new introspection is J. Ronald Engel's *Sacred Sands,* a pioneering exposition of the spiritual, religious, and political emanations from that unique stretch of wind-formed dunes along the southern shore of Lake Michigan in Indiana.

Engel's is a serious effort to proclaim the gospel of place in historic terms, not so much as the focus for an individual's sense of a particular environment, but as a focus for community affection and action. Love of one's place in the United States has been uniquely expressed in citizen and community movements. This attitude fostered within the nineteenth-century Progressive Movement a "sense of responsibility for the land" and what Engel calls "the religion of democracy."

The story of the dunes is not yet over. This transitory, ever-changing, and threatened scene is perceived by Engel as a pageant, continuing the actual Dunes Pageant of 1907. In this pageant, "the passage of humanity across the landscape is meaningless apart from the great struggle for community—the struggle between those who sought to cooperate and use the wealth of the world (i.e., the dunes) for the good of all beings, and those who sought to use it selfishly for their own aggrandizement." In the 1890s, when the Indiana Dunes were the focus of an intense movement, the study of dunes ecology fitted into the then-current ideas of progressive social evolution. The idea of "community" became enlarged to include the environment, and the new study of ecology began to emphasize the unity and interdependence of all forms of being.

Engel's use of the term "religion" in his book goes a long way to explain the fervor that penetrates the conservation movement and occasionally fuels debates between conservationists and developers.

All the foregoing suggests to me that "sense of place" is a sociological invention, informed by interactions that are socially determined. Cripples who move amongst us with shudder and shake are hidden away by many societies so that they interact only barely and briefly with the outdoor environment. They know an environment far differently from the way a peasant knows his. Thus, knowing one's place is culturally learned. To know one's place is to know one's self in the fullest sense of the word. Places where one lives and works in a place-conscious society have much to do with shaping one's view of the world. As we enter the nonplace realm of computerized inputs, are we not in danger of losing that most primitive of all abilities—to know one's place in the world?

And poking over the horizon, the ancient Japanese art of ecomancy and the Chinese profundities of geomancy have for long been sending out early signals to the West. Returning scholars have been bringing back ancient wisdom from these two vast bodies of place-awareness. Niccos Rossides, writing about ecomancy in *Ekistics* (July-August 1982), noted that "ecomantic principles and techniques have their roots mainly in the Chinese disipline of fung shui, which can be defined as a body of rules designed to adapt man's habitat to the mystical forces of the universe." Its basis lies in the Taoist resonance theory of the universe, which holds that the cosmos consists of one interrelated field of energy. The ecomantics are, in fact, trying to discern what we might call the energy fields of nature, and insist that no study of place is complete without an understanding of the solar, stellar, lunar, and compass points to which a place or site is aligned.

This may seem less than pertinent to hardrock rationalists. But I recently learned of a large property on the Ohio River that was purchased by a Hong Kong investor. The deal was consummated only after his family's "spiritual advisor" (read geomancer) had arrived from Hong Kong, obtained the exact latitude and longitude of the property, in minutes and seconds, and only then was he willing to interpret and approve—as you may have guessed by now—the spirit of the place.

Books mentioned above include:

*The Sense of Place,* by Fritz Steele. Boston: CBI Publishing Company, Inc., 1981. 216 pp. Illus. $21.50.

*Genius Loci: Toward a Phenomenology of Architecture,* by Christian Norberg-Schulz. New York: Rizzoli Press, 1980. 213 pp. Illus. $19.95.

*Place Makers: Public Art That Tells You Where You Are,* by Ronald Lee Fleming and Renata von Tscharner. New York: Hastings House Publishers, 1981. 128 pp. Illus. $9.95 (paperback).

*Maintaining the Spirit of Place: A Guidebook for Citizen and Professional Participation in the Preservation and Enhancement of Small Texas Towns,* by Harry Launce Garnham. College Station, Texas: Texas A & M University Press, 1976. 83 pp.

*Places: A Quarterly Journal of Environmental Design.* M.I.T. Press/ Journals, 28 Carleton St., Cambridge, Mass. Initial subscription, $25.

*Places: Public Places for Private Events and Private Places for Public Functions.* New York: Tenth House Enterprises. Biennial. 220 pp. $16.95.

*Sacred Sands, The Struggle for Community In the Indiana Dunes,* by J. Ronald Engel. Middletown, Conn.: Wesleyan University Press, 1983. 352 pp. Illus. $22.95.

---

# Prairie
# Preservation

Flat out on the prairie 35 miles west of Chicago's Loop, spread across a landscape that looks like a giant farm gone to grass, sits one of the largest manmade structures in North America, a nuclear accelerator ring and its laboratories. They stretch nearly two miles across the green horizon—land, lakes, greenbelt, laboratories, and other apparatus covering 7,000 acres.

"Never again," we are told, will this be farming country. The rich, deep black prairie soil is now said to be "permanently" under grass, forest, and the control of federal agencies and contractors. That old fluke of national atomic policy that spread more than 200 million federal dollars across this landscape also sets it up as a peculiar federal reserve, somewhat open to the public, and labeled as a "permanent" greenwedge.

As our sightseeing bus, filled with planners from a Chicago
conference and labeled "Mobile Workshop," approaches the National Accelerator Laboratory from the south, we pass Fox River
East, a 4,200-acre shopping center and housing development by
Urban Investment and Development Corporation, Chicago, "one of
a series of mini-towns," says its design director. ("Another thunder-
bolt they're throwing out at these small towns that don't know
what's hitting them," growls a local planner on my bus.) We view
huge stockpiles of black topsoil, eventually to be converted into
berms, mounds, and other forms described as "new landscape
features." For the moment they have become much-used by local
sportsbike riders who careen up and down the steep slopes.

Now we approach the heart of NAL turf—a new buffalo herd on
our right, possibly a future meat supply? Soon we see remnants of
Weston, Illinois, which is now called NAL Village, consisting only of
strings of gaudy-painted houses, primary blues, reds, oranges
never seen on the real prairie except on barns. Oddly scattered on
our left are old farmhouses, assembled from some of the former 81
farms on the site. They seem to stagger drunkenly across the
landscape, turning their corners to the road, something to be

examined more closely once we get off the bus.

Visual confusion persists as we move northwest on Batavia and D Roads. The 17-story central laboratory office structure looms above the prairie, located as formally as if this were a Versailles palace for electronic Ph.D.s. Outbuildings seem to tumble playfully about like painted children's toys rolled out on a giant's lawn for visiting cousins.

Later I return for a closer look at those white farmhouses so queasily perched about the prairie. Indeed they do appear foreign to this place, plunked down around a new curving, 1970-type subdivision road in positions that none of them would have occupied on their original farmstead. Some squat in low spots—which a good Illinois farmhouse never, never does—suggesting wet floors and accumulating snow. Only one house rests on its original location, high and dry on a slight rise. Most of the others slant away at odd angles from the main road, slaunchwise, out of context, alien to their new locations. No barns, no outbuildings, and few trees yet to anchor them familiarly to the land. Even though this is essentially a land of Swell and Swale (to borrow the title of a beautiful prairie flower book by photographer Torkel Korling, who lives in the

2–2. At "NAL Village," of the farmhouses reassembled on the Illinois prairie, only one house (right) still rests easily in its original location. Most of the others slant away from the main road, out of context even to their new locations, having no outbuildings and few trees to anchor them familiarly to the land.

western suburbs), whoever cast about with these houses could not tell the difference between swell and swale, high and low, fit and misfit.

Later when I describe this to Prof. Amos Rapoport at the University of Wisconsin-Milwaukee, he snorts with scorn and recalls how the Danes recreated a farm village near Copenhagen by salvaging old farmhouses from an urbanizing landscape. They had taken care to recreate the original landscape in which those houses set, down to such details as manufacturing a knoll and swamp so that the displaced farmhouse would exhibit its historic relationship to its classic flatland setting. One of those farmhouses, I recall from my own visit, had been turned over to the family of the metropolitan park district's chief landscape architect. They fitted in beautifully.

Merely to save old buildings out of some nostalgic impulse is not enough. Nineteenth-century farmhouses grafted onto suburban lots lose meaning and associations, which are the precise qualities for which they were to be moved and saved. In such details, as in the larger landscape, this vast NAL spread is the result of high-level decision making that lost touch, perhaps never had the slightest grasp of those details that normally unify buildings and their landscape—slope, local drainage, microclimate, existing trees and vegetation, and the details of local building tradition.

All across the Midwest, cities still expand, sending out their "thunderbolts," their land-buyers and commuters, to alight in small towns and impact the open countryside. Wherever they alight, it makes good sense to build upon existing settlements, to expand them carefully and to pay attention to the way things were—which were the way-they-were usually for quite practical reasons. The study of landscape history, which I gather is coming to be a hot academic subject with many future jobs in prospect, offers lessons for all such urbanization—not slavish imitation of some romanticized past, but careful digging-out of the reasons, the rationale, for settling these places in these particular ways. Such lessons went unheeded in the creation of this oddly beautiful and equally disturbing NAL countryside.

# Savannah
## Miasma

Fog in the early morning blocks my view of the flat road through the pinewoods. I am in a thin, vague line of motorists, feeling our way. We slow to a hesitant crawl, our lights gleaming through the murk and my eyes not yet fully attuned to this in-between land of half-light.

Still rich in memory are South Carolina's wide beaches, dotted with their colorful vacationers, and the brightly zip-a-toned land-use maps on the office walls at Hilton Head Island, where the developer, Charles Fraser, is expanding his Sea Pines Plantation. All of us consultants from near and far have been caught up in the enthusiasms of a promoter's golden dream come true. Fraser's properties are selling like hotcakes, and only much later would he find himself over-extended when the Arabian oil embargo suddenly punctured the enthusiasm that fueled the Sea Pines lot sales.

And so, the beaches far behind, peering intently at the grey scene ahead, I speed up toward the distant airfield at Savannah, hoping to catch the nine o'clocker for Atlanta.

Finally, we come out of the fog and drive over the wide expanse of salt marsh, with Savannah's modest skyline like dominoes along the river bluff ahead. And all across the marshes, a thin but growing cloud of . . . fog? As it grew nearer, I marveled again at the great green expanse of tidewater marsh, for scenes such as this one had fastened themselves to my emotions long before. As a child I had vacationed at St. Simonds Island on the Georgia coast, and shared a frightened family "escape" across the marshes just ahead of a hurricane up from the Caribbean. I recalled many a trip from marsh to mainland and back when I was in my early 20s, girl-chasing in Savannah.

Now the grey cloud poured through my car, filled my lungs, its smell catching in my throat, rousing fierce memories. What stench is coming off this lovely expanse of green? I slowed the car, peered across the marshes, and finally made the connection. Way yonder was the source, the largest kraft paper mill in the world, Union Camp's huge enterprise downriver from Savannah.

Without warning my eyes filled with tears. I pulled the car off the road to a complete stop, shut the engine, crying uncontrollably. For minutes I cowered there in the front seat, self-conscious as other drivers slowed and peered at what might be just another drunk. The fumes stayed with me. Gradually the shock of finding such a place of beauty so overrun with the stench of the beast ran its course, and finally I could wipe away the last tears and shake off the remaining shudder, and start out again through the white cloud that spelled Progress in Savannah.

Much later the story came out and a familiar one it was. How Union Bag and Paper Company, as it had been called, had moved into Savannah in the 1930s, buying up the cheap lands off to the horizon, some bought outright, some leased for forest cropping. And the key to the pungent grey cloud lay in the agreements signed by Savannah's officials back during that Great Depression, anxious to get and keep jobs that Union Bag would provide. Savannah agreed to hold the company exempt from municipal attack for its polluting clouds. If there were lawsuits, the city and not the company would pay damages.

"Welcome to Georgia," says the sign as I cross the Savannah River, and the clock tells me I have an hour to kill before plane-leaving. And what better to do in Savannah than to saunter as slowly as a car can saunter down Bull Street? Here is the city's historic spine with city hall at its river end, and the pineywoods and a military airfield far to the south—Savannah's history as a garrison town (the first Georgia colonial settlement set up by England in 1636).

Old houses, preserved houses, freshly painted houses (one of them, I learn, in a bright burnt orange that is called Savannah Peach Melba), and Historic Houses proclaim their presence. Then south on Whittaker, one of the Great Old Streets, still lined with Historic Houses already marked on the nation's first Historic Register. The Peter Meldrim House, where General William Tecumseh Sherman put up as occupying commander in 1864(5) . . . At Gaston Street and Bull, the former home of Henry R. Jackson was Union Army headquarters during the Civil War occupation, and is now the Oglethorpe Club, Members Only, a handsome two-story brick house, raised one level above the street.

## TO TURN IS TO LEARN

But the trip grows monotonous: all this history and unending Improvement. The western side of Whittaker opposite Forsythe Park is Mansion Row, a fine array of houses left from those great rice and cotton bonanzas between the Revolution and Civil wars. It has a distinctive English, rather than French look. But I've had enough of all this, and turn off, onto a side street to head west.

I am in another world within a half block. Huntingdon Street has turned from brick to dirt, and as I drive slowly west the car bounces from chugholes. There are junked cars in the side yards, totally empty tenement houses. I circle around the block to double-check these first impressions on Barnard, Tatnall, Gaston, Park, and other streets. The pattern repeats: Off the grand avenue opposite the park the faces go from white to black, the cars from new to rusty, the street from brick to brickbat; the trees grow sparser, grass turns weedy, the gutters trashy, and the evidence is clearly that of a low-income neighborhood cheek by jowl with the high-prestige district along Forsythe Park. "Yes, it's great that rich and poor can live so close together," a well-dressed Savannah woman has said to me at a party in Hilton Head. "But we do send our children to separate private schools. I haven't got the courage to change that yet."

Much later, I describe this experience to a psychologist, for by this time I had gone back over my own tape-recorded comments as I had turned off Forsythe into the lower-class side streets, and was astounded at the suddenly increased volume of commentary.

"Of course," said the psychologist. "You were in strange territory. No doubt you felt it to be hostile country. If we'd had you properly hooked up, we'd have a perfect record. Your pulse was probably faster, your pupils dilated, skin moist, breath shallow . . . Your whole metabolism was geared up for the unexpected. . . . "

Soon the plane was off the runway, the pineywoods stretched away to the horizon, and Savannah far behind, the Union Camp's feathery plume of grey still spreading over the marshes of green.

---

# Trekking
# on Down
# to Kodachrome
# Town

Packed into Anne Hathaway's cottage in Shakespeare Country, I stand behind Spaniards, more arriving by the busload. Waiting to cross a London street, I am warned to "look left" for traffic. At country intersections, yellow-painted "AA" emergency trucks wait for me to get lost or into accidents while ads and signs in several languages warn or entice me, special maps guide my path, and special guides map my sights.

I am a tourist, one among millions on their worldwide pilgrimages, equipped, propagandized, shepherded, processed, and inducted, as our group has been, into the mysteries of Great Britain's landscape. Little has been left to chance as this landscape has been converted into a Sight, where John Bull has turned hotel-keeper, where Merrie England has its latch string out, its out-stretched hand to catch the touristic dollar, dinar, yen, mark, and franc. (When I was a tourist, the dollar was falling, but could still buy a pound at $1.84.)

Like Moslems to Mecca, Crusaders on their treks, today's sight-seers "doing England" are being subjected to well-organized doses of that worshipful form of religiosity known as Tourism.

Tourism has taken over the roads, inns, and the basic economy so as to arouse the envy of other nations hankering for a bigger slice of the touristic dollar. Tourists spent around five billion pounds in Britain in 1978, some two-thirds of it by foreigners. Londoners have been the first to complain that their streets, sidewalks, hotels, restaurants and whole districts are now usurped by inflationary tourists who not only spend more money, but occupy more public space per person than natives.

In five visits since 1958, I have watched Britain become a world model of tourism development, its landscape increasingly regulated, ordered, managed, tended, repaired, planted, and maintained for show.

The English landscape works in other ways, of course; its farms are intensively managed for high production, little of its land is under-used, and the intensity of land use is increasing. Fields of buttercups and poppies are a vanishing sight, according to the Countryside Commission's 1977 study, *New Agricultural Landscapes*, and farming practices within the main agricultural regions are becoming more uniform. Fires are highly visible. Burning of wheat chaff is widespread; an American tourist in September will be reminded of the U.S. South in winter, when pine forests are burned after the quail hunting season to promote new grass growth for cattle. Many of Britain's wheat farmers combine today, burn tomorrow, and cultivate for a new crop the day after, so that smoke on the horizon means wheat in the bin.

2–3. Originally designed to keep
marauders at bay, the Roman wall
around the historic English town of
Chester was reconstructed in the
Middle Ages and now provides
tourists an upper level route around
the half-timbered shopping district,
right. The town is gradually
undergoing "Middle-Aging" in
conformity with historical
guidelines.

Bright blue on many a farmstead stands the tall Harvestore, a
metal glass-lined silo. Silage cutting and storage are on the increase,
as is the feeding of cattle year-round in buildings, and beyond such
processes the British farmers are increasing the size of their fields,
cutting old hedgerows, filling or straightening ditches. Such
changes since 1945 are "almost as extensive as those which have
occurred during the 'enclosure movement' (sixteenth to eighteenth

2-4. Happy the land where productive Holsteins graze on newly expanded, mechanized farm pastures, against a backdrop of smaller fields that remind visitors of Wales's ancient walled field pattern from the Middle Ages.

centuries)," according to the 1977 Countryside Commission survey. In parts of Britain you can readily imagine Illinois and Iowa, the scale is that large. As in Iowa or Illinois, the high-yield farming districts are so mechanized that to see a walking farmer in a field is a rare thing indeed.

### STAGE BUSINESS

Yet, even in the high-yield farming districts, yard and field work has become a form of stage management. Farming must not be merely efficient; it must also look right. For in a nation that counts on tourism for income, landscape becomes an essential stage setting that must be managed for touristic expectations. In one sense, that is what much of town and country planning is all about in Britain today. Support for the heavy burden of land-use regulations comes from millions of Britons who now depend on tourism for income. Picturesque pays.

As evidence of conflicting pressures, the editor of *Country Life* magazine as early as 1974 was complaining that English farmers—discriminated against by Common Market regulations—were being forced to plan accommodations for tourists "when they ought to be concentrating on the production of food."

The ubiquitous stone walls—along thousands of miles of roads and fields—speak clearly of a landscape that was organized first for defense and small-scale farming but is now being reorganized to accommodate the pervasive invasion of tourists. Many landowners raise new fences or tend old ones to keep out picnickers and day-trippers. Above all, it is a landscape that has been scrupulously examined and mapped: America has nothing to compare with the Ordinance Survey maps at several scales—my favorite for auto travel being the One Inch Series (one inch on the map equals one statute mile on the ground). They're for sale at most bookstores, as are Automobile Association ("AA") maps, which put most products of the American Automobile Association to shame.

A huge publishing industry has expanded around tourists—maps, pamphlets, signs, posters, guidebooks, specialty books on endless subjects. Towns such as the Roman city of Chester have Official Guidebooks of high quality; a good bookstore will yield a dozen histories of any middle-sized city. Airports are something else; tourists may encounter huge military airports that do not appear on most maps.

From antiquity the art of landscape observation and analysis has been highly developed. I picked up a 1939 reissue of *Brittania*, a handsome book of John Ogilby's maps of English roads in 1675 that must have been a godsend to the few tourists and travelers of that time. Today hundreds of towns, counties, and special districts have their own historical maps for the tourist.

Thus all of touristic England is being organized into Settings. Such stage settings or touring districts cover thousands of miles. Their numbers vary. The British Travel and Holidays Association in 1978 listed 11 (Lake District, Shakespeare Country, West Country, North East Highlands, Lowlands, Wales, Northern Ireland, South Coast, East Anglia, London and Around London). Each of these regional showplaces has its managers, its special audience, its claque.

## SIGHT COUNTRY

One such setting that has long aroused my interest was The Cotswolds, a region of low rolling hills some 20 by 65 miles in area, bounded by the Severn and Thames River valleys, 80 miles north-

2-5. Although located off center on the Welsh coast, the stage setting resort of Portmerion—the lifetime hobby of architect Clough Williams-Ellis—is a favorite for honeymooners, filmmakers, and architecture buffs. Its bits and pieces of castles and forts form a pastiche of composed vistas, clinging to steep slopes.

2–6. Preservation pays developers: in this case, new houses arrayed in clusters vaguely reminiscent of seventeenth century English villages, but conforming to historic preservation rules for stone walls and site plan.

2–7. Free flows the water through a disued industrial canal at Salford, near Manchester, England. Once 50 cotton mills flourished here; now tourism is a growth industry. So old canal paths are cleared, and hardstands are paved for busloads of camera-toting visitors.

west of London. Farming for 1,500 years has ironed out the wrinkles, smoothed the fields, tidied the edges, straightened the ditches; 80 to 100 generations of savages, Romans, medievalists, and today's commercial farmers have walled, barned, housed, hedged, and fenced the countryside until it looks exactly like the postcards that mirror these stage sets functioning as landscape.

There are no billboards, no littered roadsides, no visible dumps, few woods. Most of the dairy cows are black-and-white Holsteins (all of England's milkers are deserting the Jersey, Guernsey, and other old breeds). The towns and walls are limestone, whole villages immured in lovely tan stone that is kept fresh for the next busload of snapshotting tourists. Special legal protections hover over all such towns and landscape. Since the Town and Country Planning Act of 1947 made planning compulsory the country over, it has been revised and tightened (although drastically relaxed since this was written.) Most of England has now been "planned" for some 30 years. Planning permission must be obtained, usually from a local authority, for any land development, and in special districts this translates to mean that nothing may be changed—no new signs, no old walls rebuilt or razed—without official hearings and all that bureaucratic jazz. Historic landscapes are especially ringed-about with prohibitions. Tourists in 1990 can expect Chipping Camden in The Cotswolds to appear almost exactly as it did in 1978—a lovely bug in legal amber.

The gospel according to St. Bartholomew the Map Maker tells us that in such touristic territory no venerable stone shall be left unidentified, no pilgrimage unmarked, no rites of passage administered without proper certification. To become a tourist one must assume a reverential stance, one that grants the sanctification of Sights as worthy of our worship.

Even though the new religion of Tourism requires that The Way encompass an eight-lane superhighway as well as narrow lanes once trod by revered early pilgrims, there is no escape from the universal sanctification that has been spread across the British countryside.

Shocking as it may be to describe Tourism as a form of religion, the parallels are inescapable. These implications have been explored more fully by Prof. Dean MacCannell, of the University of California-Davis, in a prescient little book called *The Tourist, A New Theory of the Leisure Class* (1976, Shocken Books, New York).

For travelers who think they're merely enjoying themselves, MacCannell suggests that tourists are really searching for modernity. The tourist seeks a universal, religious experience of being up-to-date as a form of expertise in an increasingly specialized world. Sightseeing is "a ritual performed to the differentiation of society . . . a collective striving for transcendence . . . an effort to pack all the differences of a complex world into a single ideology . . . a collective quest for a higher moral authority in a godless universe."

Thus millions of us get caught up in what MacCannell calls "extensive ceremonial agendas involving long strings of obligatory rites." Instead of using the Bible, we prepare for our journeys with Baedeker, Murray, Blue, and other guides to holy lands. We read up ahead of time on Sights; we memorize the names of places Everybody Must Visit; we join like-minded groups of worshippers, travel in caravans, read from catechisms (guidebooks), respond to the guidance of the priest (tour guide); we dismount, stand in reverential awe at appropriate relics, take out special equipment (cameras) for memorializing the Sight.

## BECOMING PILGRIMS

Ordinary citizens from halfway around the world are transformed by propaganda, advertising, and national promotions into pilgrims seeking the personal, certified validity that comes from Having Been There, of being an eyewitness participant in a significant happening. The biweekly Changing of the Guard at Buckingham Palace causes one of London's largest recurrent traffic jams. Many such events are now scheduled, advertised, and reshaped for larger crowds. But our expectations and perceptions are also different. As certified Tourists we require not simple scenes but landscapes filled with symbols, signs, and activities. Mundane scenes are transformed for our benefits; here come the Ancient Bellringers, the costumed Militia, reenacting some Historic Moment.

Thus engaged in an active rigmarole of communing with historic landscapes, our pilgrimages require endurance and ready cash. And the owners of these ritualized sites cash in on the bonanza, just as merchants in Mecca or hoteliers in Washington, D.C., benefit from the pilgrims who come to worship at holy or patriotic shrines. Instead of bringing back Crosses, we snap Kodachromes and buy postcards to prove our presence at holy places. We are thus transformed as much as the sights themselves, becoming more complex persons with needs for cameras, campers, walking sticks, hiking shoes, foul weather gear, maps, signs, schedules, and guides to ease us through the ritualistic encounters.

What is lacking in MacCannell's ingenious exposition of tourism-as-religion is a theological base. It has no true saints, no Savior, nor a God. Yet tourists act as though they were responding to the same powerful stimuli that drove Crusaders marauding across the Middle East. Conversely, the literature of preservationists who oppose touristic developments is full of Crusader-type zeal against savages, infidels, heathen, and other lower orders who despoil the virginal countryside, besmirch the holy places, snatch the holy relics.

I have not watched this process with much care lately outside North America and Great Britain, but there is accumulating evidence that as tourism expands worldwide, this transformation of plain, everyday landscape into significant Sights is well under way. Several landscape architects in Britain have described the requirements for managing landscapes converted into Sights and Settings.

There is, in fact, a fine little paperback book of instructions for those whose job is to prepare buildings and countryside for touristic viewing. It is *The Countryside on View* by Elizabeth Beazley (Christopher Davies Publishers Ltd., 4/5 Thomas Row, Swansea SA1 1NJ, 1971, 206 pp., $4.95). It describes "some of the many ways in which those going into the country may find out about what they have come to enjoy," and offers helpful hints for locating information centers and routing tourists in and out of Sights with minimum delay and damage. And, commendably enough, the author offers advice on how to stimulate the tourist to "go out and see for himself" rather than lounge about indoors.

For the stage managers, a whole new level of expertise is required, and a knowledge of history—of how the Sight and Setting came to be—is now essential. "Civilizations which respected the past have also respected nature, and wonderfully adapted their settlements to the landscape," wrote historian Golo Mann not long ago in *Encounter* magazine; even as a German, he could surely have been speaking of the English.

Like all holy mysteries, this one has plenty of hokum, bunkum, and mush for the outsider and nonbeliever to sort though. But I have no doubt, looking back on my somewhat agnostic comments on this worldwide crusade, that the world that tourism has made is indeed being transformed before and behind our very eyes.

2–8. 'Twould never do for visitors to
find unkempt the bright civic flowers
of coastal resorts in Wales, especially
since this oceanside promenade at
Llandudno is overlooked by blocks
of tourist hotels' verandas.

## A REJOINDER

Grady Clay is half-right about the English landscape. But what he has wrong about it could further the demise of the countryside he believes is so well-managed for tourist shows. The admired English landscape is the product of loving care over many centuries. But it is increasingly difficult to protect this landscape against those who exploit it for purely productive uses.

Tourism is not only one of Britain's strongest and fastest growing industries; it is the major factor in Britain's favorable balance of payments. And as Marcus Binney and Max Hanna show (*Preservation Days*, Save Britain's Heritage, London, 1979), Britain's architectural and landscape heritage is the main drawing card for overseas visitors and natives alike. Visits to historic buildings and areas in 1977 netted Britain at least half a billion pounds, the central government collecting 60 million pounds in direct taxes.

Nothwithstanding this tourist bonanza and increasing domestic interest in preservation, Britain provides only token support for conservation. Total grants from the Department of the Environment's Historic Buildings Council in 1977-78 were only 4.6 million pounds, less than one-tenth of the government receipts from tourist taxes. The sums available for managing ancient monuments, for listing and recording historic buildings, and for matching grants to local authorities for conservation have actually declined over the past two years. In the face of imminent threats to country houses, churches, and cathedrals, official apathy is notorious. Industrial archeology has begun to attract widespread public interest but is largely ignored by government. An exhibition of Pennine Woolen Mills (Satanic Mills: Industrial Architecture in the Pennines, R.I.B.A. Heinz Gallery, London) showed that Britain is in danger of losing its most magnificent and evocative relics of the Industrial Revolution, which transformed the whole world. In all these areas of preservation, Britain, so rich in historical resources, lags far behind the United States.

It is in the British countryside, though, that the risk of destruction is most grave. Planning controls in cities and towns may act as a brake against untoward development or deliberate demolition, though they are powerless to prevent loss through neglect and decay—more than 1,000 buildings listed by the Department of the Environment as having special architectural or historic interest have disappeared in the past three years, and more than 25,000 listed buildings are derelict and in desperate need of help (George Allan and Timothy Cantell, "Left to Rot," *Architects' Journal*, November 22, 1978). But no planning controls whatever govern farming and forestry operations—the activities that dominate most of the English countryside. Unlike householders or factory operators, farmers and foresters are free to make whatever changes in land use and management they wish. Hence the shocking changes Grady Clay reports—uprooting hedgerows, enlarging fields to suit mammoth machines, draining wetlands, transforming much of England's small-scale patchwork quilt of arable land, pasture, and rough land into a monotonous, featureless, Illinois-type prairie.

Even in Britain's national parks no extra controls over farming exist, though park authorities may require farmers to give notice of intention to plow up moorland (Britain's national parks remain mostly in private hands). But the national parks are primarily in upland areas, where mountain and moorland landscapes are less threatened in any case by modern agriculture and are less crucial to the national heritage than the traditional landscapes of lowland England. Most valued by overseas visitors and Britons alike, lowland England is almost wholly unprotected against large-scale agricultural change (David Lowenthal and H.C. Prince, "English Landscape Tastes," *Geographical Review,* 1965). "Most of Britain has been 'planned' for some 30 years," claims Grady Clay; but countryside planning is a mockery of conservation. The designation of specially attractive landscapes, mainly in the lowlands, as "Areas of Outstanding Natural Beauty" provides no safeguards whatever against alteration. Indeed, it is easier to get planning permission for development in some AONBs than in areas not specially designated (Mark Blacksell and Andrew W. Gilg, "Planning Control in an Area of Outstanding Natural Beauty," *Social and Economic Administration,* 1977). Cotswold villages may be pickled in amber, as Clay suggests; but Cotswold landscapes are fragile and highly vulnerable. Not only is the cherished countryside being rapidly transformed, it is becoming increasingly inaccessible to most of those who cherish it. (Mason Shoard, "Metropolitan Escape Routes," *London Journal,* 1979.)

## THE DESTRUCTIVE AGRICULTURALISTS

Where does Grady Clay find the "millions of Britons who now depend on tourism" who supposedly support the fictitious "heavy burden of land-use regulations"? Apart from a few towns in Bath and York, where tourism is so obviously vital to the local economy that even the city councils now realize preservation pays, most of the country, public and private sectors alike, remains unenthusiastic about assisting tourism, even out of self-interest. Canterbury's cathedral and other historic buildings brought local merchants and hotel keepers 6.8 million pounds in 1975, yet tourist-hating locals sport buttons proclaiming, "I Just Live Here." Some towns and villages reject designation as conservation areas for fear they may become "popular" with visitors, even though such designation would make them eligible for maintenance and other grants. And private landowners often go to extreme lengths to resist public access, claiming against all the evidence that countryside visitors jeopardize their livelihoods (Marion Shoard, "Recreation: The Key to the Survival of England's Countryside," *Countryside for All*, Countryside Commission, 1978). Far from managing landscapes for appearance, most farmers view conservation and recreation interests as antagonistic to their own.

Grady Clay thinks tourism has transformed Britain's environment. It is true that some sites are so heavily impacted as to detract from the environment itself—as at Stonehenge—or from the quality of the experience, as at Canterbury Cathedral. One reason is that lack of access to, and information about, much of the country concentrates visitors at the best-known sites. Were Britain as a whole managed as Grady Clay thinks it is, the effect of visitor pressure would be reduced by being spread over more of the country. But at present the niggardly treatment of conservation by government, the absence of planning controls in the countryside, and the selfishness of entrenched interests—notably agriculture— threaten to destroy the fabric of the English landscape and to deprive both tourists and inhabitants of a most precious heritage.

*David Lowenthal*
*Department of Geography*
*University College, London*

## AUTHOR'S RESPONSE

Writing in *New Society* magazine, Michael Wood, after describing the changing mosaic of Mexico City, says, "But then I discovered that my sense of what was lost was getting in the way of my sense of what was left, and this must be a pretty common city experience." I myself have bristled at visiting critics' impressions of my own city, of my own familiar countryside. They see it as it appears at the moment, but I have watched it change through time and, the more the visitors exult over their discoveries, the more my sense of outrage grows. When I visit elsewhere I find myself exuberant—about the beautiful greenbelt over the Rockies front range at Boulder, Colorado; or about the incredibly uniform expanse of green, white-fenced thoroughbred horse farms around Lexington, Kentucky. But in each city the natives insist on telling me about how much more wonderful it used to be before the developers, those bastards, moved in.

And so perhaps the distinguished American geographer David Lowenthal and I are fated never to see the same England, even if we toured it together, he knowing every fall from grace, spotting every opportunity missed, and I goggling at the incredible reality of the momentary scene, when England still appears to have learned more about landscape preservation and all the stage-management that goes with it—than any country I have visited in the Western Hemisphere.

# Remembered Landscapes

All across a continent the bulldozers wait for spring. In the drafting rooms, the landscape architects trace out the contour lines of vast new neighborhoods, the surveyors stomp indoors with muddy boots and notebooks full of figures to be translated into a new suburban landscape.

Wherever frost, mud, and ice prevail, an entire industry marks time until it can open up another building season and carve its desires upon the landscape. In the South, the earth-movers never stop for weather; but farther north, men must wait, repair their scoops and scrapers, their dozers ands diggers, and stay indoors until the season opens.

And finally, by the season's ending, another million or so acres will have been subjected to the currently most-favored treatment, urbanization. Another million acres, more or less, will have been converted from open farmland, field, swamp, and wooded hillside into a newly urbanized landscape. The contours will have disappeared; man will have cut down the intervening hills, dug into the resisting slopes, filled up the marshes and swamplands, smoothed out the rough spots, and installed in their place a new angularity, a new geometry.

This will be a rawer, yellower, dustier landscape by midsummer; a landscape of houses and sidewalks, For Sale signs, airport runways and hardstands, express highways cutting precisely across random wilderness, slicing exactly through older cities: a landscape of asphalt, concrete, angularity, predictability.

Already the promises are being made, the options taken by the advance men who draw pretty pictures of Planned Industrial Districts, or Your Home in the Country while they act out the ancient pageantry of the salesman-developer of land. "Without the jobs we bring, you won't be able to afford all this," they argue, waving their hands over the suburban map, while a reluctant planning commission listens wearily. "Let us in, and your land will be worth double," they confide to possible objectors in the neighborhood.

In the face of all this—the bulldozer in the wings, the advance man, the job promise—the opposition crumbles, the trees and grass disappear, the random quality of the countryside becomes more predictable. We know that around the next corner will be neither cornfield nor open plain but more developments, more structures.

## KNOWLEDGE UNDERGROUNDED

And yet, deep within many of us is the knowledge, carefully and deliberately pushed underground as we grow older, that the miracles of lush grass, tangled undergrowth, a running brook, a tree to climb, a view to enjoy—these somehow should be protected and preserved for yet another generation as our worlds move ponderously toward total urbanization.

This feeling, this knowledge, is an esthetic one, and has been discounted by land developers until lately. Now, in this "tight-money" era, they are discovering a wide resistance among millions of families shopping for new homes, new neighborhoods. "We want more trees," clamour the housewives attending a "Women's Congress on Housing" in Washington. Even the highway builders, notorious for, and proud of, their disregard for trees and running brooks, are now being admonished by a Federal Highway Administrator to improve the looks of their roads because it is "just as cheap or cheaper to use the advantages nature has given."

Man's need for a bit of wilderness among the concrete, for a respite from angularity and aridity, is a deep need, long recognized by poet and artist, and noted by sensitive men for ages. But a research project at the Massachusetts Institute of Technology has produced some findings that may impress even developers, men who never believe a fact unless it is statistical.

Back in the summer of 1955, a class of architects and planners at M.I.T. wrote short papers on their memories of their childhood environments. These papers tempted two men, Alvin K. Lukashok and Kevin Lynch, to undertake a series of detailed interviews with 40 persons, none of them professionally involved in urbanism or design. These ranged from 18 to 32 years in age, had come mostly from the Boston area, but included a few persons from New York, and as far distant as Vienna. The Lukashok-Lynch study grew out of one assumption: "that present adult memories reflect actual childhood preoccupations." In other words, that memories of childhood are important emotional underpinnings of modern man's life, and are to be laughed away or disregarded at our peril and great loss.

What they discovered would gladden the hearts of all concerned with creating a decent, pleasant environment out of America's crowded and ugly cities, and of insuring such surroundings in the new Outer and Inner Suburbias.

### AH, DISTINCTLY, I REMEMBER . . .

For these people remember most vividly those elements of their childhood that involved landscape: lawns and pavement surfaces, foliage, woods and green hills, and water in the landscape. Among these childhood memories, lawns were associated with spaciousness, a sense of freedom. "I was very happy," recalls one of those interviewed. "I remember the first day we got there I was running over the lawns, up the slopes because it was so much of a change."

Of the various types of (landscape) floor coverings mentioned, grass is the best liked, then dirt that can be dug or molded, and after that, any smooth surface that allows roller-skating or bicycling. "The floor surfaces a child seems to dislike are asphalt on open spaces that otherwise would remain grassy, and brick, gravel, and cobblestones placed where he can suffer a fall. Of the few people who mention brick-paved surfaces, none talk about the visual quality of such surfaces, all dislike the uneven texture it provides . . . This surface, rarely the conscious concern of the designer, so often left to the contractor or to sheer custom, thus turns out to be the most important sensuous element of all."

Trees, trees, and more trees reappear in these childhood memories, and are mentioned with great warmth. For children, trees offer ideal places for play, shade, climbing, carving, hiding, and for creating wonderful childhood fantasies. Hardly a single interview failed to reveal this affinity for trees.

"We had a big oak tree in front of our house which was sort of a favorite. Then they were planting these small ones which were supposed to grow into these big ones someday but never got a chance because we would hang on them or try to climb them and break them off. During the latter part of the spring, when they used to get real bushy, they almost covered the street in a sort of tunnel. It gave a nice feeling of security. You could walk on the outside of the trees and be blocked off from the road. Yet it wasn't the same thing as barriers you encountered in Brookline, it was sort of a friendly thing. We carved our initials in them. You could do a lot of things with them, climb them, hit them, hide behind them: You could see out between the trees, but none could see in, and we used to hide in there and watch people. . . . I always liked to watch people."

Or: "I can remember in summertime it was beautiful along Saratoga and Bennington Streets because it was shaded. We used to play on the front stoop of somebody's house, and it was so nice to get under the trees for shade."

Or: "There were maple trees along our street. It's about the only tree I've ever been conscious of; it's the first tree I remember the name of, I've thought of it all my life. White birch trees, too, have a special meaning. But when I think of Scarsdale, I think of maple trees."

This may cause shudders among professional recreationalists, for these interviews showed clearly that children seem to prefer to play anywhere but the playground. Some comments: "We would rather play in the foliage. . . . Our idea when I was nine or 10 years old was not to play on the playground, but to find some place where there were rocks and broken bottles . . . a lot of trees and holes to fall into. . . . Out in back was a big field where the grass was over your head. They have cut that down now, and made a playground out of it so it isn't as romantic."

And: "I remember Riverside Park before it turned into developed areas . . . I remember there being a lot more space to play in. The big change, the big spurt of playground building had gone up. I was sort of pleased with having all these nice places to play in, the nice things that moved and worked, etc., but there simply wasn't enough space just to go and play in and do idiotic things in. You couldn't dig, for example; I like to dig. There weren't many places to dig because of the hard asphalt on the playground."

"So many people remember with pleasure, the overgrown lot, thick brush and woods," say the authors. "It is sufficient to give us pause in our treatment of 'waste' or 'untidy' areas or in the design of play spaces.

"On the whole, people remember keenly and with pleasure the hills that were in the vicinity. . . . Because so often a hill is not the best site for a building, it is the last part of an area developed, allowing it to remain wild and therefore attractive to children."

Oddly enough, none of the persons interviewed complained about too much space. Most professional designers nowadays seem to avoid excessively big, open spaces, in replanning cities ("prairie planning" has become a dirty word among many American planners, especially those influenced by the [European] C.I.A.M. city-square tradition). But few children remembered too much space—perhaps because there are so few urban spaces with "too much" open space. In fact, the authors conclude that "there is so little open space left in our cities that, in their hunger for it, most people cannot afford to be concerned with the quality of the space, they are grateful that it is there." And, as one of those interviewed put it: "Boston Common is one of the best parks in New England. They'll never get that."

## STATUS SIGNALS

Finally, "The feelings and key elements that run through all the interviews on childhood memories have strong similarities. The . . . children were sharply aware of lawns and floor surfaces; they delighted in foliage, woods, and green. There is a strong and pleasant memory for hills and for water in the landscape. A somewhat ambiguous fascination with the big transportation vehicles is equally clear. There was conscious alertness to spatial qualities, a definite preference for openness and spaciousness, and distaste for crowdedness. Even in childhood, perception is strongly colored by associations of social status: by 'niceness,' by cleanliness, by upkeep, and by money."

To my mind, the most disturbing thing coming out of this study was the authors' conclusion that most of the people interviewed "rarely conceive of the city as something that might give pleasure in itself. They hardly expect to have an enjoyable city environment, as if a mild civic nausea were a normal burden of man's existence."

If this conclusion may be justified in America, what must one expect from the great booming cities of the world—Johannesburg, Singapore, Agadir in Morocco, Sao Paulo, Hong Kong—where a flood of villagers and farmers is inundating whole square miles of cities, wiping out the green corners, the open lots, with overcrowding of appalling intensity?

One is forced to conclude from the M.I.T. studies, if not from a knowledge of the world as it exists without benefit of such research, that somehow the delights of waste spaces, of odd lots, of tangled woodlands left in the midst of housing developments—somehow these must be protected and preserved. For the city—not merely the Exurbs, the Suburbs, the Rolling Knolls and other high-income area neighborhoods—must keep these delights if it is to keep the affections of its people.

Under the impact of housing shortages, of get-rich-quick pressures on city officials, the urban green spaces are disappearing at an appalling rate. And with the disappearance of these "wastes" we lose trees, hills, water, fields of tall grass, the hidden and hiding places of the world, and in the end, an important part of life itself.

---

# Poland:
# Tunnel Vision
# Along
# the Vistula

Now that Poland has begun opening its doors more freely to Western tourists,[1] what is only a trickle may well turn into a torrent, and would-be non-Polish tourists would be advised to enjoy with reservations this latest addition to their available world.

For my part, I can only report on the side effects from that more specialized form of tourism known as an international seminar, this one dealing with the possibly arcane subject of historic preservation, at which the Poles have become world experts. God knows they had plenty to rebuild after the Nazis got through dynamiting, flame throwing, and systematically beating the hell out of the Polish townscape during World War II.

You need a visa, and they're not all that easy to get, but if you're willing to wait awhile, and add as many official or semi-official reasons for your trip as possible, it's not much tougher than going to France. Once there, just be sure you don't get caught money changing on the black market, however appealing getting an exchange of 2.5 to one may be. The language is tougher, which means you'll need an interpreter unless your folks were Polish, which can't be managed as an afterthought.

Poland is Behind the Iron Curtain. Once you've said that, forget it and look hard, ask questions, and read what's available, but don't count on your local U.S. tourist agent who operates as though this were still 1934 and Poland were nothing more than the origin of bad jokes, which is a bad joke itself. (It pays, however, to recall that Poland has no supreme court able to overturn executive or legislative acts.)

Poland has 33 million people, extends from the Baltic Sea southward to the Carpathian Mountains, where it enjoys a border with Czechoslovakia that for some 125 miles has stayed in place (unlike its east-west borders) since 1634.

Poland is industrialized, socialistic, traditional, varied, and its people still traumatized by the Nazis' efforts to wipe both nation and culture off the map in the 1940s. It is Soviet Russia's best trading partner within the socialist bloc; there seems to be plenty to eat, a boom in jobs, so much coal they're exporting 500 million tons to the U.S., so much efficiently extracted copper they've undercut world prices, and the same goes for sulphur.

What follows is a series of looks at the Polish landscape, chiefly physical but inevitably cultural/economic, etc., and limited by that particular form of tunnel vision accruing to official tourists. There were 24 of us Americans assembled in late 1974 by the National Endowment for the Arts. The trip was paid for by the Smithsonian Institution using American funds that could not be taken out of Poland, but could be used in-country. All our travel was by Orbis (government-owned) bus, and most of the seminars consisted of Americans listening to Polish experts, including some of the great figures of the resistance to the Nazis and of rebuilding what the Nazis wrecked. One of our group, Prof. Kevin Lynch of the Massachusetts Institute of Technology planning faculty, told us of enjoying a bibulous evening with a former student and his family in Warsaw. We spoke to few ordinary folks, but were able to walk freely, photograph indiscriminately without censorship, searches, etc. Twelve of us abandoned the prepared schedule so as to visit Auschwitz, the camp where Nazis exterminated four million persons. Most of us, I think, want to return to Poland for more rambling and casual inspections. It is unexplored territory for English-speaking scholars—there are no published works in the West, for example, on Poland's fantastic wealth of well-preserved log villages.

Why would a socialist state pour its millions of scarce funds from 1945 onward into restoring gutted palaces, replanting royal bosks and alleys, and at great cost training hundreds of craftsmen and women in such lost arts as weaving tapestries, peeling paint off

2–9. Off hours at the restored (i.e., almost totally rebuilt) medieval market square of Warsaw, Poland. No houses here survived Nazi demolitions at the end of World War II. Now fully rebuilt, they enclose space alternately busy with tourists in roving clusters or nearly empty, as in this 1974 photo.

hidden frescoes, and digging—everywhere they're still digging—under houses, castles, courtyards, to find medieval or earlier evidence of Polish History, much of it royal, aristocratic, elitist? They dig with great machines, they dig with trowels and whiskbrooms and put the findings in thick notebooks and museums. Why? To restore evidences of the historical greatness of a country that was denied statehood from 1793 (the last Great Partition) until 1919 (the Versailles treaty), and almost wiped out by World War II, having only past history to be proud of until the present became available.

Only in this context does the occasional great Renaissance garden, preserved and/or restored in socialized splendor, make any particular sense. A recent book, *The Picturesque Garden and its Influence Outside the British Isles*, states that "the arrival of the English Garden in Poland is by now well-documented," and that is without doubt, but I would not recommend this as preparatory reading for a trip to Poland. For the Picturesque Garden never caught on here except among a tiny but incredibly rich elite. (The Potockis, who had a fine Picturesque Garden at Lancut Castle near Warsaw, also had 360,000 acres of land, which is larger than a typical county in the U.S. Their county was expropriated, and no wonder.) Unless you make a point of visiting along with hordes of Polish tourists and school kids the few remnant castles and palace grounds, you'd never know the Picturesque got this far east of the Palace of

Versailles. The Polish landscape on the whole is not Picturesque.

Garden preservation is no easy breeze, as I was reminded during a leaf-scuffling and tape-recorded walk through the grounds of the romantically beautiful Lazienkowski Palace in Warsaw. (The palace itself was once a sort of one-man Playboy Club, the then King given to splashing around a great tiled bath with the ladies, accompanied by offstage poetry readings.) My walking companion was director in charge of the palace itself; the grounds—unfortunately, from his viewpoint—are owned and managed by the city of Warsaw. He manages the palace as a national museum with care and precision; "they," on the other hand, want to add to the palace grounds new buildings, recreation facilities, parking space, activities. "I will fight for the protection of this garden," he observed. "There are many conflicts because we have different conceptions. We want to create a garden like a museum, an object of art, connected to the palace, not separated. It is all the same conception. They have other conceptions and often there is quarreling between us."

No such quarrels mar the management of Baranof, another vast and far more isolated castle arising like a great stucco whale from the drained marshes along the Vistula River about three hours drive south of Warsaw. Its formal parterres, clipped lawns, paved terraces, and outbuildings are carefully maintained by the huge state-owned company that is exploiting vast sulphur deposits nearby. (One of our U.S. group, a Texan, observed that the town of Pecos, Texas, economically hooked to marginal sulphur mining and processing, was thrown into a depression when this Polish mine began producing with high efficiency, undercutting the world price of sulphur.) Baranof was restored both by the Ministry of Culture and the sulphur company, the latter using the basement for educational exhibits, and the castle at times for company meetings and entertainment. The company manager spoke to our group after dinner: Mr. Efficiency, full of affability, productivity, and talk about world markets, rather much what you'd hear at an international seminar at M.I.T.

## DRIP-DRIED POLAND

It is as though Poland had been hung up on a huge clothesline to drip dry slowly, over generations. But now, instead of the old windmills that have become touristic curiosa, the countryside has machines big and small, digging, ditching, dredging, recontouring,

2-10. Salvaged from World War II
destruction, these stone remnants of
former royal buildings in Warsaw
await identification and replacement
by restorations—part of the
"boneyard" vital to history buffs.

drying the country out. Baranof Castle (c.1579) was located in what was a vast swamp, isolated and thus protected from its enemies by recurring floods from the Vistula River. Today the Vistula is leveed, its flooding reduced, and Baranof Castle is surrounded by a network of ditches and canals across dry land. The name of Wavel Castle, on a bluff in dried-out downtown Krakow, means "a dry, raised place surrounded by water."

In some 300 miles of travel, mostly in open country or villages, from the Baltic Sea south to the Carpathian Mountains, we were seldom out of sight of new ditches, newly installed drainage works, or new utility lines. I kept seeing an omnipresent type of machine I never encountered in the U.S.: a small clamshell bucket digger, of about two cubic-foot capacity, with a 10-foot reach, run by a gasoline engine (under 10 horsepower, I guessed), mounted on a maneuverable four-wheel frame easily towed behind a truck, tractor, or horse. They are the mechanical arms Nigel Dennis wrote about in *Eden Was No Garden*, loading sand, gravel, and building materials, digging ditches, filling and excavating on farms and building sites (half the farms seem to be sprouting one or more new brick buildings), along roads.

Dessication, while a wetlands solution, can become an urban problem. The director of a geographic research institute told us that in scores of historic places (out of 1,400 known), the collapse of medieval sewers has altered many underground water levels, as has the installation of new sewers in hundreds of towns; the drying out process destabilizes old foundations, which require shoring up. In the medieval hilltop town of Sandomirz, ancient sewers are settling, causing wholesale wall-cracking among handsome three-story brick houses, some built in the fourteen century. For blocks all we could see was scaffolding, blockades, repairs, setting the stage for future tourists, another mini-Williamsburg, Virginia, in the remaking.

At the outskirts of every city and town, the new housing proliferates in dull, gray, concrete four-story walkups and 12- to 14-story elevator apartments. Almost every official we met apologized for the new monotony, saying, "It is not a Polish solution, it is a world solution," and there are of course truth elements tracing through such statements for, disregarding details, one could indeed think he were in a renewal area of Detroit, Cincinnati, St. Louis, Stockholm, or Paris.

## MASS-PRODUCED SITES

Since the 1930s, when two-thirds of all Poles were on farms or villages, the pattern has reversed, so that today two-thirds live in towns and cities, most of the newcomers since 1946 in mass housing projects, which one might expect in any westernized nation today. Those projects I saw from a bus were on mass-produced (i.e., butchered) sites with few traces of original landscape.

Most surprising to me were stringtowns of suburban villas strung outside towns and cities, sometimes for miles in open country, scenes of startling continuity and vitality. This is suburbia without autos, its habitants mostly using the public bus system permeating the countryside, many bicycles, motorbikes, and railroads. (Some 140,000 workers a day commute into Warsaw by rail, many from towns, villages, and stringtown villas.)

The typical villa is brick, fairly new (since 1946), two full stories above a raised basement or ground floor, on an intensively cultivated, long-lot plot of two to 20 acres that is generally fenced;the fence resting upon a perimeter concrete footing around the smaller tracts. The narrow frontage always faces the road. Many villas are owner-built; we saw hundreds in mid-construction, some being built on weekends, many with bricks, etc. stored under sheds next to a just-planted orchard.

"Socialized" does not describe the countryside. Eighty-five percent of Poland's total farmland is privately owned, the other 15 percent in state farms generally confiscated from giant landowners at the end of World War II. Last year that 85 percent produced 88 percent of the nation's food and fiber, a U.S. farm expert told me. It seemed clear, from the number of people working the fields, that high production is achieved at the cost of hard labor by entire families, seven days a week. Poland's is an inhabited countryside: people working in the fields cutting and pulling turnip tops in rows, women leading cows to fields, women tethering cows, older men and women driving tractors or V-bodied wagons behind a pair of horses. Two weeks after leaving Poland, by way of contrast, I spent a day with soil conservationists inspecting the "richest farming country in Wisconsin." On a six-hour bus trip, I saw not a single solitary person in the farming landscape. Not one.

Pressure from the Polish government, on the one hand, seeks to shoehorn more farmland into the big state farms by offering aging farmers liberal lifetime pensions if they bequeath the farm to the state. On the other hand, small town and farm families can get permits to build larger houses than can city families, a policy that encourages them to settle outside the cities in the countryside. Could it be that the socialized left hand knoweth not what the agrarianized right hand pursueth?

## WHEN IN DOUBT, DIG!

Wars and other disasters leave unexpected and often unmanageable tracts of exposed landscape, and Poland had far more than its share of scorched and otherwise devastated earth. The results are strangely visible, even though great portions of the medieval and Renaissance centers of towns and buildings have been restored— carefully, with extraordinary attention to historical accuracy.

What survives from World War II in many of the towns and cities we inspected are unexpected open spaces. They now have become part of official turf and are decorated with various civic impedimenta—rather mundane patriotic posters, monuments, walks, benches, and acres of pavements. Every village has its rectangular bosk, its tree-lined main street, its scurrying civil servants.

One of our party photographed an elderly woman sweeping horse manure from a town street, only to find himself receiving a patriotic lecture from the sweeper (through our group interpreter): She was doing important work, necessary to the city's proper care, and didn't want her significance to be missed by camera-happy tourists. Thus alerted, we noted signs of what must be a large national army of sweepers, cleaners, clippers, and maintainers. As we toured the Royal Castle in Warsaw, a small troop of bandanna'd and heavy-booted women in their fifties and older moved in on frostbitten begonias in nearby round planters and in 10 minutes had most of them replaced by chrysanthemums.

"When in doubt, DIG!" seemed to be the motto among preservationists. Consequently, historic parts of towns and other places in Poland still resemble construction sites. Diggers in supposedly sixteenth-century buildings uncover medieval foundations. Diggers in Torun, the birthplace of Copernicus, uncovered a complex network of wooden pipes and cisterns under the Copernicus house, revealing an unsuspectedly sophisticated neighborhood water system at least 400 years old. As Greek and Roman archaeologists have long been telling us, every civilization, even a red-brick one, rests

2-11. Among Crusaders who occupied parts of Poland, Teutonic Knights of the twelfth and thirteenth centuries built great hospitals and castles, this one in Torun eventually thrown into ruin by Turks. The ruins are still preserved where they fell 400 years ago.

upon the remnants of earlier cultures and their technology.

Uncovered foundations, then, have become objects of civilized attention and occasionally, as at Krakow's Wavel Castle courtyard, become planter-bed reminders of some princely era long gone. Most staggering discovery to the writer was the Teutonic Knights' Castle, wrecked and burned by angry Torun citizens in the thirteenth century. Some of the brick towers are still lying exactly as they fell 600 years ago, still unpillaged and unvandalized. How to ensure the maintenance of such visible and accessible evidence for 600 years is one of many mysteries to be unraveled only on future visits.

---

# Kerrow
# to the Gap

I am where the geographers say such journeys should begin: where two Great and Mighty Rivers come together; where history tatters itself into crime statistics; and the only town to stand here at mid-river in mid-continent bears the crusts, the shards, and scars of a century of floods.

To cross the middle of the North American continent, you may choose among hundreds of routes, but my wife and I have chosen to start this exploration at Cairo, Illinois, which is pronounced Kerrow by Kerrovians, and has been victimized as often by the bordering and flooding Ohio and Mississippi Rivers as by the criminalizing refugees from Cicero and Chicago to the north.

We are starting the second leg of a thousand-mile cross-section of Kentucky, having driven westward down the Ohio River valley to Kerrow, and now turn our faces to the east. Travelers are warned, as they leave Kerrow, not to smuggle cigarettes across the Great Water into Kentucky, for such is a crime punishable by law if discovered. And this, a friend suggests, means running afoul of the police for another offense, say overtime parking, and having one's car and baggage searched in process—an invasive procedure recently made legal for lawmen by a Supreme Court decision.

Centuries of history lie between our starting point and our distant finish, between Kerrow cowering behind its floodwalls, which bear marks of past floodings, and those dim and distant mountains of Appalachia waiting some 400 miles to the east. Before we leave, we look out over deltoid flatlands, which once were, for thousands of years, trade and war routes for native Indian tribes. Far to the north and up the Illinois River, Northwestern University students have uncovered stratified remains of buried Indian villages, their origins going back some 8,000 years.

Why, then, does the first roadside sign on Kentucky highways thrust a running horse into our vision—a horse running fullstride against, and not with, the flow of traffic? Does this follow some arcane rule-of-painted-thumb among sign painters? Is there a hidden dynamic that bids the painter to run his horse off the road, and thus more surely to capture our attention?

Amid such speculations, we stop to hunker down and picnic on the Mississippi riverbank at Wickliffe, a quiet spot far below the floodmarks on cottonwood trees and temporary-looking sheds and shops that have that distinct meant-to-be-flooded look. From where we picnic, we watch distant tugboats (called "tows" in these parts) shove their long, low barge flotillas downriver and disappear over the murky distant horizon. Ghostly and afar lies Missouri yonder, separated by historical ages from Kentucky. For nearly a hundred miles up and down the Mississippi, Kentucky and Missouri look askance at one another across this wide, wide river, no bridges and only two ferries between them, as if to make permanent the gap that separates the two cultures—Midwest and South—that spring away from these two riverbanks.

Picnic behind us, we proceed. Then and now, past and present, two cultures comingle along the roadside. We stop to inspect a spanking new mobile home, a "twelve-wide" it is called, with its white, windowless, baked-enamel side facing the roadway. Next door stands a U-Haul trailer at the ready, an escape mechanism come the next flood. Looming behind is a huge steel grain bin waiting for the next barge to take away its bellyfull of corn. And in the front yard, a rusted metal wheelbarrow stands profiled to the road with magenta petunias nodding from its load of dirt. And beside it still another nostalgic reminder of pre-aluminum times: An old mouldboard plow leans wearily against the corner foundation of the trailer-house.

## TELL-TALE TOKENS

From this point eastward, we continue to run into the same front-yard telltales: the old plows, rake harrows, disc harrows, wagon wheels, buggy wheels, tractor wheels, mementoes of farming days long gone, tools long out of use. On other cross-section trips I have encountered similar reminders—a giant loggers' cart in a suburban front yard north of Jacksonville, Florida, left from early days of logging off the giant pine; a pioneer-type wagon on a Midwestern front yard; and prettied-up wagon wheels guarding the gates of suburban houses from Florida to British Columbia. Handed down from pioneering ancestors? Discovered in Granpa's barn when the family homestead was sold off? Rescued from a dump heap, or bought at auction? All this and more, for evidence mounts during the journey that we are watching the dregs of a one-man-one-plow culture being resurrected as last-ditch front-yard reminders of a small-scale way of family farming life now on the skids. Later into the trip we stop at a roadside flea market and talk with three men loading a large mouldboard plow into a pickup truck. An old family relic rescued from the sale? No, he said. "It's like the one I learned to plow with when I was a kid." Where will it go? "We gonna fix it up and set it out in the yard."

Down at the next crossroads an array of giant combines, some of them the four-wheel-drive variety, an Allis-Chalmers with air-conditioned cab, stares down at us from a roadside array of equipment. These are the engines that run the new farming countryside. Costing $30,000 and more apiece, they can deep-plow their way through tough sod or bottomland clay yet never stop their sloshing be the land muddy or boggy, extending the season, and plunging their owners deeper into debt. Later we are to see the evidence and hear the tales of soil erosion throughout the Upper South and Midwest, aggravated by these huge machines, which stand in bright paint on the small-town sales floor, as awesome evidences of what is called The New Tomorrow Agriculture.

Flat as far as the eye can see, the Western Kentucky landscape that confronts the traveler is an extension of the flat-square corn-wheat Grain Belt—minus the square. Hardly ever in crossing Kentucky east-west does one encounter that fixity of Midwest geography, the mile-square grid. On the better maps (but not on the thin and withholding face of oil-company maps) the facts come out: Kentucky and Tennessee stand as the westernmost outriders of that higgledy-piggledy every-whichaway disorder by which the Eastern seaboard states' lands were laid out and sold off to early settlers. Old roads follow old paths, which ratified old hunting trails; up, down, around, and about.

Only a suspicious lack of population on what appears to be rich land hints at that great historic blood-letting that followed the early nineteenth-century battles over land titles. We later turned to the historian Steven A. Channing's detailed account, published in 1977, which tells of the chicanery and stupidity by which early land speculators and surveyors confused and disrupted the early land titles. As a result, thousands of original settlers quit in disgust over lost titles, and moved on west. Others moved out in dismay over a generation-long legal dispute in which two state courts of appeal disputed their respective legality. From 1815 to 1818 there was a rash of openings of new banks, most of which went bankrupt by 1820. Thousands of depositors and others ended up dead broke and moved west. If anybody has measured the long-term losses due to these early out-migrations, local boosters do not pass along the story. Yet I cannot escape the sense that this history helps explain the exhausted and ill-cared-for look of many stretches of the Kentucky landscape.

## FENCEROW TO FENCEROW

Our move across the hundred-mile granary coincides with the annual double-cropping drama that has swept through mid-America. Farmers have been harvesting wheat in late June, immediately planting soybeans for a fall crop. "Wheat is big here—back to what it was in the 1870s," comments a guide outlining our path across the grainbelt.

Soon we pass imperceptibly out of the grain belt into what is affectionately, if compressedly, called The Pennyrile, an Anglo-Saxon corruption of Pennyroyal mint, for which the region was once noted. The region sweeps southward into Tennessee, but such is the insistence of parochial patriotism, one would think that soil types changed from black to white at the state border. Tennessee has no such name for its companion region across the state line.

It would never do, we tell ourselves, to cross this great coal-rich scene without glimpsing open-strip mining. We've watched television present the scene as a vast and pitted moonscape. But watching from the road, we visitors find ourselves screened off from strip-mining countryside as though this were another Potemkin Village, its summery green facade hiding the machines loose in the garden. Once the facade breaks, once we can peer through an opening in the trees, we watch the machine snorting and kicking up dust. Smoke-belching trucks haul off the overburden, so that great shovels can gouge up the coal that already has been priced to sell at the nearby Paradise steam-generating plant for distribution as electrical current flowing southward through the Tennessee Valley Authority's lines. Now we are behind schedule, and look for the nearest thruway-tollway-superhighway to get us quickly eastward.

Bloodlines, rather than other power lines, are what counts in the

2–12. Keeping its distance from strangers, a typical Kentucky Bluegrass horse farm surrounds itself with layers of fences, pastures, gated approach roads—symbols if not specific signs instructing outsiders to keep their distance.

Kentucky Bluegrass, which we can reach painlessly and by a dulling of the senses via one of those interminable cross-state tollroads that grew popular in the 1960s. Distinguished in no way from thousands of miles of other interstate highways, this one delivers us without advance warning, except for changing its name to become Bluegrass Parkway, into the Bluegrass region of Thoroughbred (the word invariably capitalized here) horse farms and deep-rooted land ownership.

White-fenced and often treeless except along pencil-thin hedgerows, the landscape begins to withhold itself from us travelers out on the road. The flow of messages from there to here diminishes. Before we reached the Bluegrass, that flow had been overwhelming. From every nook and cranny of crowded roadside, the messages had poured out: from mailboxes, signs, signs, signs, junkheaps, ruins, front porches. But in the Bluegrass, all is ordered and reserved. Messages are few and far between. They come in muted tones, genteel accents; they keep their distance from the road and from strangers.

Large manor houses, some of them gleaming new ("That's the new coal money coming out of East Kentucky," snorts an old-family Bluegrass acquaintance), horse-barns on faraway crests. There are no stage hands to run this stagesetting, no farmers walking the fields. We are distanced by owners who tell us only that they are rich and we are passing.

Through Lexington, we pass that rare remnant from Old Virginia—the brick-walled garden. Even in suburbia it comes between us and whatever intimacies are played out in the shady side and rear yards. But outside the imitative gentility of these garden wall lies New Money.

Platoons of new wealthy, some with oil money from the Red Sea and Mediterranean shores, others swollen with capital gains from coal deposits, have prompted Lexington into displays unthinkable among the old gentry. A golden-mirrored downtown bank, twin towers for housing students at the state university (almost duplicates of others at the state university near Albany, New York, also by the architect Edward Durrell Stone), and extravagant horse barns at $20,000 and up per stall—all this has altered the Lexington scene.

While money sweeps across the countryside, local custom rides herd on the way it sprouts. For generations, whitewashed or white-painted fences marked the contours and ownerships of these horse farms wherever the legacies of slave-days and cheap labor did not leave behind the grand miles of grey stone walls. So powerful is the white-fence image that it now jumps at us from cigarette and clothing ads, as from the countryside. And so pervasive its power that the same combination of white-fence, hilltop house, and barn follows our route out of the open countryside of the Bluegrass and into the notches and confines of the Eastern Kentucky mountains and coalfields. Old wooden barns hang close to the road only a few steps from shelter to the pavement. But the new metal barns respond to Bluegrass images: They stand well back and highly visible, on sites that have been made accessible by the ubiquitous bulldozer. No matter how inappropriate a "Bluegrass Barn" looks on these steep slopes, owners carry out the ritual and import white fences and Colonial plantation houses into the steepest confines of Appalachia.

## THE NOTCH-AND-MOAT LANDSCAPE

Now we are into Eastern Kentucky, where the hills rise into mountains, and valleys become dark and narrow, the coal boom has done its work. Here seems to be emerging what an embryologist, Richard Goldschmidt, has called "hopeful monsters"—one of those mutants that emerge from extraordinary geographic bottlenecks— these tortuous, narrow valleys where railroads, highways, flooding creeks, and family homesteads nestle and jostle for space. And the most monstrous force at work is coal—the human and economic energies let loose by the world-wide demand for coal that lies in billion-ton seams under these mountains.

Along these narrow and notched valleys is growing up a continuous, high-density and high-activity ribbon of human settlement. For hundreds of miles—dodging about a bit—we confront the same scene, which I can only describe as The Notch-and-Moat Landscape. It appears and reappears, mile after mile, the same set of objects and situations:

First, there's the narrow valley that had little but a narrow rocky or creek-bottom road until the first railroad came in around 1905, its roadbed consisting of a narrow strip cut into one side of the valley. Next to that railroad cut there's a narrow strip of land that is packed, or littered, with houses, trailers, sheds, shacks, shanties, machines, trucks, cars, spare parts, lumber, coal, building materials, firewood, junked cars, equipment for sale or being repaired, animals, and people. Lots of people.

These stringtowns are busy, active, changeable. As they unrolled before our eyes, I came to see them as extensions of the mid-American production line, working overtime and on weekends, part of the production line out of which comes thousands of hopper cars of coal, headed north, south, east, west out of the coalfields. These notch-and-moat valleys and their people are an essential part of the mass-production process. These houses, surrounded by

2–13. The "notch-and-moat" landscape of Appalachian valleys, in contrast to horse-farm country, crams all human activities into a narrow set of strips and ledges in the valley bottoms: vehicles, walled creek, bridge, house, outbuildings, neighbors, trailers.

2–14. Generations of shelter nestle in a narrow patch between highway and creek: a tiny log storage barn following eighteenth-century models alongside a late-model house trailer (a.k.a. mobile home).

trucks and jalopies, by coal piles and spare parts, struck me as being items of capital investment, rather than as consumer goods like Kleenex.

The full flow of regional traffic goes past every house and front door every day. Every house now has a recognizable address, and its people can tap into the regional networks of mail, deliveries, utilities, visitors, strangers, outsiders—and new ideas.

Such communities present themselves as a kind of stage setting, continuously unrolled before an ever-changing audience. There is no hiding place, no retreat from the gaze and judgement of the passing throng. Will this long-term surveillance force Stringtown to look like and act like the rest of the world?

It takes specialized, locally owned and constantly available machines to make this scene work. The major scene-shifter is the bright yellow backhoe. It keeps open the ditches, pulls wrecks out of creeks, regrades the steep terrain, hustling up and down the road for hire.

The whole scene carries one step further the interchangeable parts system—once called the American System—which gave us the cotton gin, the textile mill, the mass-produced flintlock musket, and now the Sony television and Toyota pickup from Japan.

Suddenly, watching this unrolling pageantry, I am mentally plunged back into an Italian valley in World War II, all the strung-out apparatus of a moving army cluttering the roadsides. And it occurs to me that much of this Kentucky scene could be picked up, hauled away, and be gone tomorrow, as sensitive to the price of coal as were those Italian valleys to the fortunes of war.

## INTO THE PEDIGREED LANDSCAPE

Soon our southward journey takes us deeper into history: The Cumberland Gap awaits beyond Middlesboro. Lunchtime along such busy highways means short-order joints crowded with the noonday hungry. We are herded quickly through ordering, seating, eating, and clean-up; an ear-piercing buzzer preempts the place whenever a customer drives up to the drive-in window.

Escape takes us into a new Pedigreed Landscape[1] (to use Michael Hough's felicitous phrase), an extraneous and exogenous landscape form transplanted into this historic valley, courtesy of the National Park Service. Here at Cumberland Gap National Historical Park, the farm scene has long since disappeared, the rolling terrain is mechanically clipped and tended. We could be in any of a hundred such scenes, made memorable (and mass-produced) by the great wave of park renewal that began with Mission 66 almost a generation ago.

Up at the Gap, we catch our first glimpse of The South. The weather seems warmer, the grass greener as we make our crossing to the southeast. Both sides of the Gap are smothering in that infamous southern export: kudzu vine.

Immediately, as a native Southerner, I feel at home, but with a wry sense of shame, as though I were suddenly to come upon some long-forgotten relative, the family stumblebum, retarded into

2–15. The kudzu vines at right recognize no historic regional boundaries, having long since left the Old South to smother roadsides, as here at historic Cumberland Gap on the Kentucky–Tennessee border.

adulthood yet still roaming benignly at large. Kudzu, kudzu, stirring boyhood memories . . . Of my father, proudly reclaiming a worn-out Georgia farm, preaching the benefits of that soil-holding new miracle plant, kudzu. Of summers spent on farm crews, grading down the steep sides of red-clay gullies, stomping pinetree branches into the bottoms, and planting kudzu along the sides. We were certain—and it did prove a certainty—that kudzu would grow fast, cover the scarred earth, and provide good grazing for the cattle. But of course none of us knew then—at a time when there were hardly 10,000 areas of kudzu across the entire South—that eventually this rampageous vine would leap the fences, climb the tallest trees, spread over old pastures and aged barns to cover more than five million acres by the 1960s.

Through the kudzu at Cumberland Gap we pass from what historians called the New West, and head down into the Old South. From this moment on, where King Cotton once was symbol of southern wealth and agricultural power, kudzu adds its constant reminder: Every agricultural scene is up for grabs.

---

# The Copper Basin
# of Tennessee

Looking outward from this small hilltop town perched amidst bare, red, eroded hillsides' at the junction of Tennessee, Georgia, and North Carolina, a Ducktown resident sees what has been variously described as:

A hellhole, a blister, a desecration, something out of Dante's Inferno, the Tennessee badlands, the ugliest place in the South, a fascinating wasteland, a wilderness, a monument to waste, a scenic attraction, a big accident, a beloved scar, a moonscape, a red desert, post-holocaust wasteland, a ravaged wonder, the largest man-made desert in the United States, a strangely beautiful landscape of historic importance—and possibly the nation's least-known, large-scale experiment in land reclamation by tree planting.

"Some people say the Devil wouldn't have it, and that's how we got it—but I love it," commented a white-haired woman I chatted with one morning at breakfast.

All these and possibly more colorful descriptions have been

2–16. The author's shadow foregrounds a longer view across the variegated semi-desert of Copper Basin, Tennessee.

applied to the Copper Basin of Tennessee, a scenic expanse of rolling hills covering some 35,000 acres and surrounded by mountains in three states that reach some 4,200-foot elevations.

For roughly three-quarters of a century—from before the Civil War into the 1920s—the Basin's forests were badly cut-over to get fuel for copper smelting and were later subjected to copper sulphide fumes generated by the open-air roasting of copper ore. After around 1907 the fumes were spread farther by high stacks.

The early fumes, according to local historians, were so thick that the mules hauling copper ore had to be belled so they wouldn't collide in the murk. And to fuel the roasting piles, which sometimes stretched 600 feet long and half-a-house high, the copper companies and their contractors continued to cut all the timber within hauling distance, which extended over 20 miles. They even ended up digging out the stumps and burning them, too.

Those fumes, hanging close to the ground, or mixing with frost, fog, or rain, killed nearly every remaining tree, bush, shrub, weed, and growing plant over an area that has been variously estimated to be 32,000 acres more or less—roughly three times the size of Manhattan Island. Only a few well-tended pockets survived denudation.

## ACID RAIN

The Basin remains therefore the clearest example in the United States of the long-term effects of acid rain. Unlike the much-debated contemporary acid rain, this early version descended close to its point of origin, was highly visible, and had an immediate as well as long-term effect. These effects were hotly disputed then and now, and resulted in many lawsuits, two of which reached the U.S. Supreme Court before 1918. Nowhere in hundreds of documents did I find any references to sickness or deaths attributed to the fumes. But I did encounter a public advertisement signed by the circuit clerk, saying that the Basin was noted for its "salubrious sulphurous fumes" conducive to good health. I leave it to some future doctoral thesis writer to plumb this mystery.

In a 1907 case Georgia's attorney general insisted to the Supreme Court that the invasion by Tennessee fumes across the state line resulted "in laying the territory of the State of Georgia in waste more surely and completely than could be accomplished by any invading army bent upon its destruction." Justice Oliver Wendell Holmes delivered the opinion, upholding Georgia's right to have "the last word as to whether its mountains shall be stripped of their forests and its inhabitants shall breathe pure air." The court's ruling forced the copper company to reduce its fuming. Fortunately the company about that time discovered a way to reclaim sulphuric acid from the fumes, and that acid is the present company's main product.

## THE GEOPOLITICS OF SMELL

The fumes had a long-term geopolitical impact. Most of their devastation denuded land in Tennessee, just north of the Georgia boundary. Gradually, mine workers retreated into Georgia, just across the Ocoee River, bypassing some of the denuded, close-in land. Thus began a long process of selective settlement "south of the border," and today a long string of settlements is festooned along Highway 5 through the Georgia woodlands southward to the town of Blue Ridge. More than half of the Tennessee company's 1,330 workers live in Georgia.

Few people of the current generation, aside from specialists and local residents, know about the Basin. I picked up 26 tourist maps and brochures at a roadside Tennessee Welcome stop. None showed or mentioned the Basin. The closest interstate highway is 45 miles west. The Basin lies at the outer edge of three states, being central to none, and thus has little political visibility or clout. It has never, so far as I could find, received extensive national media coverage. Even during the decades of the 1960s and '70s when environmentalists raged at polluters, the Basin stood raw and red, oozing and overlooked. It was old stuff, a scene perpetrated by persons dead and gone, a place where old residents are accustomed, and sometimes quite proud, to live in a uniquely devastated part of the world. "I get more emotion from tourists than from local people," according to County Executive Charles Stevens.

Not even the most avid booster, however, can claim that this is truly "the largest man-made desert in North America," since *BioScience Magazine* (Vol. 25, No. 12, p. 758) published some updated comparisons. In the Copper Basin, it reported, "smelting destroyed 28 square kilometers of forest and replaced an additional 40 square kilometers of forest with grass species," while near Kennet, California, "all vegetation was destroyed by smelter fumes on an area of more than 271 square kilometers," and in Sudbury, Ontario, "three large smelters are causing severe tree injury . . . over a 1,900 square kilometer area."

But in the green, tree-covered Appalachian highlands of Tennes-

2-17. Early pine-planting efforts by
the Tennessee Valley Authority in
the 1940s show at upper left, part of
many struggles to get pine trees to
cover the denuded basin.

see, Georgia, and North Carolina, denudation causes visual shock.
The Basin continues—in spite of substantial tree planting since the
1930s—to shock visitors and especially white-water enthusiasts who
come in swelling numbers to shoot the nearby rapids of the Ocoee
River. "They all ask me 'Who did it?'" observed outfitter Rodger
Lozier of Ocoee Rafters, Ducktown.

Whitewater paddlers who arrive when the Ocoee River's three
lakes are "down" are equally shocked at the expanse of silt that has
covered the upper part of Ocoee No.3. On inquiry they learn that
the Basin has contributed millions of tons of topsoil to the streams,
lakes, and bottomlands that lie downstream. Thousands of acre-feet
dropped in the Ocoee lakes; untold volumes continued downstream.

### NUDITY AT LARGE

As a result one headline writer around 1900 called this "The Nude
Basin." In many parts of the basin the ground crunches, clinks, and
clanks as you walk on it. It consists of shards, flakes, chips, and

2-18. A century of erosion from copper sulphide fumes left only shards behind—a surface that clinks when you walk on it.

2-19. Ducktown, Tennessee, surviving through the worst of the destruction from sulphide fumes, used imported water to stay green during three generations of devastation of this wide valley.

chunks of rock. No top soil. No mud. Just rocky debris left behind as the soil moved slowly toward the Gulf of Mexico.

My visit to the Basin aroused various reactions. Friends puzzled about my wasting time on an unknown place, expecting a journalist to look for places "in the news." One local resident asked if I were planning to "do something" about the basin. One veteran forester, William Mercier, who'd spent years planting trees and grasses on company land, was shocked when I told him I found the orange-red-yellow scene both mysterious and beautiful, worthy of preservation. "I don't know how somebody like you can talk like that," he reacted.

My visits also happened to coincide with a turning-point in the Basin's history. For the Tennessee Chemical Company, which owns some 20,000 acres of land and 5,500 acres of mineral rights, had decided to sell off major parts of its land holding beginning in September, 1983. Its profits from land sales would then count as capital gains, since it bought the property from Cities Service Company in September, 1982. It promised to give first choice to company employees and retirees, many of whom lease isolated tracts from the company, where they live in a surprising variety of structures ranging from temporary-looking shacks to substantial houses. About 7,000 acres where the company continues active underground mining, smelting, etc., will not be sold, according to company president Bruce D. Davis.

Also, it happens that in 1983 the company began mining in what is called Fractional Township No. 16. This quarter-section (160 acres) of land was reserved for school purposes when Tennessee joined the Union. And that year, for the first time, TCC began paying to the Township Commission over $200,000 in annual mining royalties based on 31 cents per ton mined. TCC's predecessors beginning in 1912 agreed to pay $12,000 per year to help out the school commission, although the companies were not yet mining school lands. The company also paid four percent annual interest. In the early 1970s the company began mining township property and drew on its earlier-paid funds to pay current royalties. These funds were depleted in 1982, so the company subsequently pays the flat royalty per ton mined.

What happens to this new money seemed likely to provoke a continuing political struggle within Polk County over how much the company should pay and how it is to be spent. For the Basin—

thanks to the mine workers' income and to the company tax payments—is the rich end of Polk County. This has always excited envy from "below the mountains," where lies the county seat of Benton and what appears to be the envious majority of the county's population. Basin people say, "Polk County's got a big cow. We feed it up here, and they milk it down in Benton."

Whitewater paddlers have enlarged their entry into the area: 17,000 of them in 1978, and more than 93,000 in 1982, fighting the 4.7 miles of challenging rapids on the Ocoee River. Many paddlers are outfitted by two new firms doing business in the basin, one of them occupying the defunct Sahara Motel. The U.S. Whitewater Slalom racing team trained here in the spring of 1983. Everybody I spoke to

2–20. The appropriately named "Sahara Motel" is now closed, its building reoccupied by a sports outfit catering to white-water enthusiasts come to shoot the rapids of the nearby Ocoee River.

in the rafting business expects the boom to continue, intensifying a struggle between the rafters and the Tennessee Valley Authority over the duration of whitewater released from one of the Ocoee dams. (A historic 4.5 mile flume normally diverts the waters from this dam around some of the finest whitewater rapids in the eastern United States. Without released water, there is no whitewater sport.)

## WATCHING THE CHANGE SINCE '67

My own observations of the Basin began in 1967, when I first climbed to the top of Red Hill for a panoramic view. Later I learned that photographers from TVA and elsewhere had been climbing that same hill for three quarters of a century, taking their own panoramas. Red Hill's top is 2,052 feet above sea level, some 500 to 1,000 feet above nearby valleys. In 1967 its top was still bare except for a few tufts of sedge grass. The redness extended for miles, with tiny Ducktown perched like a hilltop oasis surrounded with raw, red desert. Looking hard, I could see a few plantations of dark green pine planted by the copper companies and by TVA during its great interventions from around 1934 to 1951. A few house owners had ventured into the desert, their lawns distinct and green against the orange-to-brown background.

On that first entry into the Basin in 1967, making notes in a pad on my car seat, I wrote: "Bizarre scene. Nothing in my experience fits this. Bushes arising from crevices. Great chasms in all directions. Houses on green pads stuck out in a wilderness of washed-away red."

Generations of new arrivals have found their emotions stirred by the same scenes. A famous traveler, Jonathan Daniels, when he was writing his 1938 book, *A Southerner Discovers the South,* described a barren Basin hill as having a "high hideousness close to beauty and wonder." But today there's a difference. In April, 1983, when I climbed Red Hill again, I picked my way through a spotty growth of young pines, many growing from tiny ridges and peaks between deep gullies. At the top I had some trouble finding a place between the pinetrees to photograph scenes that had been wide open in 1967.

The shock of the raw is less today than even a decade ago, for two modern state highways now cross the basin near Ducktown. These imported into parts of the Basin their standard, even-graded, grassed, and mowed roadsides and ditches, so that travelers now see the denuded hills against a foreground of tax-supported

2–21. Kudzu, one of few grasses and
plants that can survive such terrain,
puts out tendrils seeking a foothold
on steep slopes.

greenery, except in the depths of the active-mining areas and close to
the copper company's processing plants. Ironically, one of the early
hillocks that had been test-planted to pine was named Nort's Hill
after a tree-loving copper company executive. Nort's Hill was later
bulldozed clear of trees and now rises, grass-covered, in the midst of
a new highway interchange near Ducktown, directly in front of the
Ole Copper Inn.

## ENCROACHING GREENERY

The desert itself is growing smaller, thanks to a half-century series of
planting experiments and programs. This could very well be called

the most extensive reclamation project of this sort in U.S. history, but for one overriding fact. Nobody knows the whole story. No source I could find—in the TVA headquarters at Knoxville, in the TVA records stored at Muscle Shoals, Alabama (and moved to Knoxville by an obliging librarian so I could inspect them), in the U.S. Forest Service office at Norris, Tennessee, or in the land-owning Tennessee Chemical Company—nowhere did there appear to be a coordinated record of all these huge experiments. Various groups have planted trees, probably since the 1920s, certainly since the 1930s, and concentratedly since the 1940s. One TVA map of 1944 showed 40 "test tree plantings" and hundreds of acres, chiefly pine plantations set out from 1939 to 1944. The company expected to plant some 285,000 pine seedlings in 1983. Over the years, the mining companies have been the most consistent tree-planters, and since the 1930s have planted more than nine million seedlings, according to an estimate prepared for president Bruce Davis—"far more than ever planted by the two federal organizations."

But in several days of inquiry, I could find no single map, no comprehensive history of these many efforts. Here, so I thought, was I in the midst of one of the great scientific experiments of our history . . . and nobody has yet begun to organize the full body of evidence.

At the company offices, Safety Superintendent Don Sisson showed me the maps he was assembling after inheriting a few scattered documents from his predecessor. He was doing his best with shamefully sparse documentation to start with.

Records of this great experiment are scattered far and wide. At TVA headquarters, Knoxville, I found a 1973 report by Cities Service Company to the Environmental Protection Agency. At that time, the Soil Conservation Service had classified 13,200 acres of the Basin as having zero to 75 percent vegetative cover. Of those 13,200 acres, about 4,600 were then covered by vegetation, with 8,600 acres or 13.5 square miles still bare, yet to be reclaimed.

This report was my first clue as to the many hands that had dipped into the copper basin. Studies, reports, surveys, and/or plantings have been conducted by three copper companies, TVA, the U.S. Soil Conservation Service, the U.S. Forest Service, the former Civilian Conservation Corps, the Tennessee Division of Natural Resources, and by other state agencies as well as the Universities of Tennessee, Georgia, and North Carolina. Some were joint ventures. Some were and are funded by the Polk County government and the Township Commission. Most of them were conducted with the cooperation of whatever company owned the mines at the time. Today TCC is the major tree planter.

## FOUR TYPES OF RECLAMATION

In the records I had a chance to examine, "reclamation" has consisted of four types of work. The most thorough and expensive (costing up to $4,000 per acre reclaimed) was a 30-acre project (codenamed "RC&D") that reclaimed a steep and bare hillside directly across Highway 68 from the company's giant smelter and acid-recovery plants. The hillsides were roughly regraded and partially terraced by bulldozer; rock check dams were built, locust seedling planted in the accumulated soil above the dams; and the rest of the hillsides thickly planted with *Ceresea lespedeza,* weeping lovegrass, and clumps of Japanese knotweed. The last I recognized as a pestiferous backyard perennial called polygonum, which appears to be the only plant able to survive on some of the barren slopes down in the town of Copperhill. All these grasses, as well as the riotous kudzu vine, have been widely planted throughout the Basin.

A second experiment was conducted by TVA prior to 1951 at two adjoining watersheds called "IE" and "IW," in order to compare siltation runoff from the bare watershed with runoff from the revegetated watershed. I saw correspondence in the TVA files stressing the importance of these experiments, as well as excellent TVA records in Knoxville showing exactly how the new vegetation reduced the silt runoff. But the company records I saw at Sisson's office did not show these IE-IW locations, and Sisson was unable to locate them for me to visit.

Third, from 1934 to 1951 the TVA planted and studied extensively. TVA's motives were clear. Just downslope from the bare and fast-eroding Copper Basin lies the Ocoee River. When TVA took over the existing Ocoee dam and lake (built by a private company in 1912 to generate electricity), TVA knew that silt from the basin was fast filling the lakes and would greatly reduce the lakes' capacity to hold water.

As late as 1945, the director of TVA's Department of Forest Relations, William M. Baker, wrote (in a letter to T.A. Mitchell of TCC.) that "the major portion of the silt coming off the entire 23,000-

acre area flows unhindered into the Ocoee River . . . Observation indicates that the denuded area is increasing in size each year and that no lessening of the rate of erosion may be expected until control action is instituted." TVA had joint-ventured with the copper company and others to replant the Basin as fast as possible to slow the erosion.

Early on, TVA joined with the brand-new Civilian Conservation Corps, which, during the Depression, built two camps in the basin and trained young men in tree-planting and other reclamation work. Photographs made from 1934 to 1942 show these strangely nineteenth-century-looking youths working on raw hillsides, building dams, planting trees, and pitching straw mulch out of mule-drawn wagons to cover the ground.

Since "the CCC" figures so largely in histories of the New Deal—and there was brief but baseless talk about reconstituting it by the Reagan Administration in 1984—I took an afternoon in the spring of 1983 to go hunting for the old CCC ruins. My USGS maps showed 16 buildings had existed in 1941. I went tramping through the thick woods, mostly tall pine up to two feet in diameter at the base. Together with young hardwoods, they were growing on slopes that I reckoned to be about six to eight percent, a bit steep for a campsite. Yet it was there that I discovered the ruins—one complete foundation of a building that, once I got hold of the 1942 TVA photo files, I could identify as a seedling storage house. I also located three perimeter foundation walls and several concrete footings, perhaps for fireplaces and a water tank, plus an array of flattened building sites cut into the slopes, one of which may have been an exercise or drill ground. Feeling much like an archeologist returning triumphant from his latest dig, I reported my "find" to several local people. It stirred their childhood memories of "those CCC boys" working way out there in the then-raw and barren wastelands.

A fourth form of reclamation is the planting by various uncoordinated individuals and groups. One Saturday I encountered the Copper Basin High School football team in pickup trucks headed for an afternoon's tree planting, paid for by the township. Another day I saw an eight-man crew planting seedlings on part of the township's "school lands." The new whitewater outfitter had lined his approach road with the ubiquitous small pine. Most of the current seedlings are spurred to fast growth by pale green pellets of fertilizer, about the size of ping-pong balls, supplied by the Tennessee Chemical Company.

As a result of all these activities, artificial woodlands are slowly closing in, not only on historic sites, but on the raw desert. For a mile east of the once naked town of Copperhill, there are hundreds of acres of now-mature pine forests, mostly off the main roads.

If there were one continuing policy evident for a half-century, it was a determined effort to find the right combination of pine, locust, and grasses to stop the worst erosion. Coupled with this was the familiar ecological principle of "working with what's there." A former company forester, Ben Crawford, told me that many tree planters had covered raw slopes with pine, knowing (or at least assuming) that gradually the pines would "pioneer out"—spread their seedlings into adjoining gullied fields. This is now happening in many parts of the Basin.

It was hard and sometimes disappointing work. Planting pine in a gullied desert subject to 50-plus inches of rain that comes in driving torrents is a high-risk enterprise. Former forester Mercier told me of planting some areas three times before getting a 75 percent "catch," or survival rate.

Erosion has certainly slowed, though exact figures are hard to come by. TCC's Don Sisson recalls growing up in the stringtown mining community of Isabella, in the heart of the ravaged Basin. "When I was a boy, Potato Creek through Isabella filled the entire valley after a rain. But now you never see that. All that (pine) planting upstream is what must account for it." I drove up that valley and found an abandoned industrial wasteland. But the pines do cover large tracts of it.

## OPPOSING VIEWS

The most intriguing aspect of the Basin's future is its value as an "historical landscape." The old Burra Burra mine, adjacent to Ducktown, was abandoned by the mining company and its 17-acre hilltop and a straggle of old buildings was given to the Ducktown Basin Museum, which is now spruced up and open to the public. The tract has been listed on the National Register of Historic Places.

David Beckler, one of the museum organizers, I found to be a clear-voiced spokesman for leaving at least the central Basin raw, naked, historic, and unforested—"just like it's been as long as anybody in the Basin remembers." He'd like to see the whole central Basin declared a historic landmark, a wish that dismays veteran tree planters.

Part of the Basin's unique quality is its extraordinary visibility.

This is part of the first shock to visitors who emerge from miles of roads that are tree-enclosed tunnels through dense National Forests. Visitors coming from the west drive for miles along the Ocoee River gorge, enclosed by steep green mountainsides. Suddenly, you can "see out." The Basin spreads out into the far distance, offering endless photogenic views, some of them covering an expanse of six to 10 miles. Many travelers report that it is "just like being out West."

The Rev. David Brown, who lives at the foot of Red Hill, recalls that just a few years back, he could watch his young boys roaming for thousands of feet in any direction. But that was before the pines came in. David Beckler recalls, "A nice thing about the Basin was you'd never get lost; as kids we were free to roam everywhere, and were always visible."

Beckler's comments, and those of resident artist Sue Mitchell (whose father was once company president), sound much like the British critics of that nation's reforestation program. The dullness, sameness, and the ecological monotony of pine-covered landscapes gives them cause for concern. Copper Basin is a long way from being covered, but from my own experience visiting and photographing the basin from 1967 to 1983, I can see it gradually disappearing under the evergreen.

Such pineywoods planting has aroused another form of antagonism that goes back to generations of individualistic settlers who burned off woodlands—anybody's woodlands—to get spring pasturage for their cattle. Tennessee historian J.B. Killebrew, writing in 1874, commented that the region already was "a barren sterile region prior to 1850." The settlers' burnings, perhaps following still-earlier burnings by the Cherokee Indians, may have contributed to the barren aspect.

Incredibly, Tennessee law still permitted the open-range grazing of cattle until 1946, when fencing laws were finally passed. TVA photos from the 1930s, which I saw at Norris, Tennessee, showed cattle roaming over the nearly bare semidesert near Isabella and Ducktown. Lowland farmers drove and later trucked cattle up into the Basin for free grazing. Until 1946 (and some say much later) they burned land, indiscriminately, to encourage springtime growth of the thin sedge pasturage. According to Nora Foehner, of Huntsville, Alabama, who did her master's degree thesis in geography on the Basin, burners-and-grazers were major contributors to Basin erosion long after the copper smelting fumes were controlled. Rancor toward mass planting of pines continues. I was told of a roadside sign, probably put up by local hunters, on land outside the Basin, now heavily planted to pine by a giant pulpwood-paper company:

"If you got the money, we got the time.
You kill off our hardwood, we'll burn your damn pine."

## A LOOK AHEAD

I must confess to having accumulated a strong bias in the course of four visits to the Basin. It exerts an irresistible attraction: one of the strangest places in my experience—difficult to "read," tantalizing in what it conceals, complex in the reactions it inspires. I could envision a new form of tourism based on exploring its mysteries, not the least of which would be piecing together its many evidences of a century of mining practices. Like the Chinese "scenes" which, geographer George Scdden tells us, have prompted the writing of instructional books for tourists, showing them where to stand, what to see, The Basin contains endless opportunities for guides, artists, photographers, map-makers, instructors, teachers. If students find it as unforgettable as I do, their teachers will have an enviable open-air classroom at their disposal.

Whether the people of the Basin see in all this the same opportunity that shines so clear to me is something else again. Whatever they may do, the one missing element in all this, as I saw it, is any effective form of long-range community planning for the Basin. No one among the many local people I spoke with works with any such comprehensive plan; the county executive proudly re-counted 18 projects he wants to foster, but they are clearly unrelated to any plan that has strong political support. A member of the County Planning Commission told me that that the commission "primarily administers subdivision regulations." He referred me to the Southeast Tennessee Regional Plan—but then, in response to my question, said the closest copy was in Chattanooga.

As TCC sells off the bulk of its planted acreage, new owners, local and absentee, will take over much of the Basin. TCC intends to plant on the barren areas "closest to our operation until we have com-pleted our program." Whether new owners will take over and continue planting remains to be seen. There's a new water supply system going in for Ducktown and its outskirts; a new "industrial park" on two leveled-off hilltops. But the Environmental Protection

Agency, which works through state agencies, may find it more difficult to require that the new scattered owners control their own erosion than it has in the past, when it worked with one corporate landlord.

For awhile longer, possibly into the 1990s, it will be possible for visitors like me to become enraptured by this unexpected aberration, with its wonderful shapes and dazzling colors. It can still generate comments such as those of a Chattanooga columnist, Alfred Mynders, who called it "definitely one of the 'sights' to see, a tourist attraction of a macabre type."

Slowly nature's forces will move in from the perimeter; rawness will recede. Public-spirited groups no doubt will continue tree-planting. The unique Copper Basin—now clearly visible in satellite infrared photos as an isolated, almost white blob surrounded by thick forests—will slowly merge, even if it does not totally disappear, into the standard Appalachian landscape. No longer will its bare surface radiate extra heat into the atmosphere. No longer will a single summery white cloud hover silent above the Basin, formed by invisible heat rising upward. At the core—several thousand acres of mining activities—the open wound may survive. But in another generation, no one will know what it is like to stand in a vast landscape that has been altogether ruined by the hand of man. This livid monument to manmade erosion at last will have been hidden away.

## NOTES

1. This is a reminder that Poland has been eagerly solicitous of American tourists in the past, and may yet again open its doors as wide as in 1974, when this exploration took place.

2. "It is what we have seen in public parks, recreation areas, civic spaces, landscaped industrial estates, and shopping centers, and in affluent residential districts. It is shaped by established design traditions. Its mown turf, selected trees, and specified shrub borders are the symbol of civic pride and care, chosen to reflect the city's public face. Their prime objective is to maintain amenities and aesthetic benefits. Wherever possible these benefits are spelled out and enumerated in Official Documents." Michael Hough. *City Form and Natural Process* (London, Croom Helm, 1984).

# 3

# Emerging Scenes

---

## What Makes
## A Good Square
## Good?

### Square One
*"Plenty of
Action on the
Square"*

One morning not long ago I stood in the ancient and rundown Haymarket of Louisville, Kentucky, watching the steady procession of shoppers, farmers, peddlers, produce hawkers, speculators, and plain drifters go by.[1] It soon became apparent that the center of the Haymarket this particular morning was a spavined, broken-down, living-room chair set up on the brick sidewalk. Alongside it was a hot charcoal stove made from a 55-gallon oil drum cut in two and set up on stilts. Plumped down on the chair was a huge man; he was carrying on a sidewalk business in Christmas trees, and he was constantly bantering with everybody in sight. It was as if they all knew him. Like his stove, he radiated warmth over a wide radius, and tapped something in nearly everyone who passed by. He was the vital center of the Haymarket that morning. Where, I wondered, would anybody like him fit into the concrete prairies being laid out for so many cities?

Since that morning I have walked for more than 40 miles through the downtown centers of 11 cities and several smaller ones, seeking answers to puzzling questions: What makes a good city center? Why are some downtown plazas enjoyable and others a damned bore? Why do some open places feel right, and others somehow lack any quality that makes the visitor want to return?

There are many answers to such questions, but one thing my travels have convinced me of: The key to the successful square is action—and this is true of the quiet ones, too. Redevelopment, I am sure, is far too shortsighted if it merely builds buildings. It must build in a host of activities as well.

One thesis: Attract the tourists, and tourists attract crowds. As crowd bait, tourists have no peers and I would venture this prescription: Build in as much "local color" as can be found, revived, encouraged, or even created. Many a civic tradition has been allowed, through neglect, to be moved indoors or to the suburbs. Many a downtown square has been divested of most of the activities that once made it a vital part of everyday life. There seems to be a great opportunity for civic improvers here: to strengthen or revive the old festivals and public ceremonies that now take place, or have occurred historically, around the city's central plazas.

City attorneys, engineers, directors of public works, and such officials must revise their attitudes toward sidewalk displays and similar activities. In many cities you cannot sell anything, promote anything, or in fact, do anything on sidewalks but walk—unless you're making the annual Christmas pitch for contributions to a local charity. Somehow the gaiety and activity that once pervaded the old market squares must be reintroduced into downtown.

Outdoor dining is one good way; it gives life to the scene, and so long as the food is reasonably edible, there will be plenty of customers. In New York the outdoor cafes in Central Park have been pulling crowds for years; in the garden of the Museum of Modern Art, where the coffee is barely drinkable, the tables are usually jammed. Farther south are many more examples: Jackson Square in New Orleans, beside the river in San Antonio, and in Florida— where it is the intelligent custom to provide movable enclosures and awnings for bad weather. (Since these comments were written, sidewalk cafes have been widely legitimatized, the River Walk in San Antonio has become world-famous and much copied, and many of the promptings recorded here have been carried out from one end of the continent to the other.)

Southerners seem much smarter than Northerners at making good weather go farther. In New Orleans, for example, the patio of Brennan's Vieux Carre restaurant is dotted with electric heaters that fill it with warmth when there's a chill in the air. Such radiation, whether concealed in sidewalks, overhead canopies, or wall panels, offers a lesson for all downtown improvers. The installation of snow-melting equipment in downtown sidewalks up North is merely a timid beginning.

Since outdoor restaurants should give life to the scene, it is important not to seclude the diners from it. The cafe in Rockefeller Plaza is a case in point. It makes a gay scene for onlookers from above, but it is disappointing to eat there; you are down where you see nobody but other diners. All the fun accrues to the people who see you. Fortunately, New York has enough first-time tourists to keep the cafe reasonably populated. Ideally, though, the participant should be able simultaneously to take in the show and to be a part of it.

## THAT ENCLOSED FEELING

To a surprising degree the amount of activity in an open space depends on the feeling of enclosure it gives people. It is a feeling much like that you can enjoy in your corner drugstores where, as you sit and drink coke or coffee, you are comfortable in your own protected "cave"—while you watch the flow of people outside the big plate-glass windows.

Open spaces can have the same quality. In most cities there is a spot, hardly ever marked on a map, that has that almost indefinable quality of intimacy, comfort, and protection. I think of the landings on the steps leading southward down Washington Place south of Mount Vernon Place in Baltimore—sun-catchers, warm on cold days, and somewhat protected from the full impact of traffic noises by berms of earth on either side; certain benches in Union Square, San Francisco; and Mellon Square, Pittsburgh, which are nicely protected from wind currents.

To be enjoyable, an open space doesn't have to be small. New York's Central Park is in aerial view far more expansive than the concrete prairies on planners' drawing boards, yet it never over-powers people with its vastness. They don't see it from the air; they see it from the ground, and thanks to designer Frederick Law

Olmsted what they have is essentially a huge aggregation of small places—a pond, a skating rink, a zoo, a patch of woods. The skyline background is spectacular but it is the foreground that gives Central Park its peculiar enchantment.

There certainly need be no antithesis between good enclosure and contemporary design. A fine example of enclosure is provided by Chicago's *Sun-Times* Building and the elevated garden just east of it. The most important thing here is a wide balcony along the entire river side of the Sun-Times Building. You now can walk from Michigan Avenue across a catwalk from the Wrigley Building to the *Sun-Times* open-air garden, thence along the balcony for a long block—and in comfort, with superb views on either side. To your left you can look through a plate-glass wall into the busy *Sun-Times* pressrooms. To your right, there's the river, some four stories below. On occasion a great boat fills the entire canyon below; everybody turns to watch this sudden apparition, larger than life, suddenly filling this canyon in the middle of a great city.

Another thing I noticed was that the most interesting open spaces were those in which several currents of life came together—working-class people, well-dressed junior executives, mink-stoled ladies at their shopping, and, above all, children, who add a quality of noise, excitement, and vibrancy to the urban scene that is altogether indispensable.

There is much talk about the problem of bums in squares. Where downtown has an ample number of spaces, however, there is no real trouble. Savannah is a good case in point; it is the only city in America with enough squares for everybody, and no one square is dominated by the homeless drifters who, in many cities, cluster around the only available open space.

## MAKING SPLASHES

Finally, let me salute the fountain, for it is one of the most promising devices for a real transformation of downtown dry spots into places of delight, of joy, wonder, surprise, and beauty. The sound of them exerts a magnetism irresistible to people; they stir man out of his lethargies, remind him of youthful expeditions, stimulate him, elevate his spirits.

One of the finest of all downtown fountains in America is the Tyler Davidson Fountain in Cincinnati's Fountain Square. Around it is a maelstrom of activity, which continues, cold weather or warm; unlike most fountains in northern cities, this one is never boarded up in winter, and in all but the most freezing weather it flows undiminished.

For another cold-weather gambit, civic improvers should visit the Eastland shopping center northeast of Detroit. The secret: warm water in the pools. The fountains stop in midwinter—but in the coldest weather the waters of the pools around them are artificially warmed. I stood one cold morning watching these pools, while frigid winds whipped though the courtyards. Children made beelines for the misty, warm pools, and dipped up handfuls of the warm water in delight.

The use of color offers another way of building more liveliness into fountains. The cascade of Mellon Square in Pittsburgh offers a prime example. The cascade—great sheets of water pouring over a series of six graceful shelves alongside the stairway down to the Smithfield Street level—provides by day a shaded, water-splashed bit of landscape; by night, lit with colored lights, an exciting display.

Even more spectacular is the fountain at Orlando, Florida. The idea for it occurred to several local business leaders who went to a Washington, D.C., convention. They were staying at the Shoreham Hotel and were much impressed by the Shoreham's 50-foot illuminated spouts of water. Why not have one for Orlando? Better yet, why not put it smack in the middle of Orlando's lagoon? It would be a wonderful pitch for tourists, they agreed, and in short order they sold the townspeople on the idea.

It has to be seen to be believed: The fountain itself rises 18 feet above the lagoon and has seven subfountains around it. All are illuminated in an electrically controlled sequence of colors that lasts 18 minutes. In the center the major fountain spurts from a green-blue Plexiglas dome lighted from within.

For a really screwball fountain, however, the place to go is Northland shopping center, north of Detroit. Here is a collection of jets and sculpture that would delight Rube Goldberg, and does delight constant streams of visitors. People flock and stand, fascinated at the interplay of small wheels, levers, jets, spurts, and streams, a fantasy of motion and invention.

Here, it seems to me, lies the promise of the future: in the application of humor, inventiveness, and ingenuity to enliven display and entertainment. The great challenge to downtown is that such inventiveness has appeared most notably in several suburban shopping centers and in a Florida resort town. Is there any reason we can't have it in downtown, too?

## Square 2
*Action*
*Revisited*

"What makes a good square good?" That question headlined an article I wrote some 20 years ago for *Fortune* magazine. It was reprinted in *The Exploring Metropolis* (Doubleday & Co., New York, 1958) and had a small part in the impact of both the *Fortune* articles and that book upon contemporary attitudes toward the giant new public and private plazas being built in the U.S. in the 1950s.

Today hundreds of those great projects have been finished; hundreds more are under construction in North America and abroad. The world is being plazafied, its cities and their centers concreted in a fashion that was already apparent in 1958. As William H. Whyte Jr., the editor of *The Exploding Metropolis*, then wrote, "The hundreds of superblocks that are being planned will irretrievably fix the landscape of the city for some 50 years to come . . . (many of the new projects consisting of) a big central mall so vast and abstract as to be vaguely oppressive."

I recall that during the planning of the book in 1957 Whyte conceived a series of time-lapse photos from the Time-Life Building looking down into Rockefeller Center so as to chart the ebb and flow of the human throng in those open spaces below.

The process he set in motion has now come full circle: Whyte has become the dominant figure in a series of continuing studies, books, films, and time-lapse recordings of street life in New York. In Copenhagen, Prof. Jan Gehl has done pioneering photographic analyses of street-life (including a photographic record of what happens when a woman slowly removes her clothing in a public square in Copenhagen; very scientific.)

A whole new science of land-use analysis has bloomed in these two decades—the work of authors Neill and Joardar in Vancouver, B.C., being an example of the techniques currently applied. (I still have my own cache of three-by-five inch cards from my plaza reportage for *Fortune* of 1958—primitive stuff compared with the computer mapping available today.) Neill and Joardar bring some civility into the big-scale corporate enterprise that dominates cities in the U.S. and abroad.

### MONOPOLY CAPITAL AT WORK

Here is indeed a big-scale question, going beyond the more limited design issue of properly designing a plaza for people. Increasingly the central core of most Western cities—including the headquarter cities of corporate power all around the world—are everywhere dominated by the huge building blocks of public and private corporations. For complex reasons, one can no longer expect that a public corporation—say a British Broadcasting Corporation or World Bank or Federal Reserve Bank—will contribute anything more to street life and pleasures than a Mobil or a General Motors. Why this is so is in itself the subject for a book.

The name of the game is Display of Power, and even when the display is discreet, the fact is that most downtown spaces in the traditional core of Western cities are being redeveloped overwhelmingly beyond human scale. The skyscrapers tower, the doormen glower, and the citizens cower in the spaces in between.

Now of course there are exceptions, and in Vancouver and San Francisco developers find it occasionally possible to encourage or allow designers to provide the so-called amenities along the public way. It is fashionable these days to speak of "enlightened developers." This I take to mean slightly less rapacious than the rest—or else compelled by political and other pressures to provide comforts and pleasures to the public, in return for the privilege of occupying monopoly locations of center-city space. It is no accident that many Manhattan plazas now provide seating for people; for not until Whyte's exposes—or, more properly, his detailed user-studies— showed the bleak and forbidding aspect of Manhattan's new plazas did that city's Planning Commission enact ordinances to ensure that the plazas would be used comfortably by the public. (Whyte's 1972 article in the *New York Times Magazine* was a superb piece of propaganda in behalf of better-designed plazas.)

## LOOKING FOR CRUMBS

If I understand correctly the politics of these matters, most of the design professions have played a cautious game, hoping that the center-city developers would throw them, and the public, enough crumbs in the form of open space, so as to keep up some semblance of civility. Thus architects, landscape architects, and others have been among the leaders in many local fights to produce a "more humane center-city plan"—one with increased ratios of open to built space.

Only rarely have I ever heard of these same professions attempting to prohibit the monopolizing of huge blocks of urban space by one owner; or, much less, to limit the amount of economic space that could be dominated by a single private firm. That is a radicalism that may once have been central to the concerns of the planning and design professions but one seldom voiced by them today.[2]

Yet if you examine closely many of the favorite townscapes visited worldwide by tourists, it is just those places, usually in multiple small ownerships, that have not been taken over by the bleak, barren, and deadening big-scale developers. Often it is those smaller, more intimate streets just off the huge new monopoly sites. Maiden Lane off Jackson Square in San Francisco; Georgetown, D.C., safely distant across the Potomac from the massive towering offices of Rosslyn, Virginia; Philadelphia's low-rise Mole Street just off Market Street (razed later for more block-buster projects), Greenwich Village occupying the swale between Manhattan's high-density districts.

But in discussing the monopoly of central sites we are not yet at the core of the issue. Any society that is organized so as inevitably to concentrate wealth and center-city power into fewer hands—as is visible in scores of Western nations—is a society that is also organized to discomfit ordinary citizens when they go out in the noonday sun for a stroll or to lunch or to shop.

And I think it proceeds from the above that any society that still forces its millions of citizens off the land, out of hamlets, villages, and small towns to pack up and crowd into cities, artificially inflating land values to be monopolized at the center, is to harass and deprive the ordinary citizen trying to live in these cities.

I cannot speak for the others who had a hand in writing *The Exploding Metropolis* 20 years ago, but I see the advent of well-designed urban plazas as only a small step toward creating livable cities. We can celebrate the pleasures of these small blessings, while remembering that they are tiny indeed compared with what is yet to be done.

---

# Swarming

I had been looking in the mid-1960s for some way to describe the new kind of place I kept seeing—huge new state fairgrounds, civic centers, community plazas, shopping centers, stadiums, all surrounded by vast parking lots. I had called them "congregation stations," an awkward phrase. Finally, it was a word from J.B. Jackson, the landscape historian, that helped me to form a new concept, a handle for the Woodstock phenomenon.

This is the word "swarm" in its biological sense, and the activity I call "swarming." In its early nineteenth-century meaning in New England, the phrase "to swarm" meant to send out a colonizing group from a parent church into the wilderness to form a new mission church, let us say in western Massachusetts. It was also called "hiving," and old accounts give these events a strong emotional flavor. (The word "hiving" also occurs in descriptions of the ancient Phoenicians' process of spinning off new communities around the Mediterranean.)

Looking at the hundreds of rock festivals since Woodstock, it is clear that these twentieth-century swarmings bring people from vast distances with their own transport, free time, and a determination to be a part of a group experience. It is massive declaration of identity—and it is continuing.

Tolstoy once defined history as "the unconscious general swarmlife of mankind." Today's swarming by groups who seek self-discovery is shaking the establishment, doing away with old geographic fixations, creating unheard of markets, finding new bases of information—all with implications for architecture. More people crowd into the business, old professions learn new tricks, competition is keen. New products flood into the market, and new media expand to cover and promote these identities.

## SEARCHING FOR IDENTITY

"Identity" has become an object of widespread research and coinage; it is fashionably multidisciplinary. Charles Reich's *The Greening of America* made it semiofficial by defining states of Consciousness I, II, and III with which all Americans could identify or argue. The search-for-identity cuts across all social groups, uniting Black Panthers and white ethnics as they work both sides of the same street.

To think about one's own personal identity is a familiar struggle for most people, but the struggle has become institutionalized as professions, business firms, political subgroups, and whole regions now go through the ordeal of asking, "Who am I? Who are we?"— and then begins the longer process of trying to peddle, market, and/

or promote this thing called identity.

In this process, the invention, production, and marketing of new identities has become an important growth industry. It is full of newcomers jostling for a slice of the market, which they conceive to be ever expanding. There is good evidence that, once one begins the search for identity, it never stops. As the world changes, one's own "fit" into the world must change and so must one's identity. It may well turn out that nobody will ever find an identity because he is too busy anxiously becoming something else, engaged in a deliberate personality-change-game all the way to and beyond the grave. But at the moment, most identity-seekers do not view it this way.

I propose to examine one contemporary form of identity as a new product in the marketplace. It includes millions of Americans. It has architectural implications. In dealing with it I will offer an impressionistic description and few conclusions.

### SWARMERS

They came to be called the Woodstock Nation, having come together on that memorable weekend in August 1969, when their campers, cars, bikes, and buses formed a bumper-to-bumper traffic jam for some 30 miles outside Max Yasgur's farm near Woodstock, New York.

The occasion was one of the most curious examples of identity-declaration in modern times. Never before Woodstock had U.S. society so clearly shown its capacity for nonmilitary crowd formation. Never before Woodstock had 350,000 young people assembled under such festive and primitive conditions, drawn one and all to seek and to declare a new identity.

Never before had mass auto-mobility combined so effectively with mass media to create instant US—large-scale communities assembled by media, by word-of-mouth, and by personal transport. We have had crowds before, traffic jams before; we have had chatauquas, world's fairs, camp meetings, conventions, and jamborees before. But this was something else.

Such swarming requires a large and mobile population from which to draw, a market conditioned by years of exposure to recordings, to personal appearances, and to television showing rock music and its personalities. Music has been the magical network of communication, "the glue holding us all together," as Ralph Gleason put it in *Rolling Stone*, the most successful of all newspapers catering to the rock culture identity.

Such tribal occasions as Woodstock and its sequel appear live and kicking on television and with great shock value invade every living room. Thus swarming has accumulated the suspicions of the square world, the attentions of its police, and the counteraction of its establishments.

Those who hold the old traditionalist-monopolist view of cities tend to see these mobile, volatile, touch-and-go swarmers as threats to all those predictable fixities-in-place on which traditional cities have for so long depended. Swarming does not hold still for scientific examination. It keeps no records. But it makes exciting movies, and some of them—like "Gimme Shelter," depicting the Rolling Stones' 1969 fiasco at Altamont Race Track, California—turn into rank identity propaganda.

To market-oriented economists, swarming is shattering evidence of the evanescence of markets. It can pick up its 350,000 potential spenders and move out—just like that. The gate potential at Woodstock, unrealized because of gate-crashing, was $5.5 million; the festival used $1.4 million in materials and over $600,000 in services. Such vast new money in town, or in the boondocks, is a radicalizing force, and many small towns and other outlandish places have been and will be radicalized. This chancey dumping of money by strangers onto small-town society is upsetting to normal commerce and society, which react adversely. Fathers fear for daughters' virginity, farmers for their crops, and sound sleepers for things that go boom in the night.

By now it has become apparent that swarming, being the essence of transience, is a threat to so-called stable community values. It contributes nothing to "normal community growth." It puts a premium on the swarmer's own mobility and self-sufficiency. Swarming descendents of the Woodstock Nation wear their own costumes, speaking a kind of sartorial Esperanto, travel light, and prefer off-the-road vehicles wherever possible.

Any day now we should expect "swarming kits" to appear at supermarket prices, a derivative of the riot coverage kit developed by the general manager of Los Angeles Radio Station KHJ for its reporters who cover the more violent outdoor events. It cost $800 and contained, among other things, a blue jumpsuit with the large words "Press" front and back. By the 1980s this was becoming suicidal, as reporters covering the El Salvador revolution discovered. Terrorists had seized on the murder of media people as just another tactical ritual.

Other early warning radar images of the swarming kit may be found in the work of the Archigram group of architects in London: A "cybernomadic living kit," a mobile air-land-sea vehicle with its own plug-in terminals for computer access; or the "informaison," fully equipped with the latest mobile telecom.

Swarmers themselves want as little as possible to do with new buildings, with cities, and with organized, structured places. Swarming does not require buildings, but it cannot exist without urban supplies and infrastructure: highways, communications, helicopters on call, instant coming-down places for bad trips.

## GENERATING INSTANT COMMUNITY

The essence of this capacity to swarm is the geographic mobility of the swarmers and the instant community spirit or communication that they can generate. The fact that drugs eased the pains of high-density overcrowding in the mud and rainstorms at Woodstock 1969 tells us something about how high-density overcrowding may be made bearable, palatable, and repeatable in the future. But it is clear that something more pervasive and powerful than drugs was and still is at work. That stimulation was and remains a searching for identity, a declaration of selfhood, a dramatic and photogenic aspect of what I call "Instant-Us Culture."

Swarming arises from new feelings and convictions among young Americans, from their search for identity and community. It is the outward evidence of a new and powerful minority group declaring its existence and its intention to become a majority no matter what statistics may say to the contrary. For the swarmers themselves, it has proved to be a powerful means of self-discovery; of finding out who are one's friends; of trading passwords, new language forms, identity tokens, and attitudes; and of making declarations about these matters to the world outside.

The Woodstock swarming is only one example of the emergence of new and often violent groups of freewheeling, independent people with their own lifestyles and values that appear to be the primitive setting up of threatening camps just outside straight society. Such occasions test the capacity of straight society and its mass media to distinguish one tribe from another without falling into the error of concluding, "They all look alike to me." One should not be surprised at future swarms of more conservative types: ecology-actionists cleaning up trashed valleys in weekend swarms or mobile Boy Scout jamborees bringing mass good deeds to the multitudes.

In *Beyond the Melting Pot*, Nathan Glazer and Daniel P. Moynihan observed: "Ethnicity is more than an influence on events; it is commonly the source of events. Social and political institutions do not merely respond to ethnic interests; a great number of institutions exist for the specific purpose of serving ethnic interests." I would extend the Glazer/Moynihan image to say that "identity is more than an influence on events; it is commonly the source of events."

In the course of declaring their identity, swarmers have met increasing resistance. As city police have armed themselves to overcome rioters, they have quickly turned on swarmers. It has grown tougher to get a permit, to get highway access, or to avoid injunctions and hassling from the nonswarming world. But the basic conditions that created the market for coming together in the first place still exist: the huge numbers of young people not yet admissible or taken into the labor market; the all-time record number in college with spring and summer vacations; their automobility and their special communications through music.

I would argue that swarming is becoming a permanent condition, and, if it is repressed, the energies it has set loose will crop up in other, maybe more dangerous form. Automobility and the vast communications systems behind it cannot be shut off.

---

# Superblockbusting

All aglaze and agog inside and burnished brightly outside for its opening ceremonies, SuperBlock looms over the main drag of this Southern Indiana town. Surely, as the word gets around, it will become yet another magnet for architectural buffs who find their way to Columbus, this "Athens of the Prairie."

This farming and industrial town of some 30,000 population has become world renowned for well-designed new buildings, and a unique tradition of local architectural patronage. SuperBlock, on Washington Street, the latest and in some ways most ambitious architectural project in local history, was conceived and designed by architect Caesar Pelli, partner in charge of design for Victor Gruen Associates, Los Angeles.

SuperBlock (as originally labeled) has now been rechristened The Courthouse Center as a verbal gesture to the handsome old red-brick Bartholomew Country Courthouse, which stands in a green lawn across heavily traveled Fourth Street. Apart from its name, however, SuperBlock has little to do with the courthouse, setting its own pace and visual standards. It is both "successful architecture" and an estranged neighbor for the courthouse.

I know of no building quite like this anywhere—nor any town, for that matter. First the building itself: SuperBlock occupies two renewed city blocks and a vacated city street, a large Sears Roebuck store filling its western block, and a block-wide civic space, The Commons, taking up the principal street frontage. Under most daylight conditions, it is a huge, dark brown, glassy building unlike anything else in the region. Seen from some angles, it turns bright as the sky reflects from its glass. People inside can see out easily but not vice versa. At night The Commons is the brightest thing on Washington Street. In the daytime, it dominates without quite overwhelming its neighboring buildings, maintaining a three-story cornice line. The concept clearly borrows from, but improves on, such older Gruen buildings as Detroit's Northland (suburban center) and Rochester's Midtown Plaza, and older public galleries in Milan, Naples, or Brussels. Nowhere else in any nonmetropolitian building have I encountered such generous and well-designed public spaces. Certainly it puts to shame the typical U.S. suburban shopping center, which is sucking away retail trade from most towns the size of Columbus, Indiana.

On a recent visit I encountered Jean Tinguely, whose new mobile sculpture was clacking and whirring away in The Commons—a mechanical structure some 30 feet high with 12 motors and a convoluted raceway for light steel spheres going their perpetual journeys up and around. The sculpture was commissioned by the local architectural and industrial patron of Columbus, J. Irwin Miller, president of the Cummings (diesel) Engine Company. The major investor in SuperBlock is Miller and Company, an investment partnership of members of the Miller and Irwin families. SuperBlock could never have come off without their money and drive.

The Commons could hold a high school graduation or two

basketball games; its delights are multiple. There is space, flooring, carpeting, displays, community rooms, children's play yard, etc.— of a quality (and apparent expense) not to be seen even in such high-fashion shopping centers as Old Orchard, in Skokie, Illinois; Irvine, California; or Columbia, Maryland. My visits took place two days before the opening public ceremonies and the week afterwards.

## TURNING ITS BACK TO NEIGHBORS

Where SuperBlock performs badly in my view it does so obviously—in its relation to its southern neighbors. No doubt Pelli was determined—so he appeared in 1971 to the city's design review committee of which I was a member—to produce both a commercially successful building and a dramatic, self-contained civic wonderland. But in doing so, he turned a two-block-long blank but well-planted (euonymus and local swampbirch) berm and wall southward to the county courthouse and civic center site, interrupted by only one opening, using "landscaping" as a condescending gesture

3–1. Caesar Pelli's superblock, called The Commons, turns its long, cold shoulder to the street for two blocks in Columbus, Indiana ("Athens of the Prairie"), opposite Bartholomew County Courthouse, at right.

to the neighbors, especially with a flippant wave of the hand (grassed and treed corner plot), to the southeast. It shows how far modern building architects can venture in solving complex urban problems—and yet continue to use "landscaping" as a placatory screening device or concession.

SuperBlock thus reflects not only its neighbors, but in another sense the dominance of building architects. Landscape architect Dan Kiley of Charlotte, Vermont, has had an occasional strong influence in Columbus, having designed the landscape for several significant buildings, including Miller's own extraordinary house. The city has followed an early Skidmore, Owings & Merrill plan for linking renewal sites with new sidewalks, wider streets, new trees carefully chosen, sign controls, well-tended verges, and quality street furnishings. But to equal the splendor of its buildings, the city's landscape still has a long way to go.

---

# Harboring
# Afterthoughts
# in Baltimore

Blackness swirls at your feet, come 10,000 miles to bobble here below. Throw a bottled message down into the dark water and away it may swirl to the ends of the earth. I stare into its blackness and dream up sea serpents and the remnants of World War II ships that never got far enough from harbor to be sunk by Nazi submarines . . . reckless coins carrying wishes down into the mire, dregs of whiskey in farflung bottles, and bones from long-dead sailors locked grim in each others grip, a knife under the ribs, a drunken fall off one of those long-gone grain ships that once clustered in Baltimore's Inner Harbor.

I wrote this rather gaudy memorandum after my last visit to the Inner Harbor of Baltimore, Maryland, partly in reaction to its Upbeat, Upscale, Boutiquey, and Hoity-toity atmosphere, coupled with some reading of the city's history. The fact that old Baltimore was a rough and rather dangerous port doesn't come through the literature of the so-called Baltimore Renaissance of the 1980s (nor is there any reason why it should do so).

The current story of that old port, that window to the world, that funnel for profits from faraway, became Big News in 1981-82. For in the years 1954-1980, before Reaganomics took hold and cut into subsidies for urban programs, no city had been more successful than Baltimore in soliciting and directing the flood of federal subsidies to solve its own deep troubles.

It happens that 1981 also was the year when the phrase "The Rouseing of America" was coined to describe the spreading influence of Baltimore's remarkable James W. Rouse. Developers from all over the world rushed to Boston to see Rouse's successful rehabbing of old Quincy Market into a vastly profitable food-and-drink emporium. Others flew to Baltimore to rush down to the Inner Harbor and see Rouse's Harborplace, hoping to "do a Rouse" back on their own turf.

Standing at Harborplace, watching today's 'recreational shopping' and promenading crowds, one is tempted to overlook how it came to be and goggle at the spectacle. But if one seeks a display of urban design ideas, fashionable in the United States since World War II, all are here. Here, too, are the latest gimmicks in modern merchandising. And, thanks to Baltimore's penchant for keeping history alive, stories of how-it-came-to-be fall readily to hand.

## THE SENSE OF THE PLACE

If gravity were the only force at work here, everything in Baltimore would slowly slide downhill to tidewater, and much of the city would end up in Inner Harbor. But gravity alone can hardly explain the fact that the Inner Harbor has become such a magnetic attraction. Only by standing in, and carefully examining the environs of "the Crotch," as the downtown intersection of Pratt and Light Streets is indelicately called, can one understand the geopolitical forces that have converged here.

The flow off the city has sweetened up considerably since H.L. Mencken complained in the 1930s that it "stunk like a million polecats." The harbor waters no longer smell of oil, offal, and sewage. The crowds are neater and better-heeled than in the 1950s, when this was still a fishermen's and produce dealer's port, and not much of one at that. Today the ocean tide counts for little except as a magnet; the human tide is what pays the new high rents.

Only two blocks away from the Harbor and uphill is Charles Center, 42-acres of new skyscrapers, tightly merged with dozens of other older towers, offices, a civic center, and a new public library to attract thousands of shoppers. These gravitate downhill to eat and

3–2 and 3–3. Part of the customary treatment for Baltimore's visiting VIPs includes this view down into the Inner Harbor from the top floor of the World Trade Center.

shop around Inner Harbor, which is now considered to be an integral part of the central business district, whereas the former fish docks were beyond the pale, part of another world.

In addition to catching the flood of shoppers, strollers, and tourists, Inner Harbor also brings the continental edge visibly into downtown Baltimore. You can board cruise ships here. Or you can reboard a training cruiser—as did visiting sailors in 1975—and sail back to Norway. Someday, according to local hopefuls, there will be hovercraft and fast ferries from here to major Chesapeake Bay ports.

Visitors first must straighten out the place names. Harborplace, technically speaking, consists of an L-shaped public plaza about 1,500 feet long, noted for a pair of two-story buildings crammed with shops and restaurants. This was opened in 1980, adjacent to Inner Harbor, by the (James) Rouse Company. "Inner Harbor" has come to mean the entire district around the water. And by that skillful public-relations feat, the larger area has been swept up in the tide of publicity that has drenched the harbor itself.

Inner Harbor has great carrying capacity. Its two bordering streets, Pratt and Light, carry huge volumes of daily traffic. It is a major turning and crossing point for local as well as for through-truck traffic. It has around it the central city's largest array of public promenades, new parks, plazas, playgrounds, and gardens. Visual and walking access to the harbor has been carefully planned, directed, managed, and merchandised by planners, landscape architects, architects, urban designers, and developers.

Consequently the array of new buildings and spaces around the Harbor is just that: a carefully managed setting. The Pratt-and-Light area comes close to being the East Coast's prime example of the Renaissance City. Here you see played out the classic techniques of enclosure, height, and setback controls, the regulation of water edges, of sight lines, of building forms, and the manipulation of street furniture and public gardens. It's a game played by experts, and all of their gadgets and gambols and gavottes fit neatly into well publicized and coherent urban plans.

Everything you see is man-made or manipulated, and subject to formal regulations. Nearly two miles of Inner Harbor are now accessible to, and owned by, the public. None of it is fenced off. You can fall, drunk or sober, into Inner Harbor for as far as you can see.

Furthermore, the place enjoys two public vantage points from which thousands of visitors snap panoramas: the city-financed top floor of the 30-story World Trade Center and city-owned Federal Hill to the south across Inner Harbor. Beyond that, several buildings on the slopes above Inner Harbor have been designed with open or glassed plazas at the ground floor. Thus you can stand two blocks back from the water and look through these skyscrapers to catch a view of *U.S.S. Constellation,* a historic naval warship, at its mooring. A Harbor View has become a valuable commodity.

Practically everything closely visible from the Crotch is new; historical exceptions like *Constellation* have been virtually rebuilt. From the moment one leaves Lombard Street, going upslope to the North, one confronts newness—one building per block and a narrow range of building materials. The old city farther uphill snuggles together with a dozen or two older masonry buildings per block. If you want to see the nineteenth- and late twentieth-century cities confront each other, Lombard is a good place to begin.

## MAGNETS, GENERATORS AND FEEDERS

One way to get a sense of the transformation at Harborplace is to take the Metroliner out of Washington, D.C. This 62-minute run ends underneath Baltimore's old Greek Revival Pennsylvania Railroad Station. A $3.50 taxi ride down St. Paul Street takes you past blocks of row houses, downtown and downhill to Harborplace, that highly touted shopping center, design-prize winner, and profit generator for the Rouse Company. Among its many honors was a 1981 honor award from the American Society of Landscape Architects to Wallace Roberts and Todd, designers of the outdoor environment into which Rouse's two sales pavilions were built.

An unprepared tourist is in for a shock, not so much at the experience of Harborplace itself—which has all those well-advertised designer goodies, ethnic foods, expensive clothing, excursion steamers, and the historic *Constellation*—but at what lies around it.

So shrewdly was Harborplace merchandised, so desperate was American media for a success story from an old city in 1980, that Harborplace became an instant star. At grand opening, Baltimore stood by enjoying the rare glow of a good press, in which some 3,800 articles have since appeared.

The Harborplace story was soon being endlessly replicated across the continent in seminars on urban problems. "Saving Downtown" is the recurring theme, with "Harborplace" the case-study to prove there's still hope for a decrepit waterfront with the right combination of local Movers and Shakers.

But the moment any of the millions of visitors ("More than Disney World!") sets foot in the Inner Harbor neighborhood, he and she (this is a mecca for couples) confront an array of other magnets, generators, and feeders. It is these that, collectively, have made Harborplace possible as well as profitable.

Actually the place—or to be even more specific, the setting—is mostly public. The site and its redevelopment were paid for by a myriad of state, local, and national subsidies and taxes. Streets, bulkheads, the filled-in and much-altered shoreline, handsome red-paved promenades, steps, all those little ins-and-outs, provide

3–4. "These are historic artifacts," local preservationists like to declare. Thus historic paving blocks are not left exposed to artifactual thieves, but kept behind heavy fence until used for repaving a certified historic street or plaza.

guaranteed access, visibility, postcard prominence, and in the end, profit-making customers. Here is as clear a marriage of public and private investments as you can find anywhere in North America.

This may come as a shock to readers of *Time* magazine's August 24, 1981 cover story on "Master Planner" James Rouse. In Timelight one might think that Rouse did it all, with a sidebar assist from long-time Baltimore Mayor William D. Schaefer.

But this is not quite the way things happened in Baltimore, nor do they dance precisely to *Time*'s tune in any other city. Rather, as visitors look around them, they see the fruits of at least 30 years of public plans and investments in the larger Inner Harbor area. Without these investments, and the formal city planning-and-design tactics that brought them about, there would be no man-made and heavily subsidized setting for Rouse's Harborplace today.

In an era of Reaganomics, it might be argued that Harborplace "proves" what private capital can do alone, unimpeded by bureaucratic regulations and federal intervention. Nothing could be further from the truth, as a careful scan of the two-mile shore will reveal.

From a visitor's stance looking outward from the Crotch at the northwest corner of Inner Harbor, the sky to one's left is filled by the 30-story World Trade Center. Headquarters of the Maryland Port Administration, the tower is otherwise occupied by commercial tenants.

Filling the southeast horizon is the handsome National Aquarium in Baltimore (8,000 specimens, 600 different types of mammals, fish, birds, amphibians, invertebrates) that was financed jointly by state, national, and local sources.

Shifting the touristic gaze 30 degrees to the right, the visitor confronts Federal Hill dead-ahead, a large green flat-top pyramid, not exactly Disneyland, but public land kept green at public expense. Here in World War II Nike missiles stood guard against German submarines.

Barely visible (binoculars needed here) at the base of Federal Hill is a new Rusty Scupper restaurant on public land, a new public marina, and behind it Joseph H. Rash Memorial Park, built in the 1970s as part of the Inner Harbor redevelopment and run by the city's parks-and-recreation department.

Once the tourist's eye has tracked westward past Federal Hill, it slides gently and inevitably downhill to come to rest on a multi-faceted brick structure which, upon closer inspection, turns out to be the Maryland Science Center. Home of the Maryland Academy of Sciences, this is "the second-oldest scientific institution in the United States," founded in 1797. It is private, not-for-profit, which means subsidized for the public good. Visitors' feet have already polished the shiny brass medallion in the lobby floor, which reminds them that the building's planning and construction spanned the terms of three governors, each contributing his might or mite to this mecca.

## HERE AT THE STARTING-PLACE

Comes next a two-block long Gen. Sam Smith Park, which rests atop the old harbor's edge where the city first began. Landfilling has pushed the edge a block eastward from its origins, adding this 300,000-square-foot building site where now rests Rouse's Light Street Pavilion. Money for this park was voted in 1948, when citizens approved a $1.5 million bond issue. The question of whether this was supposed to "remain forever parkland" was buried under pressure to get the Rouse project under way.

Just beyond the park—assured of a permanent view of the harbor that gleams beyond the park—rises what seems to be a scaled-down replica of LeCorbusier's famed Marseilles Block, but is really part of the Christ Lutheran Church's complex of housing for the elderly. One can sit in the green quadrangle and look through the building's open ground floor to the harbor.

As if all this were not enough public investment to make any private real estate entrepreneur jump for joy, President Franklin D. Roosevelt recommissioned an ancient (1797) frigate as part of the U.S. Atlantic Fleet. Thanks to Congressional appropriations to the U.S. Navy, the U.S.S. "Constellation" stays afloat and agleam for tourists (admission $1.50 adults, 50 cents for others).

Not visible to the naked eye, the U.S. Engineers keep the harbor deep enough for seagoing craft, a long series of political deals having prevented the harbor from being blocked by an interstate highway bridge. Thus the "Tall Ships" entered the harbor in 1976 for the harbor's first of many grand openings. And thus the harbor was made a quieter place for future dwellers in the long-discussed high-rise apartments that have appeared in every plan since 1965.

Within a five-minute walk of the Crotch are several million square feet of new and old office buildings, many of which are in Charles Center, the 42-acre redevelopment built almost from scratch since

3–5. A familiar townscape device used to connect the Inner Harbor with the nearby financial district is a series of carefully prescribed openings in new buildings, so that boats and the water's gleam are visible for blocks away.

1958 as a federally assisted urban redevelopment project. One block west lies the new Convention Center that covers two square blocks. People attending conventions can walk via skywalks east of Harborplace, or north into the financial district.

Inner Harbor also enjoys the nearby presence of Little Italy, a short walk to the east, and not yet touched by the developers' wrecking ball. Just east of Inner Harbor, where the street pattern breaks off at an angle, this tangle of oddly shaped blocks is an urban village of mostly two-story frame and brick houses. Its restaurants are heavily visited by noontime lunchers and tourists. Not yet does it have the earlied-up look of Otterbein, which is an older and once-beat-up section of brick houses and cobblestoned alleys west of Harborplace. Otterbein Homestead, a short walk from the new scenes of action, is being fast renewed; several blocks of restored houses and new town-houses are available from $97,500.

Local planners long ago discovered the value of catchy names. In addition to "the Crotch," there is also "the Knuckle"—the tall USF&G building just uphill to the northwest. These anatomical junctions form a new sort of "100 percent location," in Baltimore. Behind the Knuckle looms a formidable array of tall office buildings merging with Charles Center.

3–6. When fair weather friends gather at Harborplace, there's plenty of action. In between times, the mayor's office shepherds tourists, exhibitionists, paraders, marathon runners, et al., through the public plaza nearby to keep the action going.

## THE MARRIAGE OF GOODS AND SEMANTICS

Several major crowd-getters have been assembled around the Crotch. Most attention lately has been lavished on Harborplace. The two long buildings of about 75,000 square feet each are crammed with 44 shops, boutiques, and eating places. With a custom-made mix of local merchants—including a more than pro-rata share of blacks—the buildings burst with exuberant selling. (First-year sales exceeded the Rouse projections by 40 percent.) Visitors are surrounded head-to-foot, floor-to-ceiling with colorful goodies. In the crowded halls there is hardly a visible square foot of wall or ceiling space not crowded with merchandise, with 'the Village look' prevailing in the clothing shops, a currently popular mix of Preppie, Tidewater-Country, and other trendy styles.

By thus manipulating the semantics of geography, the Baltimore planners and Rouse have created a tourist destination that expands the city's older and once-ailing retailing core. People come for weekends, "even from New York" (as the exultant local newspapers reported) to "do" Harborplace; in so doing they leave huge volumes of money for Rouse, hoteliers, taxi drivers, and all the nearby beneficiaries of the incoming trade. The city of Baltimore's share is a 400 percent increase in property taxes from the area.

"The Crotch Show" is not what its name might imply, but rather a carefully staged series of events on the plazas at Pratt and Light. Here the city's convention and tourist bureau stages shows, exhibits, charades, and parades. On the bright spring day of one of my visits, firemen were installing tall flags for a new convention, local marathon runners streamed through the place for a quarter-hour, a juggler and a fire-eater did their things, and a small marching band came through. What appears to the casual eye as a wonderfully happenstantial place is, in fact, as carefully arranged, timed, financed, and accounted for as a Hollywood movie.

And the scene is by no means finished. In conjunction with Bloomingdale's and RTKL, the nationally famous Baltimore firm of architects, the Rouse firm was, at my last visit, starting a new office-department store-garage with hotel on the top. Facing Inner Harbor across Pratt Street, this new building is being fitted rather strictly into the cornice-line-and-setback mold of nearby structures. Several other structures are also to be added to the frame; construction on the nearby subway also continues.

One of the few remaining "sleepers" (i.e., unexploited zones of real estate with harbor frontage) lies east of the aquarium in the form of disused commercial piers. While I was in Baltimore the local AIA chapter—in an effort to attract more attention to its local members' design abilities—held a competition for future development of Piers 5 and 6. One proposal by Peter Doo showed long glass conservatories down each pier. Cho Wilks and Burns, with James Reed Fulton as landscape architect, proposed combining the piers, the most thoroughly detailed of all the plans I saw. Another by John Rode, Siming Tan, and Randy Kuser called for a multinational community, with a "Son-of-Inner-Harbor" in the middle.

And of course, with the long-range vision that planners are supposed to enjoy, Baltimore's planning director Larry Reich looks southward. He sees the harbor of the Middle Branch, Patapsco River, with eight miles of shoreline, lying comparatively untouched—old industry needing upgrading, etc. All of it ready for the next great wave of development that Reich sees coming down the road—someday.

## THE LINK WITH THE FEDS

The view of Baltimore from Washington has long been clouded by class bias, civic prudery, and other myopias. Usually this is summarized in quips about Baltimore being "Washington's industrial suburb."

I recall the scorn that greeted my own suggestion, in one of those self-conscious task forces that swirled through Washington in the years of the Johnson presidency, that Washington needed a mixture of industry to balance its domination by the federal bureaucracy. No bastard at a family picnic could have gained more instant scorn. "This is the National Capital!" my associates shouted. "All that blue-collar stuff goes to Baltimore."

That was in 1965-66, when the Potomac Planning Task Force was formulating policy for Secretary of Interior Stuart Udall, and it offered me a quick picture of what Baltimore, in the eyes of Washingtonians, was "supposed to be."

As it turned out, Washington was not a bad spot from which to view Baltimore. The latter city and its leaders perfected a unique set of political and social linkages with the federal bureaucracy and the Democratic Party during the crucial 25 years of urban growth and renewal following World War II. And they made the most of it.

This early link with the "Feds" proved to be crucial. One of the
pioneer linkage practitioners was G. Yates Cook, who made a
national reputation in the 1950s for Baltimore housing code enforce-
ment and modest but rare improvements in existing housing. He
later became an executive for the Federal City Council in Washington. James W. Rouse headed a commission set up by President
Dwight Eisenhower to formulate national housing policy, and
maintained a high profile in Washington. Guy O. Hollyday, another
Baltimorean, became head of the Federal Housing Administration.
Richard L. Steiner moved from Baltimore's housing-urban renewal
agency to become first U.S. Urban Renewal Commissioner, taking
with him a young Baltimore newsman, Martin Millspaugh. After
two years learning the federal ropes, Millspaugh returned to
Baltimore to become long-term head of Baltimore Charles Center-
Inner Harbor Management, Inc., the chief coordinator-promotion
group for these projects. Robert Embry, Jr., moved from directing
Baltimore's housing and urban renewal to become assistant secretary of the federal Housing and Urban Development department
(HUD), thus perfecting still further the bi-polar connection.

This is not the place to write a history of Baltimore renewal, but it
should be observed that, without the close personal links between
Baltimore, "the Feds," and Congress, there would have been a mere
trickle instead of the flood of federal taxes that poured into Baltimore
in those years.

By July 1982, the public funds pumped into Baltimore's downtown Charles Center and Inner Harbor redevelopments alone had
totaled $199.8 million (according to Mayor Schaefer, in a letter to the
author), of which $137 million, or 67 percent, had come from the
federal treasury in grants and subsidies. The one crucial federal
grant was $17.7 million to get the Inner Harbor going in 1966, and
that was 14 years before Harborplace's gala opening in 1980.

Back of this golden flow stand several key men, all of them
Baltimoreans of long standing, or adopted citizens who have made
Baltimore's physical reconstruction their life's work. But the key to
the whole enterprise is James W. Rouse, whose personal genius
tends to become shadowed by the "millionaire" publicity. I once
interviewed the first Mrs. Rouse back in the 1960s, when she recalled
that, when Rouse entered the mortgage business in Baltimore, "it
was the dullest business in town."

Rouse quickly outgrew the mossback legend. He came from an

old Eastern Shore (Easton, Maryland) family of devout and public-spirited people. His brother, financially astute Willard, was a noted Baltimore charity fund-raiser. James Rouse formed a research company that dug up so much new information about shopping center locations that soon Rouse knew more about these new monsters than their owners. He quickly went into shopping center development, succeeding where others failed; by the 1950s, he had a national reputation as a trustworthy developer-evangelist. President Dwight Eisenhower pulled him to Washington to head an urban housing policy task force. Rouse and Nathaniel Keith wrote a persuasive report, "No Slums in Ten Years." By 1953 Rouse, his partner, Hunter Moss, and a young planner named David A. Wallace had become three of a seven-man committee including Mayor Thomas D'Alesandro to draft a plan for Baltimore's ailing downtown. In a rare case of longevity, the Rouse-Wallace teamwork has continued into the present.

Rouse seems to have been one of the first nationally known people, along with geographer Jean Gottman and planner Christopher Tunnard, to perceive the reality of the East Coast Megalopolis. Rouse became the leading mortgage lender in the Washington-Baltimore corridor, and his was the firm that secretly bought up more than 15,000 acres between Baltimore and Washington to build what is now the city of Columbia, Maryland.

## THE RISING STAR OF WALLACE

Wallace, who was recruited from the University of Pennsylvania in 1957 at the suggestion of famed engineer Abel Wolman of Johns Hopkins University, became planner for the planning committee of the Greater Baltimore Committee. Such a dull-sounding name concealed tremendous political clout and design skills; the plans that Wallace and others drew in the late 1950s gave early vision to what thousands of visitors see today.

It would not be overly simplistic to say that Baltimore's renaissance rests on two forms of human skill: physical planning that includes superb graphic presentation and negotiations based on long-standing personal trust. As I comb through some 25 years' experience in urban reporting, I can find no city that combines these skills as does Baltimore.

Skills come and go, and Baltimore has enjoyed its share of outside designers, brought in for dazzling solutions. One such was the brilliant Pietro Belluschi, who was imported to do a Harborside Civic Center plan in 1953. Here one can see early versions of Harborplace today. Such plans and models, in a generation-long stream, formed a repetitive and pervasive set of mental images of what Baltimore could become. Wallace recalls especially an early article by Jane Jacobs about Charles Center. "It made people's chests stick out . . . changed the self-fulfilling prophesy of defeat."

Wallace himself shares with Rouse a brilliant mind, an instant command of complex figures, and by now a perfected spiel on Baltimore's recent history. His talks and writings enjoy large audiences and wide circulation.

High on the list of designers who have come and gone is one who stayed in Philadelphia: Tom Todd, a partner in the firm that was once Wallace, McHarg, Roberts and Todd of Philadelphia until the departure of partner/landscape architect Ian McHarg. Todd was a skillful designer; his sketches and plans stand out for their clarity and for what advertisers call "jump." His sculptural fountain designs now dominate two corners of Pratt Street near Harborplace and are pointed to with pride, although some may find them rather ponderous and overdone, as I did.

Integrity and trust are two words that a visitor encounters time and again in unraveling "the Baltimore story." The city enjoyed a power structure with remarkably few mavericks or entrepreneurs totally lacking in civic spirit. Many of these leaders moved in and out of public office, returned to lead local fundraising and civic commit-tees.

A sense of honesty and continuity so pervades the place that visitors from more rank and corrupt cities marvel at the history of 'no scandal' that surrounds city hall. Its present Mayor William D. Schaefer[3] appears to live, breathe, and sleep with the city uppermost in his psyche.

All this turned into past history when the Reagan administration began cutting federal programs of aid to cities. Baltimore's basic economy, still based on old-style heavy industries, is in bad shape, and this old industrial port is struggling for modern sources of income. A reporter from the *Manchester* (England) *Guardian* came, saw, and was repelled by what he took to be "gold fillings in a mouthful of decay."

But if trust and a capacity for long-range planning, coupled with top-quality urban design, have any usefulness in adapting to a new future, Baltimore seems to be well-equipped.

# The Street
# as Teacher

It is the Road which determines the sites of many cities and the growth and nourishment of all. It is the Road which controls the development of strategies and fixes the sites of battles. It is the Road that gives its framework to all economic development. It is the Road which is the channel of all trade and, what is more important, of all ideas. In its most humble function it is a necessary guide without which progress from place to place would be a ceaseless experiment; it is a sustenance without which organized society would be impossible; thus, and with those other characters I have mentioned, the Road moves and controls all history. (From *The Road*, by Hilaire Belloc, 1923.)

That we have traveled a long distance from such deterministic views, and a long time from 1923, when Belloc wrote these words, does not reduce their power, nor conceal the strategic mind at work in a large field. One of the great English essayists of the first half-century, Belloc was nothing if not absolutely certain, and a master of the sheer crescendo of utterance in argumentation. His grasp of geography, though bearing traces of the British empire-building tradition, is often firm and occasionally brilliant.

Modern readers must struggle with Belloc over many a detour and diversion, for the English personal essayists, of whom few still practice the art, were devotees of the telling aside, the by-the-ways and by-ways of exposition. Belloc's intriguing book, *The Path to Rome*, first published in 1902 and repeatedly paperbacked, tells us as much about Belloc's encounters with folk, drink, and quirk along the way as it does about the way itself. That was Belloc's way of operating: anecdotal, diversionary, reflective from various distances and viewpoints.

He would be among the first to welcome with erudite derision the modern wave of analysts of the street, road, and highway. Of their preoccupation with efficient movement, their charts and questionnaires, of their paradigms and parameters he would have little but epigrammatic scorn. Yet without my attempting to push him ahead of his times, he was, I think, offering a rare insight into the cultural functions of street, road, and highway that would do us well to consider today—not the least of which was his plumbing the depths of the historical process by which tracks became trails became paths became pathways, ways, wagon and carriage roads, well-traveled routes, and eventually today's autoroutes across Europe and interstate highways across the United States.

Above all, it occurs to me after taking a second look at some of Belloc's work, he was viewing street and road as a palimpsest of past and present, a teller of tales for all who care to look, a schoolbook both continental in scope and transferable across cultures. Without this conviction I would be foolish indeed to bring Belloc kicking and screaming across the Atlantic and into the great North American scene of street, road, highway, and multimodal transit systems. (However, I expect Belloc must have welcomed the no doubt considerable royalties from his book sales in North America.) Belloc's closest model in current literature is James/Jan Morris, whose mastery of the long-distance trip in essay form for *Rolling Stone* and other media is as well-fitted to modern dress as was Belloc's to more old-fashioned modes.

From Belloc's pioneering Road to the modern American street is not as long a leap as one might suppose, given certain universals about all linear means of transportation, and most especially about the street as it is situated in contemporary urban territory. In undertaking this essay, I assume that the street is the great common carrier of information for a democratic society, an educational device of huge dimensions, giving off great volumes of lessons, examples, warnings, admonitions, penetrating all phases of life, a living and inescapable classroom. My view is further conditioned by assuming that our knowledge about the Street (in which term I include Road and Highway) is socially conditioned, so that only by supreme effort can we think of it much beyond its simplistic function of getting us from here to there.

We have been brainwashed by at least a half-century of "research," all of it designed to prove that getting from here to there quickly by personal vehicle was the fundamental human activity of the twentieth century. Vast sums of money have cascaded through state highway departments, research institutes, and the universities to ratify trends, rather than to explore alternatives. My own bookshelves—reflecting an abiding interest in highway development—are crowded with studies such as "Impact of the Houston Freeway on Land Values," reinventions of the wheel to suit every local whim and budget.

## THE MULTIPLICATION OF PRESENCE

If one of the major revolutions in history was the multiplication of the amount of food one man can produce in one day's time, then another revolution surely is the multiplication of places that a human being can occupy or modify in the space of a day's travel. That first revolution lay in the multiplication of sustenance; the next was the multiplication of presence.

In this multiplication table, the street speaks a universal language: Its signals are part of everyday learning; its rules for movement are among the most widely understood of all public codes of conduct; and even its most bizarre variations offer, upon close examination, familiar goings-on.

The School of the Street offers kindergarten-to-graduate-level curricula, evidence, texts, and tests. To "matriculate" in the School of the Street, one must take determined steps that go beyond merely venturing down the sidewalk of one's own street—even though Jane Jacobs showed masterfully what a large curriculum is offered by any complex street system and how much is to be learned in front of one's own house. (Her pre-Toronto location, Hudson Street, Manhattan, has gone down in urban history as one of the great Learning Streets: See her *Death and Life of Great American Cities* for a more complete lesson.)

Marshall McLuhan reminded us in *Understanding Media* that "for the West, literacy has long been pipes and taps and streets and assembly lines and inventories . . . things in sequence and succession." The road and the printed word he dismissed as "our older media." Implicit in McLuhan's writings—as in those of his mentor, the Canadian economist Harold A. Innis—was his conviction that transportation and personal movement-through-territory was a dying form of communication fast being supplanted by TV and the electronic grid forming the Global Village (his capitals, not mine). The world he attempted to describe would soon be moving information to the body, rather than vice versa.

But now, 30 years after *Understanding Media*, the mass movement of persons from Here to There persists, and neither McLuhan's brilliant insights nor the rise thus far in the price of oil seems able to diminish the world's appetite for movement—by personal vehicle if possible and by any means where necessary. Human movement itself shows such power as a learning device that I doubt it can ever be fully replaced by electronic substitutes. Street scenes will change, perhaps beyond all recognition, but differences between places will continue to require human movement to exploit or escape those differences—as tourist, as entrepreneur, as military invader, or as refugee.

Photography changed the presence of places by moving them to the easy chair, the desk or slide-show, and later to the TV screen. This truncation of places-in-the-round to places-on-a-flat-surface left out feeling, smelling, movement, experiment—all those elements of "being there" that were the essence of there-ness.

## MASSAGING THE MEDIUM

But in considering how such a scene, this locus of movement—the North American street—can operate as a fully rewarding educational instrument, we must approach it in a structured way; organize it as a replicable experience; and record it in ways that prove meaningful and useful beyond the classroom's walls. In this essay, I wish to examine Street-Road-Highway collectively as a public educational medium, and do so in three ways: first as a mode of communication in which the language we use is an essential part; second, by taking a look at special methods of examination; and finally by speculating upon Street-Road-Highway if they became laboratories for universities.

Along the way, we must take note of "down time"—stretches of the urbanized environment where learning is at a minimum, where street frontage gives over to parking lots, to parking garages with impenetrable street frontages, a form of design called "Riot Renaissance" because there are no stores, no shops, few doorways along this street, none along the next block. Along the way, we also observe the rise of the new Citadels—those multipurpose megastructures containing convention halls, hotels, indoor race tracks, sports arenas, and parking ramps—self-consciously designed to capture customers and keep them spending their time and money indoors, well removed from the street. Few major American cities are without these new zones of confinement, which reduce the sidewalk population of the streets around them. Scores of them have been deposited at the edge of town, or used to clear away slums adjacent to the old downtown—with devastating impact in their neighborhoods.

Let me now reinforce this discussion with the lamentation that our language is still imprecise and deficient in dealing with Street, still stuck at the level of pre-scientific discourse that preceded Carolus Linnaeus's great codification of plant and animal names in the eighteenth century. Here before our very eyes is a definitional entity that we name Street: "a generally leveled, linear, artificially lighted, and paved surface, extended across territory in a continuous and often straight direction, bounded on either side by curbings or other tangible limits, and offering unlimited or partial access to its surface from adjoining properties" [my construction]. Having said all that in school-marmish fashion, I am obliged at once to utter qualifications and emendations. For thousands of small-town unpaved, rocky streets in the Americas admit to no such rigidities— being dusty in summer, muddy in winter, impassable after rains, of random width and direction. I am being deliberate in using such a formal definition of the urbanized street, for reasons soon to come.

Meanwhile, what about the nomenclature for all those variations and sub-species of Urban Street? What of those things called Main Street, Main Drag, Shopping Strip, Back Alley (Laneway, in Toronto), Front Street, Back Street, Side Street, Dock Street, Structural Street (a nice example from Allan Jacobs's book *Looking at Cities*)?. What about Connector, High-Tech Corridor, Mansion Row, Skid Road popularized as Skid Row, Cross-Town (with Connector understood but silent), Fashionable Shopping Street (as in Worth Avenue, Palm Beach; Regent Street, London; Rodeo Drive, Los Angeles; Rue de Faubourg, Paris; 57th Street, New York City)?

Not to mention those endless subdivisions into Fire Lane, Express Bus Lane, Fast Lane, Deceleration Lane, Bicycle Lane, Loading Ramp, Runaway Truck Ramp, No-Parking and No-Standing Zones, Towaway Zone, Carriageway (also known as Cartway), Verge, Gutter and Valley Gutter, Access Road, Pull-Outs, and then off to Easements and Rights-of-Way of infinite variation, Driveways, Sidewalks and Walkways. And as we proceed into the outskirts, here again we confront Trails, Paths, Cowpaths, Ways, and the increasing obscurities of hinterland routes. Here beyond the outskirts is where the Dirt Tracks, Raceways, Racetracks (dog, horse, and auto), and the Drag Strips flourish, where specializing hobbyists pursue each other in gymkhana, autocross, point-to-point races, cross-country steeplechases, fox hunts, and drag hunts off to the far horizons. Closer to the Main Road, we encounter the large acreages where Motel Complexes flourish, where a dozen dealers jostle for customers in the new Auto Shopping Complex, with its own internal Streets, Ramps, Hardstands, etc.

All this nomenclature suggests that the School of the Street properly begins with the language of the street, and here I do not mean the language of the gutter. (There's enough shit flying around not to go for more of it.)

## THE GREAT COMMON CARRIER

For I look upon the street as an educational enterprise, partly institutionalized and part open to the most outrageous assumptions and interventions. It is the great common carrier of information in a democratic society; an education device of gross dimensions, exuding volumes of lessons, examples, warnings, admonitions; penetrating all phases of life, a living and inescapable classroom. Its rules of movement are among the most widely understood of all codes of public conduct. Within this broad context, one should view the trip and the walk as mechanisms by which each of us learns to adjust, cope, memorize, habituate; to replicate experience and to generalize from it; to invent experience and go with it.

Linnaeus, the great Swedish botanist, spoke of "the sovereign order of nature," which he organized by a naming system that still spans the natural sciences of our day. If the study of urban objects and processes is to advance beyond its present contentiousness, then the sovereign order of the man-made urban environment will need all the intensity of gaze and discrimination of nomenclature that we can muster. And for our study to proceed much beyond name-calling, we must recognize that the order of the street is continuous; that the street exhibits the ancient order of history that Hilaire Belloc reveled in; and that it displays emerging orders of both magnitude and specialization that we have only begun to put into some useful order.

One of the more intriguing aspects of street evolution is that its evolutionary order is far more apparent to the naked eye (though not to the naked mind) than was the evolution of plants and animals. Unless we live on a farm, go to the zoo, to the jungle (with an exemplary guide to chop a path), or to laboratory and textbook, we see too few examples of animals in an ordinary life to arrive at evolutionary conclusions from visible evidence.

Not so on the street. A single daily commute from suburb to city center, an eye-filling trip to the airport, or a strongly held gaze at the passing roadsides can uncover more historical evidence of evolution than the mind can digest.

Evidence of this evolutionary process, however, is scattered far and wide among many disciplines, and in recent years much of it has been generated by the historical preservationists. Off in other directions, the environmental psychologists are taking their own cut at the subject, while traditional planners and designers each pursue their own objectives, using their own special lingo. Street literature and research methods run in all creeds and colors. Where does one find a multidisciplinary university course in Visible Evidence? Where does one find the same intensity of broad, scholarly gaze fastened upon a famous street (Fifth Avenue New York, Market Street San Francisco, North Wells Chicago, Peachtree Atlanta) as is regularly fastened upon single buildings of renown?

Without attempting to lay down my own favorite tactic upon so volatile a subject, I do suggest that use of the cross-section trip through metropolitan areas is as revealing to the modern observer as was the first cross-section of human tissue to the anatomist Andreas Vesalius, or as the Valley Section was to the botanist-ecologist-planner Patrick Geddes, to whom we shortly return.

As we move down the street itself, 10 generations of cars pass by a hundred generations of advertising fashions, and a thousand variations in roadside building styles fill the windshield in an hour's trip. The evidence is so thick we recoil, we blank it out; school is over, the mind closes shop for the rest of the trip. William Ewald, in his seminal book, *Street Graphics,* recounts a 1968 study of Baltimore County drivers: "Under normal driving conditions, the occupant of a moving car can seldom handle more than 10 items of information at a time." Yet both driver and passenger at 30 miles per hour (2,640 feet per minute) are confronted with 1,320 items of information—words, phrases, signs, symbols, diagrams, directions, admonitions. This comes to approximately 440 words a minute—about double the average person's reading speed. No wonder most road-users learn to blank it all out, to write it all off as a confusing blur. (Ewald's conclusion, which need not detain us unduly, was to ration roadside messages by zoning, so as to protect drivers from excess diversion from the road itself.)

## AN EMERGING ORDER

But behind all that razzle-dazzle of the street-road-highway, an emerging order exists there waiting to be found.

Linnaeus would remind us students of street life that certain criteria hold true for the searching gaze. We must consider birth, nutrition, aging, movement, and internal propulsion—and all of these criteria, it appears to me, operate as observably in street life as they do in animal and vegetable existence. Street evolution is far more clear in the school of the street than is biological evolution, yet the former has attracted little of the scholarly apparatus that surrounds the latter. Should we not think of today's street as the link between ancient paths and trails and tomorrow's megastructure? The street itself will take many forms beyond those envisioned by architect Louis Kahn when he said, "the street wants to be a building"—one that Kahn himself would design. But the ancient pathways persist over most of those human settlements we call cities. And in the evolution of those paths—once sufficiently recorded—there lies a new form of evolutionary theory waiting to be discovered. When such a theory finally develops, I suspect it will revolve around a single vital criterion: access and accessibility, from which all other attributes flow.

The street itself is a place of complex behavior and specialization and cannot be understood apart from its denizens and their habits. Increasingly street space is preempted by the "world car" of the 1980s.

These look-alike contenders jostle for right-of-way with mobile earth-movers, garment-workers' carts, motorized deliverymen, mobile-home transporters, backhoes and front loaders, gas-guzzlers, and a host of incipient mini-vehicles. While the city street grid attempts to accommodate all these special vehicles, specialized streets and streets-within-streets arise as demarked by Express Lanes, Bus Lanes, Truck Routes, Mass Transit Streets, Loading Zones, and special rights-of-way. Small personal vehicles—the horse, bicycle, and motorbike—have long demanded street and parking space. Now come the "Trike," the three-cylinder commuter car.

But perhaps no one (to my knowledge, at least) has put upon street life the burden of explication that Linnaeus 200 years ago[4] put upon life in its bio-zoological senses. There is yet to be found a fully documented and logical order of streets.

Contrast this, if you will, with the intensity of gaze fastened upon the street's mechanical denizens, the automobile, and especially via the sports car magazines. From years of captivity to this narcotic subspecies of literature, I can testify to the endless permutations of specialized language—terms, depiction, description, comparison, and codification that are bought, sold, traded, and given currency by both practitioners and observers. From the fastidious Museum of Modern Art down to endless locals, public museums give testimony to the object, the car, with their predictable Exhibitions of The World of the Car. That world turns out to be mostly the car itself, its couture, and that of its drivers: a celebration of mechanical commodity. Few museums or historians, until lately, have paid much attention to the world beyond the car. No doubt it was the 1974 Arabian oil embargo and the first brisk whiff of shortages that encouraged a new wave of road historians to begin publishing their observations on the road, highway, motel, and tourist facilities in the 1970s, encouraged by J.B. Jackson's early essays in *Landscape Magazine* (1960s) on The Stranger's Path and The Evolving Strip. Closer to the racetracks, the great Henry Manny III, columnist in *Road & Track* magazine, was one of the most versatile linguists of that field, relishing the wordplay involved in a run through the gears, the run-in, the test run, trial run, or trial spin, running off the track (as distinguished from an off-track run), or a run for your money (as distinguished from a run for The Money).

## GEDDES'S VALLEY SECTION

Beyond learning the language of the street, future theorists of street meanings can find no better mentor than the great Scottish biologist Patrick Geddes and no better example than his Valley Section, adapted to the modern metropolis.

Geddes's Valley Section was first exhibited in a grand civic panorama, designed for the now-famous Cities Exhibition at Chelsea, London, in 1911. His painting showed a typical seventeenth-eighteenth century valley in cross-section, with a fishing village-port at the right, and the landforms slowly ascending to the left through town streets, outskirts, hopfields, vineyards, market gardens, cattle, arable and sheep farms on higher grounds, then upland hunters, foresters, gold miners, and quarry workers and onto the mountains. It was the perfect epitome of the perfect town form. From the woods came game and pelt, off the pastures came the cattle down the paths and streets into the slaughterhouse, the cobbler's shop, and onto the ships. Off the fields came the harvests for miller, baker and town grocer—a progressional pageant from start to finish, a complete "story" in one picture.

But even the most cursory study of the Geddes epitome showed that such a cross-section as an educational device can tell only partly the story of the modern city and its street system. Geddes's town was an old-fashioned processor of raw materials. Today's American city has become a processor of power and information, and to understand that power first-hand, to tap that information, one must traverse the whole city, the whole metropolitan area as a continuous experience from outer trail to path to road to street, into the very city center, and out the other side. This completed experience forces the student-learner to confront the Whole Thing, the "city" as a complex educational enterprise, with various forms of learning available at each stage. The processing of local crops in the Geddes diagram is but a small part of today's picture.

There was no way, I concluded from a study via cross-section of 33 North American cities in 1972-3, that one can come to grips eye-to-eye, first-hand, with the complex metropolis, short of inventing and then following such a cross-section trip in a single, unifying journey. This approach could be considered Montessorian, handy for dealing with an environment rich in manipulative materials. One should look to it as a form of transactional analysis, a running encounter that requires both homework and on-site skills. It is a learning experience of high order, although it can be much simplified in scale and adapted to grade-school children, as has been done by members of the British Town and Country Planning Association with their Town Trails.

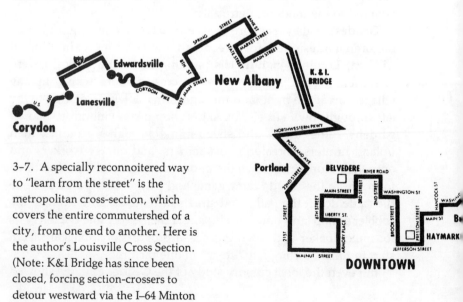

3–7. A specially reconnoitered way to "learn from the street" is the metropolitan cross-section, which covers the entire commutershed of a city, from one end to another. Here is the author's Louisville Cross Section. (Note: K&I Bridge has since been closed, forcing section-crossers to detour westward via the I–64 Minton Bridge.) Map by *The Louisville Times*.

## THE GRADY CLAY URBAN CROSS-SECTION

In order to make the most of a cross-section analysis as a learning device, one must consider and plot out a route that performs as follows:

1. It must follow one general direction, not doubling back upon itself. In this way it resembles the familiar geographer's traverse, a time-tested learning device for recording a linear experience through new territory.

2. As a corollary it must form a continuous, easily described experience, using certain routes as a "spine" for the trip.

3. It should span the full range of daily commuting, exploiting the full size of the "commutershed"—so that the cross-section route begins at the outer limits of commuting (generally considered the zone in which at least five percent of job-holders commute into the metropolitan area) and then ends at the opposite outer limits—usually but not invariably 180 degrees in the opposite direction.

4. It should deal with the Center, whether the historic city center, the Civic Center, or the geographic center where all roads once came together at a historic crossroads; it could be the original Town Landing, the Zero Milestone, Court House Square, or other designated central place.

5. It must cope with the zone or neighborhood from which comes major flows of exportable goods and services, and therefore the essential source of local income from distant markets.

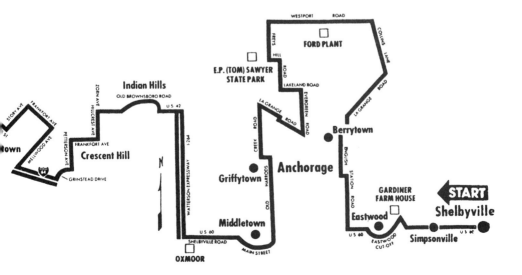

6. And explore a dying area—slums beyond recall, an abandoned warehouse district based on cost advantages long gone, a mill district undermined by foreign competition, Mansion Row on the skids.

7. It should encounter at least one growth area where booming firms burst through their walls, and workers' parking expands all bounds; where land development is under way; where roadside billboards announce zoning changes and new construction to come.

8. It should offer transactions with the Best Address, where fashion and ambition dictate that the new wealthy jostle for space with old families, or carve out their own turf, where Volvo and Mercedes agencies cluster, where the spoor of status-striving rests upon vegetation, house style, and decor.

9. And it should bring us into at least visual contact with the major geographic feature of the area, be it the closest navigable water, the dominant local peak or escarpment.

10. The ideal cross-section will touch an historic part of the city, perhaps an entire district, sufficient evidence to tell the studious what might further be pursued.

11. Necessary to a full understanding of the city, one's route should pursue at least one Main Drag, preferably that special variation I call Alpha Street—the one that starts down by the original Town Landing, meanders through the dying Mill District, then through the city center, office district, court house square, proceeds uphill along the decaying Mansion Row (See the Men's Club, watch the funeral parlors take over the old mansions), and then out the Auto Strip toward suburbia. Not all Main Drags will be so accommodating, but they bear close inspection. (Since I fastened myself upon it, Alpha Street has assumed an utter and predictable reality for me. I take delight in looking for the Alpha Street wherever I travel. I can be sure that it will not be listed in the city directory, and that few if any books—beyond anecdotal tracts pitched to visiting conventioneers—will be available. So one is left to dig it out of the city's fabric as a current discovery: Genesee Street in Utica, N.Y.; North Main in Canandaigua, N.Y.; St. Charles in New Orleans, Main Street in Houston; Meridian Street in Indianapolis, and Third Street in Louisville.

12. Finally, the course should be fun. This is the wild card in the deck, the subjectivity among those objective criteria. My own tactic has been to notice my own attention span, my own capacity for

boredom. If the route turns boring, turn off. And this opens up another axiom: To turn is to learn. Moving off a predictable or familiar route increases the intensity of one's gaze, the receptivity of one's senses. If one turns into threatening territory, pupils dilate, muscles tense, sweat exudes—and learning speeds up.

In common with many educational experiences, such a full cross-section trip does tend to screen out the hard parts: It smooths everything down to automobile grades. Any cross-section traveler may find himself choosing routes that eliminate the dead ends, the rough terrain, the spectacular views. No matter what one may intend at the start, beginning cross-sectioners unconsciously tend to follow straight lines and hence become captives to a geometry that may not correspond to a city's basic structure. But of course the truly experimenting student will stop the car, get out, and explore as necessary afoot and afresh. Often the hidden spaces just off the main routes tell a different story, allow the student to compare what's up-front with another reality out-back.

## THE UNIVERSITY-OF-THE-STREET

But beyond such personal or schoolish adventures, should we not ask ourselves: How can universities themselves tap into the School of the Street—beyond supporting all those hundreds of forays by click-counting and tape-recording students, following the footsteps of William H. Whyte, Jr.'s marvelous movies of people-on-the-street?

Private universities that own their own streets are prime candidates for such experiments as I envision. They can manage certain streets as open-air laboratories for experiments in crowd, vehicle, space, and learning-experience-management. Most such spaces, as I have encountered them, became experimental only during the riots, protests, and mass meetings that surrounded Earth Day and the Vietnam war protests of the 1970s. American streets seldom become educational media except for two forms of messages: commercial (advertising) and control (government rules and regulations). To encounter six blocks of a major thoroughfare that have been exclusively reserved for one set of messages is almost unthinkable, on-campus or off, and I will admit that the first examples that come to mind flourished during a semidictatorial election campaign in Mexico City, where some major highways were dominated by Get-Out-and-Vote billboards. But we need to know such things as: How can the street be made to perform more fully its many educational functions? And where better to begin than on the university campus itself? In such fashion the school of the street could become far more the mixed-media than we have so far explored. It would be instructive, just for starters, to see how students of engineering, urban design, architecture, and public art would handle a given block-long "street" of their own designing. So far as I have observed, all such experiments have been confined to special Events (The Big Game, Homecoming, the Beaux Arts Ball, etc.) with little effort to examine the evidence for its larger lessons. My own experience, as an outsider being ganged off of Madison, Wisconsin's State Street which, unbeknownst to me, had become university student Turf, offers a memorable example of special purpose. Looking further, how can that after-hours white elephant, the multilevel parking garage, become an extension of the classroom? A TV and computer hookup for every car, piped-in heat or cool for the car occupants, pick-up and delivery service by trike or bike?

We continue to go through each new Age of Confinement and its ensuing reactions. Sociologist Robert Gutman sees television "which takes people off the street and into their homes" as just one aspect of forces inhibiting street life—an inevitable follow-up to early sanitation laws and social reforms that swept beggars, peddlers, garbage, kids, and tramps off the streets and into institutions. The department store and elevators conspired to pull adults off the sidewalks into buildings; the modern "citadel" that I referred to earlier reinforces the trend to depopulate the street. Traditional architects and their buildings are so inward-directed that street life around buildings is a second-class activity.

But to lament all this merely reinforces our need to view the street from the reformist tradition. It is not merely the inevitable by-product of our latest mode of transport, but a vital part of the learning and testing system for the larger society. We can look back at the outpouring of federal, state, and local funds into traffic/transport/movement studies since World War II as an expensive episode in single-purpose thought. Such a look gives us time both for reflection and for preparation for a new wave of studies and examples to show how the street can perform to the fullest extent its many educational functions.

## NOTES

1. Architects of the new projects for downtown are planning vast and symmetrical open spaces. These will certainly offset the buildings; whether they will also be enjoyable to people is more of a question. To see what lessons might be learned from the squares and parks we already have, *Fortune* called on a perceptive observer, Grady Clay, real estate editor of the *Louisville Courier-Journal,* and asked him to do some walking. (*Fortune* magazine, 1958)

2. See Leonardo, Benevolo. *The Origins of Modern City Planning* (Cambridge, Mass.: The M.I.T. Press, 1967).

3. In 1978, after serving as mayor for 15 years, Schaefer was elected governor of Maryland.

4. Carolus Linnaeus, *Philosophie Botanique,* Section 33; and *Systema Naturae,* page 215.

# 4

# Prospects

---

## Vantage Pointing:
## The View
## From on High

Whenever continent-droppers gather to tell of their travels and travails, someone always demands to know "What is your favorite city?"—usually as a prelude to telling everyone in earshot about theirs.

But talking about "favorite cities" is more than an exercise in one-upmanship, for it is quite as likely to be occasioned by nostalgia. Most Americans tend to judge all favorites by that one and inescapable place in which they grew up, where they came of age, suddenly aware of a magic in their surroundings, the remembered luminosity of a familiar view, or the glow of an insight arising from a now-revealed complexity in their surroundings.

So I resist the notion of "a favorite city," and instead, have a large and sometimes unmanageable collection of unforgettables: of places, views, scenes of arrival, moments of insight. All these can be found on my own mental maps. And on these maps are places of high visibility, where sooner or later the whole greatness of the place comes through the eye and into the mind. Clarity, clarity, clarity above all. Clouds may come and go as in Vancouver, and fogs as in San Francisco, and the deadly pall of smog as in Los Angeles, and the intervening mountains and hills as one attempts to fathom Seattle.

But for me the capacity for a city to lay itself at one's feet, so to speak, marks that city for a kind of quality beyond compare. Not for nothing do I and others of like-mind search and probe—sometimes to the point of trespass—for those high points from which to peer out and about for the city's more visible secrets. Not for naught have I followed the topographical maps as well as my own nose for cities, finally arriving at the end of the valley, the nose of the hill, the edge of the dump, the rim of the escarpment, or even a fire escape or rooftop, there to grasp that one encapsulating glance at that one irreplaceable scene made visible from this particular point and from no other.

And thus my own searching as well as my insightful viewing is essential in a city's finding favor with me. That city does me the favor of unfolding itself; it grants me access into its many selves; it bestows upon me ungrudgingly that sudden slice of visibility, or "outsights," from which comes so many insights.

Cincinnati, "The Queen City," needs to be approached warily from the south, for it affords the traveler only one 10-second long-range view of itself through a curving notch in the bluffs through which Interstate 71 descends from the Kentucky highlands down to the Ohio River plain. Ten seconds in heavy traffic on a steeply sloping curve. But, there you have it, suddenly revealed through a hillside notch, quickly snatched or gone for good.

San Francisco is the city of endless views, to be captured at some expense. The standard airport arrivee's first glimpse will do, unless you're equipped for eye-catching treks. The airport bus winds past San Bruno Mountain, edges the Bay, mounts the pass between Portrero and the Mission District, and suddenly the city's sky-scrapers and downtown hills stand out ahead. A fast mile of glimpses and then the bus ramps down, the view is blocked.

Am I so topographically deterministic that I favor the view of Baltimore from Federal Hill over the much higher view from the multistory World Trade Center skyscraper across the Inner Harbor? Why so incomparably better? Perhaps because Federal Hill was always and unavoidably there, long before it was federalized, a rough rock-ribbed place to which the city accommodated. Baltimore has wound itself around its base, standing back from it in something approaching reverence for its history. And in standing back, Baltimore organized itself to be seen best from Federal Hill, rather than from the newcomer skyscrapers.

4-1. A view of Baltimore's Inner Harbor from Federal Hill.

## FLEETING GLIMPSES

Evanescent and fleeting are some of my favorite views. When in 1973 last I saw Denver from its far northwest suburbs, I was 11 miles distant from the center, parked off the road and strolling around the intersection of West 84th Street and Federal Boulevard. All four corners of the intersection were then open fields except for a small Spanish house at the southwest. From this high point I seemed to be surrounded by the old range land now yielding irrigated crops of hay. It was midday in open country. Sixteen cars had stacked up behind a red light. Land clearing was beginning a few hundred feet away, so that I have no doubt Denver's latest boom has now reached out and obscured that once-wide view.

> Facing northeast, this is an excellent spot for capturing the State of Tennessee Amphitheater, the Sunsphere, and the overhead tram all in one shot. Look southeast and get a nice low-angle view of the U.S. Pavilion. Use tree branches to frame your photo.

4–2.  Advice from Eastman Kodak Company.

To love at a distance is not enough, as geographer David Lowenthal has reminded us by his writings, and many an urban designer has now provided man-made promontories for splendid official views. Visit any of the major upscale redevelopment projects of the past two decades and you will find genuine, documented Renaissance Views, photographed in trade magazines from certified Renaissance-determined positions.

So why do I find myself resisting them, almost without exception?

Why have I avoided (now that I think back on it) that celebrated terminus designed by I.M. Pei in Washington, D.C., the L'Enfant Plaza overlook? Is it that, having written so much about the neighborhood, having, as one of the jurymen, studied intently the competition for the Portal Site nearby—having ingested this glut of information about the place, I am now reluctant to expose all that I already know to all that I can see—fearing that it can't possibly measure up to Pei's drama on paper? Of course, I should overcome this sense of ennui and go have a look, for God's sake (and Pei's)!

In all such expeditions as this we say farewell to those flatland cities, those all-laid-out-and-easy-to-read cities: the Indianapolis, Phoenix, Urbana-Champaign, Chicago-type cities. Yes, they have their edges (and as Kevin Lynch reminded us, their paths, nodes, districts, and landmarks). But they contain few geographic surprises, and few if any natural topographic points of view. And hence we must invent viewpoints, we must manufacture viewing platforms—revolving restaurants, soldiers-and-sailors monuments, and high-rise rooftop clubs so as to see-out-upon the city made memorable by the act of seeing-outward.

No sooner do I finish these comments than a wave of afterthoughts descends: What about all the exceptions? What about one's ability to view the city now via satellite, or omni-dimensionally as a revolving image on the computer terminal screen? All well and good, say I. But not to be compared with the experiential feeling, that inescapable grip of discovery that comes only from being there afoot and preferably afresh, looking with every core and fiber of insight from on high. Is there anything more suited to the consummate act of finding favor? Now I ask you.

---

# Zero Runoff:
# All Rain
# That Falls on Me
# Is Mine, Right?

As a solution for floods, soil erosion, drought, and other afflictions, "zero runoff" has a fine ringing sound. You keep the water that falls on your land from running off in all directions. All rain that falls on me is mine, right? Sounds reasonable and democratic.

Zero runoff is a term that began getting increased attention in the 1960s, at a time when the ever-normal granary first showed signs of being an exception, rather than something ordained by God and an everlastingly dependable climate. The term was further dramatized by the Texas Soil Conservation Service, which began helping the owners of some 500 cattle feedlots to redesign their land and its drainage so that no manure-fouled waters would run off their land. This seemed at the time a neighborly thing to do because it protected downstream landowners from befouled waters.

All of which goes down well enough for the individual landowner—but only in "good years," which means years when the creeks don't dry up. It works only so long as all the upstream owners don't keep all that rainfall unto themselves, and don't leave the downstream folks with zero water . . . ZERO WATER?

Now, hold your hosses just one cotton-picking minute! Let's take another look at this Texas proposition. The prospect of millions of landowners in North America scrambling singly and collectively to achieve zero runoff for themselves during the coming decades gets pretty spooky.

Suppose you are one of 2,000 landowners in the upper reaches of, let us say, Beargrass Creek, which is an urbanizing stream that first emerges from the ground as a former spring now carrying a tangible flow of runoff from underground septic tanks in the new suburbs. Thus fed, it quickly becomes an extension of suburbanites' alimentary canals. Suppose you and your 1,999 fellow landowners along Beargrass Creek begin to run out of cheap, clean water from the Creek—to water your cattle, sprinkle your garden, or to embellish your back yard. So you organize a Suburban Water District to capture all the rain that falls on your land—Your Rain! And you float a bond issue to build retention ponds, catchbasins, diversion ditches, seepage pits, reservoirs, in-soak areas, and protections for the underground aquifers. Your local state representative is a helpful fellow, so he sneaks a bill through the legislature to register all well-drillers in your watershed. There! You've become the master of your fate: Your Rain!

## PRIOR AND OTHER APPROPRIATION

But what happens when the people downstream find that, except after unusual rainstorms, there's no stream left?

What usually happens is that they hire a lawyer—the one they neglected to consult while you were busy setting up your retention ponds, catchbasins, etc. And they go to court, since it is well known that either under the Western (originally Spanish, called prior-appropriation) water laws or the Eastern (originally English) version of riparian rights, downstreamers can protect themselves against exactly what you've been messing around with upstream.

Consequently, zero runoff has served to exacerbate an already critical situation, by diverting water to the Haves (you and your neighbors) and depriving the newly created Have-Nots of what they now consider to be Their Water.

And so the managing of water-rights lawsuits and the writing and processing of new legislation has become a minor growth industry—and not merely in the litigious West. I recall coming home to Kentucky from an early trip to Denver in the 1950s, saying to friends, "Any young lawyer today would make a fortune going West, learning water law, and coming back East in time for the next round of lawsuits, when the East begins running out of water."

That day arrived, of course, in the 1960s, by which time Eastern water empire builders were colliding in court all over the place. Along the way, the various professions—lawyers, engineers, landscape architects, land planners—were involved in hundreds of local struggles, not so much with each other but to sort out the rights of all parties, including the right of the water and landscape to survive men's uses of these limited assets.

It was no accident that in a national design competition for landscape architects in the 1970s, the jury chose among 18 winning projects, 11 of them having to do with water-related development of the landscape. It was no accident that the world's first desertification conference was held by the United Nations in Nairobi, also in the 1970s—or that water shortages as well as record-breaking floods and famines plagued many parts of the world with sudden intensities, not the least of which was in Ethiopia.

All these events and pressures derive from our growing use and waste of water, our steady population drift toward the shores of water bodies large and small—and thus from the increasing value all of us now place upon access to this marvelous, miraculous liquid that unites all of life on earth.

Our attitudes toward water have been oddly warped by our history. Much of early American life east of the Mississippi consisted of getting rid of surplus water. The pioneers' East was full of swamps, muck, and mire, their early lives miserable in the mud, their feet chilled, their travels a struggle through mudwallows. Successful politics in the Eastern colonies and later states consisted of providing roads, drainage canals, wooden sidewalks, and pumps to get whole towns out of the mud. The Good Roads Movement of the late nineteenth century was enlivened by the slogan, "Get the farmers out of the mud!"—with access to all-weather roads. West of the 20-inch rainfall line, or the 100th meridian, which roughly demarks the irrigation-dependent West, laws were passed and then perverted so as to water the Great American Desert—a dry and dusty reality that generations of Westerners pretended wasn't there by wiping the term off their maps and out of their histories.

## HYDRO-CULTURAL CONFLICTS

By the 1970s, legal battles over water rights had steadily moved from West to East, so that by 1977 the citizens of Washington State voted on a revolutionary proposition to put a 50-year limit on irrigation water rights, those rights that normally ran with the land in perpetuity, or so long as they were "constructively used" by their owners.

Along with the discovery that water was a diminishing resource, even in the humid East, came the widespread realization that waterfront was growing more scarce and that derelict old water-fronts deserved to be reexamined as assets too long buried under-neath dumps, railroad tracks, and bulk-using industries. By the mid-1960s, hundreds of federally aided urban renewal projects had begun to reclaim bits and hunks of old waterfronts made derelict in the previous century: Harborplace in Baltimore, which we examine elsewhere in this book, is a spectacular example.

Quickly it became apparent that urban waterfronts, whether natural or artificial, had become prime real estate and essential ingredients to the new industry of image-formation. Photographers clustered to find just the right skyline view to decorate the new chamber-of-commerce brochure about Our Waterfront. And all up and down the whole creation, local ballets, orchestras, mimes, festival managers, regatta promoters, and others ganged up behind the latest Waterfront Plan. And thus the recycling of waterfronts became a widespread civic enterprise, just as recycling water itself had become necessary to many a water-short community.

## HYDRAULIC CULTURES

Peter Drucker, the noted economist, has written brilliantly about "the first great revolution technology wrought in human life 7,000 years ago, when the first great civilization of man, the irrigation civilization, established itself. First in Mesopotamia, and then in Egypt and in the Indus Valley, and finally in China, there appeared a new society and a new policy: the irrigation city, which then rapidly became the irrigation empire." Drucker, following an earlier line of thinking set up by the specialist in Chinese "hydraulic history," Karl A. Wittfogel, saw irrigation civilizations as "the beginning of history" inasmuch as they brought about the inventions of writing, standing armies, the concept of man as a citizen, organized trades and organized knowledge, and, not least, the individual as a focal point of the emerging concept of justice. Not a small yield.

What can we say of today's society but that it is struggling to become a recycling civilization? We are fast learning how to recycle hundreds of basic resources, principal among them water and water-serviced areas. And nowhere on the American scene is this transformation so apparent as in water-related developments in cities and suburbs. Here is where many professions combine to produce new analytic studies of landscape dynamics—including the carrying capacity of each particular place. Some of these places had been close to death: a shoreline badly battered by flood or hurricane, a marsh foolishly filled in by a generation of dumpers, a watercourse concreted and turned into an open-land sewer by the earlier and cruder forms of engineering, or riverbanks wasted and littered for a long century before.

After all this, a new kind of Place has emerged—the watershed. Hardly before the 1930s was there much talk about "managing" a watershed, although there were plenty of *causes celebres* brought on by destructive upstream practices—such as hydraulic mining in the headwaters of streams that emptied their loads into San Francisco Bay.

The Tennessee Valley Authority tried to tell us about watershed management in the 1930s, as did Sir Patrick Geddes, the famed Scots biologist of an earlier generation, but few would listen. Today, the tune is different; the times demand new forms, and hundreds of urban edges to rivers, lakes, and tidelands are being reexamined, not only for recreation potential, but for their long-term capacity to generate marine life.

Not all these waters' edges can or should be developed. It takes the wisdom of artist and technician to offer us that most difficult of all lessons—where *not* to build, where *not* to capture the water. Those of us who have watched these projects develop over the years hope they can awaken the public to the scarcity, fragility, and wonder that is to be found in water. Zero runoff teaches us the limits of human intervention; floods and hurricanes add their warnings. Living in the presence of water has its risks as well as its great rewards.

---

# War Monsters

It came as no surprise to anybody close to American land development practices in 1967 to observe a 400,000-square-foot building built from scratch in 60 days near Charleston, South Carolina. Of course it took a bloody war in Vietnam to produce such blind speed. The plant was built by Ruscon Construction Company using Armco Steel components in a crash job to get housing for helicopter engine production. The building could hold 10 football fields under one roof, housed 1,000 employees, and in three years was designed to hold 5,000, making it Charleston's largest industrial employer.

The land? Oh, that. It was there, open and fairly flat. In the name of a national emergency (and with a presidential election not far off), anything could be put anywhere, and this new factory adjacent to, that is, across the street from, a recently finished housing development proves the point. War triumphs over all. So long as the nation is on a war footing, (whatever that may mean), we may expect variations of the above scene anywhere in the nation.

The landscape . . . what's that? The idea that anybody should be concerned with what is outside the helicopter engine plant is of course foreign to the minds of the men who use the 'copters, to those who build them, and to the architects and engineers forced to get that goddam thing built and off the ground and running in 60 days, no excuses, no sleep, no evasions, get it done.

One might dismiss this as an inevitable side-effect of war: just another suburban tract development, this one under one roof. Sorry about that . . . Quit bitching and get going. . . . You a Commie or something?

But if one stands back a moment and considers that today's wartime expedients become tomorrow's peacetime routine, that today's "emergency" gets built into the structure of tomorrow's government, it becomes quite clear that the 60-day, 10-football field building is just around the corner for every community, and not merely those impacted by defense or war or "preparedness" contracts. Inflation is forcing the developers of buildings or land to speed up, to rationalize, to choose the critical path, over-invest in expensive machinery, and pass the costs along as best they can. This is the reality of a country caught up in warlike fervor.

What this means, too, is that every large and readily available tract of land outside every major city is in the target zone for future large-scale and quickly built buildings. Ten acres or 100 acres under one roof. Thousand-acre sites, fantastic runoff after every rain, traffic spillovers drenching the roads for miles around. It happened after those Korean war restrictions were lifted and federal housing subsidies were unleashed in the fifties, promoting one of the quickest speculative booms of those decades for men able to grab large hunks of buildable land in a hurry. It happens in every wartime moment, whether the war and/or the national emergency is "declared" or not. The money machine is greased, long-term as well as construction financing can again be assembled in a hurry, and the quality of the environment during and after construction is nobody's concern. Who the hell cares? There's a War On—that's the familiar cry. If the war grows hotter, if the U.S. gets drawn deeper into Asiatic or Middle Eastern fighting, only well-established and deeply embedded protection could prevent landscape from being converted willy-nilly into war production sites.

Very quickly, in a real war emergency, my kind of talk would become unpatriotic, if not illegal, liable to arouse mob spirit and vengeance, if not police handcuffs. So the questions need to be raised ahead of time, in the so-called safety of pre-World War III days: Who is going to take care of the environments for miles around, and for hundreds of miles downstream from those giant paramilitary or industrial eruptions? Before it's too late for another hundred or so cities, somebody's got to ride herd on the rough riders themselves, hold local zoning regulations, require good land planning, ensure siltation and runoff controls, insist on reasonable long-range plans that ensure long-range protection.

More important than that—and of immediate pressing concern—is the necessity for Congress to pass legislation that will prepare long-term protective measures for the nation's soil supplies, to identify and protect the irreplaceables (which, once bulldozed away, can never be recreated). This should give scientific identity and eventual legal status to those resources which, once destroyed, might never return: historic, lovely springs buried by reckless urban expansion, farmland of deeply unique soils, and even deserts beyond the city's edges that might form vital greenbelts, wedges, or permanent open spaces to help shape urban expansion.

Every building and land developer worth a hoot in today's competitive market is bustin' to get at the big-scale stuff, land by the square mile, buildings by the acre, uninterrupted in-line production, Everybody Stand Back. If the countryside around every city is not to be trampled in this process, its citizens must put pressure on their congressmen, their city councilmen, et al., and on local planning and conservation groups to first secure the ecological inventories that will identify local natural and scenic resources, and then the political protection that will shunt and divert big-scale development off to more suitable sites.

Otherwise, the careless, heedless, and single-minded developers with war money, scare tactics, and old-line "don't stop progress" arguments will have bitched up the country so it won't be worth coming home to—either during the afternoon rush hour, or from distant and undeclared wars or military adventures.

---

# Competition and the Symbols of War: A Look Behind The Vietnam Veterans Memorial

For reasons that seldom get mentioned in the heat of aesthetic disputation—and certainly did not much figure in vituperations over the Vietnam Veterans Memorial in Washington, D.C.—any architectural competition can upset the status quo. It can exhume, even if it does not create, deep-seated myths and realities.

For a winning design that emerges from an open competition may contain revolutionary ideas and stir primitive emotions; it may and sometimes does embody a thought ready to be born, a vision of transforming power. The essence of competition is risk—for those who compete and for those who consume the product.

The notion that we should plan and pick and choose our new

public environments—whether they be bicycle routes, housing projects, courthouses, or war memorials—by means of an open, non-commercial competition held in full view of the public has been slow to catch on in the United States.

I wish to explore the anomaly that in a capitalistic, industrial society that prides itself on competition in business—sink-or-swim, every man for himself, compete-or-die, fight your way to the top— the notion of open competition, of results openly arrived at, has been, historically speaking, almost unheard of in the world of fine arts.

Why should this be so?

First, the fine arts in America—most notably painting and sculpture—are still the domain of the private artists, galleries, publishers, and patrons even though in recent years governments have begun to pour funds into these arts and artists. Consequently, the power of the fine arts patron is still pervasive and effective— even in a society that claims to be egalitarian and is deeply pervaded by a populistic spirit. The royalist tradition continues, whereby individuals of great wealth and power, the local Medici, control or seek to control the giving of favors, the awarding of arts commissions or contracts, the selection of artists. This occurs in ways quite reminiscent of Renaissance Italy and France. Even though one of our most famous public places—New York City's Central Park—was built according to the design chosen in a formal competition in 1857, the very idea of aesthetic competition had to overcome the vested interest that gave wealthy donors first choice in subject-matter and the artist(s) to be commissioned. The game is still played in the United States somewhat as in eighteenth-century Europe, when royal power called the tune. Many so-called competitions of those times were mere screening devices to placate the public while the real deals were concluded behind the scenery.

That condition continued well into the 1960s, when the idea emerged—as a cultural transplant from Europe to the United States—that key tracts of land, proposed for urban redevelopment, should be sold or leased, not to the highest bidder, but to the bidder with the best new redevelopment design chosen by an impartial jury acting in the public interest. At first highly suspect, this was an idea whose time had come.

The 1960s offered a fascinating testing-ground. Dozens of cities were razing slums, planning new civic, medical, and office centers.

Billions were being spent for highly visible public works. What was more logical than to conduct a so-called developer competition in order to choose the best plans for new public spaces and the best teams of designers and developers? Of the hundreds of projects coming out of that competitive process, I would put the Golden Gateway in downtown San Francisco at the top, with Society Hill of Philadelphia a close second, and "The Farm" in Brookline, Massachusetts, as one of the most bizarre and highly politicized.

What also emerged from the mid-sixties was a hard core of potential hot-shots: hundreds of designers with the heady experience of forming teams to compete openly for large commissions, for conspicuous locations and ownerships, and much publicity. Every wave of competitions became the testing ground for the next generation of big names, and for new designs that could solve pressing problems of circulation, land use, and urban design. The times, federal subsidies, and new risk capital converged.

## FIRST RUN AT THE F.D.R. MEMORIAL

The preliminary skirmish occurred in 1961. Many architects, landscape architects, and planners of the sixties and seventies had jumped into the Franklin Delano Roosevelt Memorial Competition in Washington. (That year of 1961, by the way, was the year of the first recorded death of an American serviceman in the Vietnam war.)

Scores of today's top names in the design professions entered. Four of the Roosevelt Memorial competitors ended up 20 years later as members of the jury for the Vietnam Veterans Memorial: Harry Weese, Garrett Eckbo, Hideo Sasaki, and Constantino Nivola.

The Roosevelt Memorial design chosen in 1962 suffered from critical review, by far the most serious coming from the Roosevelt family, still politically powerful, and reinforced by Franklin Roosevelt's wishes expressed before his death. It was never built. Instead, Congress authorized a new design, this one by Lawrence Halprin of San Francisco, who had been one of the 1961 competitors. The bill was signed by President Reagan and work is under way. Halprin's design carries out at least one of the themes of the unbuilt winning design of 1961—the so-called "Instant Stonehenge"—in that it consists of large stone masses through which the walking public may proceed. Beyond those processional similarities, they are, however, quite different.

Further, Lawrence Halprin was one of many sculptors and

landscape architects who were busily writing a new agenda, not only for memorials but for the larger landscape. No longer were they content to serve up classical statues, mounted horsemen, mythic gods in stone. The landscape itself and its larger systems— wind and water, erosion, growth, and change—offered an aesthetic alternative to single metal or stone pieces plunked on a gallery floor or lawn. Gallery art was becoming pilgrimage art: Halprin's Lovejoy Fountain in Seattle was something the public could walk through wringing wet; Robert Smithson was doing "Spiral Jetty" in Great Salt Lake; Dennis Oppenheim, Michael Heizer, Mary Miss, and many others were designing their unconventionals in the open air. Something big was brewing, but it was hardly expected that the symbolistic explosion would take place in an open field next to Constitution Avenue in Washington, D.C.

The Vietnam Veterans Memorial, which now occupies that particular site, began with the determination of a young U.S. Army veteran, Jan C. Scruggs, who returned wounded from Vietnam with shrapnel still in his body, and a resolve in his mind that those who fought in that war should get more than the scorn and disregard that had greeted so many of them. He formed a committee that later became the nonprofit Vietnam Veterans Memorial Fund, or VVMF. They got a bill introduced into the Congress to provide space for the memorial in Washington, the memorial itself to be built with private contributions. The bill went through Congress in 1980 without a dissenting vote.

The VVMF began fund-raising and hired the well-known landscape architectural firm of EDAW, Inc. to analyze and compare 10 possible sites in the Washington area. EDAW recommended a two-acre site at the western end of Constitution Gardens, about three-quarters of a mile west of the Washington Monument and a short walk from the Lincoln Memorial.

At this point, VVMF turned to the author of the leading reference book on competitions, architect Paul Spreiregen of Washington. Spreiregen and the VVMF set out to write a program and to pick what they called a "world-class jury." The eight members were Pietro Belluschi, architect, of Portland; Garrett Eckbo, landscape architect, of San Francisco; Richard Hunt, sculptor, of Chicago; Constantino Nivola, sculptor, of East Hampton, New York; James Rosati, sculptor, of New York; Hideo Sasaki, landscape architect, of Berkeley, California; Harry Weese, architect, of Chicago; and the author of this account, a consulting editor and author of Louisville, Kentucky.

The VVMF decided, quite deliberately, *not* to appoint a Vietnam veteran to the jury, on the ground that other jurors would tend to treat any Vietnam veteran as a "representative" of all veterans, and would defer unduly to that person's preferences during the judging.

## STATEMENT OF PURPOSE

But before they could start, the fund had to make a formal public statement of the purpose of the memorial, as follows:

> The purpose of the Vietnam Veterans Memorial is to recognize and honor those who served and died. It will provide a symbol of acknowledgement of the courage, sacrifice, and devotion to duty of those who were among the nation's finest youth. Whether they served because of their belief in the war policy, their belief in the obligation to answer the call of their country, or their simple acquiescence in a course of events beyond their control, their service was no less honorable than that rendered by Americans in any previous war. The failure of the nation to honor them only extends the national tragedy of our involvement in Vietnam.

And then the statement continues:

> The memorial will make no political statement regarding the war or its conduct. It will transcend those issues. The hope is that the creation of the memorial will begin a healing process, a reconciliation of the grevous divisions wrought by the war. Through the memorial both supporters and opponents of the war may find a common ground for recognizing the sacrifice, heroism and loyalty which were also a part of the Vietnam experience. Through such recognition the nation will resolve its history fully. Then the Vietnam Veterans Memorial may also become a symbol of national unity, a focal point for remembering the war's dead, the veterans, and the lessons learned through a tragic experience.

Well, no matter how grand and even precise its purpose, any competition, to be a success, rests entirely and often precariously upon the formal, written, published program. In my view, the program produced by Paul Spreiregen and the VVMF was the most comprehensive and accurate that I have ever examined, which is a rather large number.

Everybody who wanted to enter was required to register intent by December 29, 1980. Copies of the competition program were mailed out the next day to the 2,573 persons registered. About 180 individuals and teams submitted over 500 questions.

Some of those questions are revealing:

Question: Can you define what is meant by a "political state-ment"? (You will recall that the program said, "The memorial will make no political statement regarding the war or its conduct.")

Answer: "For purposes of this competition, a political statement regarding the war is any comment on the rightness, wrongness, or motivation of U.S. policy in entering, conducting, or withdrawing from the war."

Question: "Is the VVMF aware of the risk taken if all possible segments of American society are not included in the participation and definition of the memorial?"

Answer: "Yes. This is one reason why the VVMF decided to have an open, anonymously juried competition to design the memorial. The number of competitors and the fact that they represent all 50 states and several U.S. territories as well as all walks of life testifies to the extent of participation in the process."

Question: (This was one of hundreds of quite technical inquiries): "Within the 4.25 acres, do topographic changes count as part of the two-acre memorial area?"

Answer: "Yes, topographic changes do count if, for example, land sculpting is a major element of your design; No if the topographic changes are moderate and not the primary element of your design. Use your judgment. Do not overwhelm the site."

After all questions were in, the VVMF consolidated questions and answers into one document, and mailed one copy to each person who had entered the competition. This process left no legitimate opening for any disgruntled competitor to claim, after the fact, that the program was flawed.

When the deadline passed, there were 1,421 entries, the largest number entered in any formal design competition in the history of the country. Less than half were registered architects.

Between five p.m. and midnight March 31, 1981, 150 last-minute entries squeezed in—an historic reenactment of the old charrette routine in the great l'Ecole de Beaux Arts tradition. "With five minutes to go, there was one woman who had her design laid out in the parking lot, filling in the return address." (*Washington Post*, May 7, 1981).

## FIVE DAYS OF JUDGMENT

Next came the judging. Each entry had to be mounted on 30-by-40-inch boards. No videotapes, no personal appearances, no pop ups, no fold-outs, no scaled models. Flat. Thirty by forty. Period.

Each entry was required to exhibit the names of all the 59,000-plus veterans killed in Vietnam in a manner easily read by visitors, the whole of it accessible to the handicapped.

By the time the VVMF got around to hiring a hall, it turned out they had to hire Aircraft Hangar Number 3 at Andrews Air Force Base outside of Washington. By the time all the display boards or panels were hung up at eye level from metal frames, they stretched for 1.3 miles up and down and up and down Hangar Number 3. The process was not helped when an Air Force pilot revved up his jet plane over in one corner of the hangar and blew down the entire house-of-boards, which had to be set aright again.

Before the jury came to Washington that spring week in 1981, our professional advisor, Paul Spreiregen, went through all 1,421 entries, grading them roughly into three groups: First, those that were so grotesque or otherwise appeared so to violate the program that it was unlikely the jury would choose them. Second, those he considered of possibly superior merit. And the remainder were all in between. We were not, of course, bound by his preliminary sorting-out, and I believe we all we made a point of looking at each and every one to decide for ourselves.

We had only five days to wade through the 1,421 entries and come out the other side with a decision and public statement. When I was chosen chairman by the other jurymen, I wanted to allow plenty of time for debate, disagreement, comparison, and final selection. I was also determined to keep my own complete journal record of all our deliberations (from which this account is written).

Hideo Sasaki, a man of exceptional experience and judgment, suggested we review the program together before looking at the entries and again after the first day's viewing—and that each of us should openly reveal our own preconceptions. We did so, and the experience clearly helped establish mutual trust within the jury.

For three days, we weeded out the worst, the most grotesque, the weak, and the indecisive. Every night Spreiregen and his crew gathered the surviving entries for the next day's examination.

By the fourth day we had cut the list to 20, with 15 honorable mentions and the first, second, and third prize winners yet to be chosen. First prize was $20,000 plus the right to oversee construction of the winning design. Second prize was $10,000; third, $5,000. One thousand dollars would go to each honorable mention.

We huddled and moved in a group, all nine of us in front of each entry. Suddenly one of the jurors—I think it was Rosati—jabbed his finger over my shoulder, pointed to one sketch, and demanded "What's that?" And "that" turned out to be somebody's very clear personal initials, drawn on the paving blocks. This was a clear violation of the traditional competition rule for anonymity. So that one was *out*.

Early on, I thought we would have trouble agreeing on first prize. As for myself, I had seen little merit in the Maya Lin entry, with its vague and almost abstract drawings. Only three of us, on our first pass, had singled it out for further review. But repeated inspection and discussion gradually made it clear that here was a unique proposal, its greatness and the strength in its deceptive simplicity grew upon us. It stood apart from all the rest in its contemplative eloquence. And we were unanimous in voting it first prize.

The morning of our final day, I got up at 5 a.m. in a Georgetown hotel room to type the first draft of our decision. We worried that the VVMF might not accept our choice. But as it turned out, they accepted it with an enthusiasm diminished only by fear that the public might not "get" the full intent of Maya Lin's design. This was forestalled by three days of intensive and secret scale-model-building so as to put Maya Lin's proposal into three-dimensional form before the awards were announced. Thus VVMF could make the announcement with a comprehensible model to show off to the public.

The winner, Maya Lin, who was then an architectural student at Yale University, was the object of intense media scrutiny, tugged and hauled into talk shows, interviews, and other intensities. Most of the early media coverage was favorable or neutral, though it was clear that many people, expecting a traditional white-marble victory statue, were puzzled.

## THE DEBATE GOES NASTY

But of course winning was only the start of the debate. Within two months after the winning design went public, several Vietnam veterans, including two well-connected Washington lawyers, attacked the design. One criticism was justified and quickly remedied: In the original Lin design there was no specific inscription that paid tribute to the dead. The VVMF quickly agreed to add such an inscription.

But a small vocal minority, led by Tom Carhart and James Webb, the author of the well-respected book, *Fields of Fire,* went public with accusatory words like "Orwellian glop . . . a black gash of shame" and "a wailing wall for future antidraft and antinuclear demonstrators" (Webb) and "a political statement of shame and dishonor" (the last from Rep. Henry Hyde, Republican, in a complaint to President Ronald Reagan).

The American Institute of Architects saw the Webb-Carhart campaign—for so it appeared to have become—as a direct challenge to the whole process of having a juried design competition. Suddenly, the design looked to be a kind of national Rorschach test.

By the fall of 1981, the few but effective critics of the design had convinced Secretary of Interior James Watt that this was a national controversy and that he should at least stall for time. So Watt, who controlled what happened on National Park land, withheld the building permit—right in the middle of the VVMF's fund-raising efforts. VVMF had already raised over three million dollars but needed seven million to finish the job—which figure included covering the very high costs of a campaign hustling private donations across the whole country.

But the critics did not stop with Watt. They went after the jury with a smear campaign. Finally, after consulting in Washington with a widely known libel lawyer, I telephoned the one person who seemed to be involved with the rumor-mongering and suggested that he check his facts, and that if the false allegations continued to circulate, somebody was going to get the hell sued out of them. For one reason or another, the rumors soon stopped.

## THE AMBUSH

But not the opposition. Secretary of Interior Watt let it be known to the VVMF that, unless they worked out a compromise with the objectors, he would deny them a building permit. This would have killed the memorial financially, since VVMF was at that moment deep into its money-raising campaign.

So the VVMF officers agreed to attend what they expected to be a small private conference to "work things out." Instead, they found themselves surrounded by more than 40 angry veterans who had been flown into Washington by C. Ross Perot, the Texas computer millionaire.

Now one must understand that Mr. Perot had come into this from the beginning as a supporter. He had given $150,000 to help finance the competition. But he didn't like the Maya Lin design, and neither did some of his employees, who included a high percentage of Vietnam veterans. He was out to stop it.

At that meeting, surrounded by angry, shouting opponents of the design, with Secretary Watt's threat hanging over their heads, the VVMF were forced to compromise. They accepted, and agreed to actively support, the inclusion of an American flag somewhere above the memorial wall and the inclusion of a combat-group statue. Perot and his crowd wanted the combat group stuck immediately in front of the apex or V-notch where the two walls come together.

Then there followed much tugging-and-hauling, back-room maneuvering. The Fine Arts Commission accepted the additions, but required that the new flagpole stay well back from the apex of the walls, and that the combat group—designed by the distinguished sculptor Frederick Hart—be kept back some 200 feet southwest of the memorial, close to the entrance, gazing toward the memorial itself. It was a reasonable compromise. So far as I know, none of the jury has publicly quarreled with that resolution, and even Maya Lin, who was deeply offended by the whole struggle, has accepted it in good grace. The money was raised, the wall built and finished on time.

Then on Veterans Day, November 11, 1982, came the climax—the parade down Constitution Avenue and the dedication, which went off with great emotion and no disruption.

The day before, I was asked by the Louisville *Courier-Journal* to meet Maya Lin at National Airport and to escort her to the memorial for photographs. We slowly wended our way through large groups of veterans. Some of them recognized Maya Lin and clustered around, with tears in their eyes, to shake her hand, to offer congratulations. Several said they had come with reservations about the design, but now endorsed it with emotion. Already the names on the wall were touching the emotions of visitors, many of them weeping against the wall.

## THE SCREAMER AT THE WALL

Suddenly, as we reached the apex at the center of the memorial, a tall young man, handsome, red-haired, wearing his Purple Heart, accosted Maya Lin and began shouting accusatories. "WHY DID YOU DO SUCH A THING? THIS IS A MEMORIAL TO YOU, NOT TO US!" . . . Towering above her, he screamed and ranted, hardly

4–3. Grady Clay and architect Maya Lin on top of the memorial wall preceding the November 11, 1982 dedication of the Vietnam Veterans Memorial, Washington, D.C.

giving her a chance to answer. She stood her ground, trying to speak. One photographer caught a picture of the three of us, with me, tape recorder in hand, acting somewhat as an ineffective buffer. Finally three young men in green berets moved in on the screamer and told him to "cool it"; as he backed off, we left. Afterwards Maya Lin confessed that she'd gone back to her hotel and wept; it was the most personal and shattering confrontation she'd had. Up till then, the controversy had leveled off at a rather professional level—a debate among specialists. This was nasty and personal. But she is a strong person. There's a steel spring inside that small body, made tense by determination. And by a strong family history of Chinese teachers, artists, poets, intellectuals.

What has happened since the November 1982 dedication is now a familiar story and television scene—the touching visitations by thousands of veterans and families. They leave their flowers, they reach out and touch those names, they fall silent in the place, they seek help and comfort from those around them. This memorial became in 1983 the second most heavily visited tourist spot in Washington, next only to the White House.

How will it survive over time? Can its powerful reach extend to future generations? In another 50 years few widows and brothers or sisters will survive to make the pilgrimage. The children of veterans will come—for awhile. But as the survivors and personal memories fade away, then what?

A lasting power clearly resides in those names. Yet even when that power diminishes, there is another force at work in this place, that mysterious force that natural forms such as trees and the earth itself and its configurations seem to have exercised far back into prehistory. For this is a place of nature, even though shaped by Lin's design—an open valley, with the memorial walls along its north side. Once you descend its easy grassy slope you are subtly and calmly enclosed; suddenly all is quiet; traffic noises fade away; you are held in the visual embrace of nature.

Sometimes this force that lays its hold upon visitors is translated as "the spirit of the place," but even though that phrase has lately become a catchword, tarnished by advertising usage, it still holds powerful meaning.

Properly to appreciate the symbolism generated by these new shapes—not only by the Maya Lin design, but many, many other landscape sculptures in this competition—we have to shift focus and consider the larger context within which most memorials occur. For our Western culture is building-bound. We create significance by enclosure—by putting a structure around it. We "save" a historic building—such as Abraham Lincoln's boyhood home at Hodgenville, Kentucky—by enclosing it in a new Greek temple. Or Benjamin Franklin's nonexistent house in Philadelphia by enclosing its disappeared reality with a space-frame.

We've become brainwashed by traditional architects into thinking of buildings to the exclusion of landscape as our special form of communication. And we have been long taught by economists that the highest and best use of open-space land was to cut it up into saleable pieces of real estate, then to cover it with buildings, and make money off of it.

## THE NEW "LANDSCAPE SOLUTIONS"

The Vietnam Veterans Memorial Competition breaks with these traditions. The so-called "landscape solutions" seem to be winning popular acceptance in the end. But that's not the whole story.

Competition consists of struggle. Aesthetic debate is hard-ball stuff and quickly turns into emotion, if not violence. The same can be said of symbols. A great work of art, even a memorial to something of the past, can uncover an emerging cultural force to which we had no previous clue. In this case, Maya Lin's great

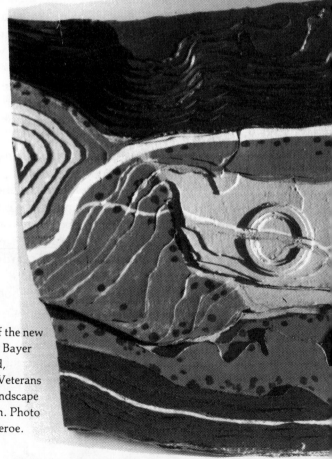

4-4. Landscape sculpture of the new wave: a creation by Herbert Bayer for a public park in Portland, Oregon. As in the Vietnam Veterans Memorial, the sculptured landscape has become the new art form. Photo of artist's maquette by Jim Feroe.

concept solidified a phenomenon—the so-called landscape sculpture trend—that had been only episodically apparent, only sporadically accepted. I think it will resemble in its long-term impact Marcel Duchamp's famous "Nude Descending a Staircase" at the New York Armory show early in this century.

Works of art have indeed escaped from the art galleries, freeing a new form of sculpture to become a part of the landscape. No longer must "a work of art" be designed, sized, and shaped to go through museum doors, to be exhibited, sold, hauled out those same doors, and set up in other rooms at considerable cost. Great works of art, it is plain for all to see, can be a permanent part of the great outdoors. This process is a part of the destructuralization of architecture, and a bitter blow to prima-donna building architects who had been insisting that The Building (Their Building!) was the keystone of

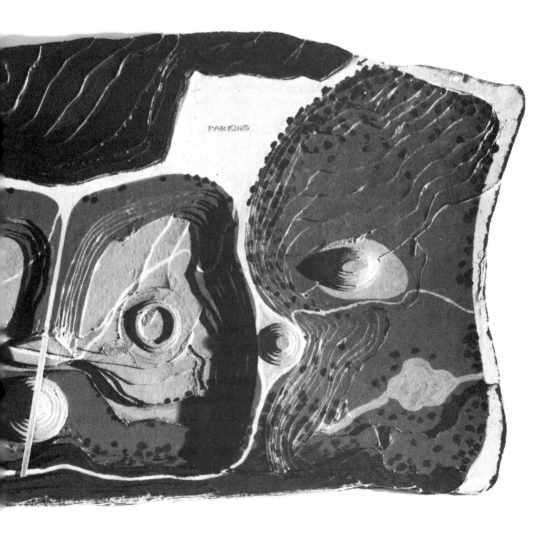

mankind's future environment.

If it did nothing else, Maya Lin's design responded to the place itself—the space, the geographic location, the setting of famous yet distant structures, the terrain, the nearby wooded groves, the presence of sunlight and shadow, and the many-faceted reflections that intensify one's emotional response to this open vale. It thus offered an overpowering lesson that modern architects would do well to learn—that of responding to subtle as well as obvious messages from the environment itself. This goes far beyond the cheap and easy "contextualism" that is rampant among Post Modernist building architects. They pick up on a moulding here, a classical round window there, a pastiche of romantic ornaments, or an old cabinetmaker's trick from a nearby building, ironwork from an old bridge—and then have the gall to boast of designing "within the context of existing structures."

Rubbish of that sort may carry them a few years. But the split between building and landscape design practitioners will not be healed by such self-serving declarations. That split will maintain its divisive force until both professions learn, as Maya Lin did so well, that the setting carries a major burden in fitting any structure, any building, any construction to its larger place in society, and to its many purposes.

Even though the Vietnam Memorial is the result of one single person's, inspiration, the competition that led to it encouraged hundreds of designers to come together in teamwork. It is to Maya Lin's credit that she personified a new spirit among young designers impatient with old-guard guild rules. This spirit can be encouraged by more competitions conducted on the Vietnam Memorial model, open to all professions, and encouraging them to work together. That is something worth waiting and working for.

---

# Territorial Defense

Visitors to Vancouver may have spotted it, a small, grassy mound rising slightly above the bustle of Vancouver's downtown Robson Square. With a magnifying glass you might have picked out a man lying on the grass, reading. But what was not so evident, either in that photo, or in the design award that went to landscape architect

Robert Zinser, was architect Arthur Erikson's fondness for grassy mounds as a personal topographic signature on many of his works. He says in an interview in the *New Yorker* (June 4, 1979), referring to that mound, "My signature—a mound, to provide a soft transition between the old and the new." In his 1975 book he confesses that "I tend to take a structural approach to landscape and a landscape approach to architecture," and is prideful of an eight-foot mound he designed in his own garden.

Punctuations such as these may be little more than a conceit ballooned into a signature, or an expensive afterthought (Erikson's mound in Robson Square was built on costly and extensive steel and concrete falsework), a "mouse under the carpet," as Lynn Miller once wrote. In short, a stunt.

Stunting around the landscape can be fun, and sometimes the results at the hand of an Erikson, an A.E. Bye, or a Jacques Simon can be pure delight, a true work of landscape art. There's a superb little back yard stunt in Colonial Williamsburg, Virginia: an ivy-covered, flat-topped pyramid about eight feet high, with steps up and trees and benches atop, a lovely little viewing platform, much used by tourists in that peaceful backwater.

In a battle, however, small elevations such as these, whether man-made or natural, can turn the tide of attack or defense. Reports from the Egyptian-Israeli campaigns have reminded us all of the life-and-death differences between being seen or unseen under enemy fire in flat country. In battle, topography makes one hell of a difference, which is something we civilians forget—how to escape an enemy or defend a place—until suddenly we're caught in a neighborhood fracas, or otherwise must deal with the question: How defensible is this space? Oscar Newman's book, *Defensible Space*, touches only the housing elements of the bigger question.

The moment social equanimity is threatened, placid landscapes are suddenly transformed and must be looked at for tactical advantages. Here is a case in point, the illegal Leningrad book market, its terrain described by Lev Lifshitz-Losev in the *New York Review of Books* May 31, 1979:

It was "in the middle of a huge vacant lot whose soil was stripped and badly eroded with numerous streams," and was thus unapproachable by police cars trying to break up the book sales. Furthermore, "a policeman on foot could easily be spotted from afar."

Police look for lines of fire, observation points; the hunted search

4–5.  Sketch by Jacques Simon from
*Landscape Architecture.*

every terrain for escape routes. All of us have something of the hunter and quarry within us, as Jay Appleton has so clearly exposed in his fine book, *The Experience of Landscape.* Are we not already culturally conditioned to look for landscapes that contain prospects—observation posts where one cannot be observed—and refuges, places of retreat and protection? Randolph Hester's account of "favorite places" [which appeared in the same issue of *Landscape Architecture* as this essay did] reveals the deeply primitive appeal of treehouses, eagle's nests (inhabited by kids), lookouts, and hideaways. It would be ironic indeed if works of topographic art by Erikson, Bye, or Simon, or Jay Appleton's book were to become references for how-to-defend-yourself in a society increasingly given to violence.

# Industrial
Archaeology

A comparative newcomer, industrial archaeology slouched onto the American scene during the 1970s as further evidence of the end of the Industrial Revolution in the United States. As a specially named branch of science, it appeared to have been identified first in England in the early 1950s by Donald Dudley, then a department director and later professor at the University of Birmingham. The best account of its rise appeared in 1979 in *World Industrial Archeology* (Cambridge University Press) by Kenneth Hudson, who observed that the field's first real impresario was Michael Rix who, in 1968, "wrote an article for the *Amateur Historian* which gave industrial archaeology, both as a name and as a range of study, to the world."

In common with historic preservationists in the United States, the early diggers-into-the past put their focus on artifacts and structures—steam engines, locomotives, the first metal-framed buildings, early cast-iron aqueducts, etc. Rix saw this as "a fascinating interlocking field of study, whole tracts of which are virtually unexplored."

Theodore Anton Sande's book, *Industrial Archaeology in America* (Penguin Books edition, 1978) perpetuated the same focus—"looking at the instruments and edifices of industrial society as culturally significant artifacts."

Sande was the founder of the Society for Industrial Archeology in the United States in 1972 and served as its first president. His book, which is subtitled "A New Look at the American Heritage," paid scant attention to the historical landscape except as incidental to structures, even though the book opens with a discussion of mines (but immediately zooms in on mine structures), and has as its frontispiece a photograph of narrow-guage concrete railroad ties in Hawaii, circa 1880. The cover blurb to his book pronounces that its focus is on "sites and structures," but sites get short shrift indeed inside the covers.

In spite of such myopias as these, industrial archeologists continued to set up their procedures, investigating, recording, collecting, surveying, and interpreting. It has been a busy although still-small world. In both Western Europe and North America, industrial archeologists continued to explore evidence of the Industrial Revolution, so familiar to our schoolbooks, which as the saying went "began" around 1700—although by now every student knows that evidence of organized mechanical and technical genius dates back thousands of years. That superb documentary from the British Broadcasting Corporation by James Burke, also published in 1978 by Little Brown & Company as the book, *Connections*, was an exemplary illumination of this vast lode. The new breed of industrial archeologists seem to have staked out modern times as their own turf, leaving pre-1700 research to traditional and/or classical archeologists.

## TECHNOLOGICAL STIRRINGS

Meanwhile, back in 1968, a tiny group of Canadian and United States specialists had come together to found the Association for Preservation Technology. They were drawn together by technical problems, arising out of the historical preservation boom, which they saw would soon burst upon the scene—thanks in part to a new generation of preservationists-scholars trained by Prof. James Marston Fitch at Columbia University. There were jobs to do, courses to organize, research projects to identify and to get funded, and technical skills to be perfected. In both countries new legislation was being passed that paved the way—not only for technicians and socially motivated preservationists, but also for investors to be lured by new tax subsidies, and city officials entranced by help from the Feds for their newest historic districts.

By 1980, A.P.T. had some 2,000 members and was able to attract some 400 attendees to its tenth annual conference, it predecessors being held alternately in Canada and in the United States. Its quarterly bulletin grew thick and, being well edited by specialists from both countries, began finding its way into influential offices.

Emerging from these A.P.T. meetings came the (U.S.) Alliance for Historic Landscape Preservation, which has been incorporated and given tax-exempt status. "Getting the people who are flocking into preservation to work both in the natural and built environments is the key to the future," commented Prof. William Tishler of the University of Wisconsin Department of Landscape Architecture. He had been an early mover-and-shaker in getting the alliance launched while maintaining close contact with the ground. "We find that landscape architects by training are comfortable dealing with buildings, artifacts, and landscape as an entity," he said. This view was in marked contrast with the one expressed back in 1960 by Profs. Stephen W. Jacobs and Barclay G. Jones in *City Design Through Conservation*, a pioneering but skewed book on methods for evaluating and using aesthetic and cultural resources. They were hooked on buildings; the man-made landscape got scant attention in this influential early work.

4-6. Angered over Seattle's decision
to demolish its old gas plant,
landscape architect Richard Haag set
up a studio in the empty plant,
invited the public, and convinced the
city to convert the plant into a
"historical sculpture" as a memorial
to old technology. It has become a
much-visited Gas Plant Park.

## THE BOOMING, LOOMING NATIONAL TRUST

Looming over the emergence of these new views is the (U.S.) National Trust for Historic Preservation, grown mightily since the 1950s, when it concentrated mainly on stately homes and the haunts of WASPish forefathers. I recall giving a rousing speech to the then-small trust at its annual meeting, in Pittsburgh in 1960, in which as an outsider, I urged them to look at the entire urbanized landscape as their responsibility. I had just come from a two-day inspection of Pittsburgh, its great rocky slopes pockmarked with abandoned mines and rundown houses, crying for some new form of preservation that went beyond saving historic structures. The late Mrs. Robert Woods Bliss, who with her husband had created and later endowed the magnificent Dumbarton Oaks estate in Georgetown, D.C., was hard-pressed to find anything polite to say about my speech afterwards. Although we were dinner partners, my speech clearly struck her as rather outside the bounds of what preservationists were up to doing.

All this has changed. Historic districts now include ethnic enclaves, transition neighborhoods of blacks, working-class districts of shotgun houses that older National Trust members wouldn't have been caught dead in. The trust itself has reached out for new members; it administers famous historic places in many states; its newsletter reaches over 180,000 persons; and it has become a mighty force in educating laymen and politicians alike to "save" historic buildings, often by restoring them to such profitable new uses as offices, commercial headquarters, and the like.

But at the end of all this promotion, all this fund-raising and fun-and-games that the preservation movement encourages, someone must get out and dig—not only into the documents and musty records in the courthouse attic, but into the ground itself, along its folds and convolutions, and below its surface.

## HOW DID THIS PLACE COME TO BE?

Sooner or later, every researcher and inquisitor—no matter from which discipline he or she may emerge—must confront a subtly configured landscape and wonder: How the devil did this particular place come to be? What hidden hands molded this innocent bank, what long-gone machines shaped that distant defile, what tools and which owners imprinted those still-visible forms upon the land?

Why are the weeds so distinctly different on this field from the one adjacent? (That particular question led ecologists in England to discover that the fence separating the two fields had been the parish boundary back into the Middle Ages, when each parish pursued distinctly different farming practices. The evidence persisted into the 1960s.)

We know that echoes, remembrances, dusty clippings, old deeds, hunches, and the hard footsteps of the investigator—all must be brought to bear. Not merely upon buildings, for the preservationists have seen to it that Great Grandfather's Stately Home, or a Founding Father's bedstead, are suitably immured and shielded from Time's grip.

But beyond the walls of historic structures, the land is everybody's game, and the bulldozer's power to rip through historic ground is all too evident. Only gradually have preservationists come to recognize that The View across the Potomac River, which George Washington once enjoyed from Mount Vernon, is as worthy of preservation as is the sumptuous front porch from which he drank it all in.

For it is the totality of the landscape—the land itself and how buildings and landscape relate to each other and to their messages— that can expose the rich history of a culture. It is that totality, rather than a single structure or artifact, that helps us understand how the landscape that supports us has changed. All of these offer insights into how we might learn to survive the transition of today's everday scenes into tomorrow's historic landscapes.

---

# Turning Left:
## Taking It
## To the Street

Street literature in the United States has been taking a sharp turn to the left. Gone are those hortatory mobility-tracts that filled official mailboxes of the 1960s, when the federal interstate highway program was booming. Gone those gaudy coffee-table reports, rushed into print by rich highway agencies and displayed by their eager consultants. Gone the heady atmosphere into which all these publications erupted, back in the days when highways and related developments triumphed over all opposition. And—not so incidentally—gone with the windy decline of the once-supreme U.S. auto industry into its present state of harsh competition.

In place of these flatulent publications has come an expanding literature of political actions; they reflect a new focus on the American street as residential turf, no longer the undisputed domain of government. This new-wave literature includes much sociological radicalism, which is opposed to the exercise of official power. No new traffic plan is exempted from these attacks; no city councilman can be certain that his latest Plan of Improvement will get an automatic majority vote. The radicalism of the 1960s, the backlash from the Vietnam war, the recurrent energy shortages, clearly set in motion the new Street Revival and its accompanying media and publishing fanfare.

The Revival of the American Street and the forces surrounding it takes many forms, but it is my intention here to look only at some specific examples of this historical turn in revisionist literature about the street. I see this as a populist revival, the latest in a century-long series of politically potent, yet still dispersed, uprisings against powerful government agencies and their captive firms.

The uprising has been scattered but persisting; and the object of this "revolt"—if that is not too strong a word—is the highway lobby. The most renowned early book of this period was *The Power Broker,* Robert Caro's 1974 Pulitzer-prize-winning and scathing biography of New York City's highwayman-impresario, Robert Moses.

During the mid-life of the Interstate Highways Act of 1956,[1] there was a widespread "run on the street," a gradual withdrawal of trust in the American urban street as a safe investment for one's time, taxes, money, and person. At the most banal level, learning on the street is a process that gradually moved indoors, where learners confronted television as their prime source of impressions, prejudices, knowledge. "Only in the slum and in the dwindling ethnic enclaves does the street still seem to function partially as a locus for public life," observed Gloria Levitas in *On Streets,* one of the new-wave books. "Visits to the residential streets . . . the real San Francisco, leave the predominant impression that the city has no street life," wrote the late perceptive teacher on city life, Donald Appleyard. "The streets are clean in the better-off districts; the houses and gardens are often interesting and sometimes beautiful . . . but the closed windows and drawn blinds exude a funereal atmosphere."

## RIPPING OFF THE MENTAL MAP

In every city where I have spent reportorial or research time—this includes five cities worked in 1980 with a television documentary crew, and some 12 cities inspected since then—it was clear to me that significant portions of such cities have been ripped out of the mental map of millions of citizens.

It is as though—if I may use the sort of metaphor beloved by street radicals of the 1960s—some malevolent hand had reached down and plucked out a street here, a boulevard there, and whole networks of streets elsewhere. These streets have grown invisible to the metropolitan eye; they are seldom if ever, traversed by strangers. Large sections of cities now enjoy an informal off-limits reputation, especially among suburbanites.

As a result of both the fear in which some city districts are regarded, and the gradual erection of defenses by residents and by developers, we have watched the rise of new citadels—such as Detroit's Renaissance Center, Syracuse's early Mid-City Plaza, Atlanta's self-contained Peachtree Plaza and its Omni. These large and forbidding mixed-use centers, as they came to be called, were carefully planned to avoid the unruly life of the street. Further, in downtown Minneapolis, St. Paul, Louisville, Cincinnati, whole networks of elevated walkways or "skyways" were supplying an all-weather circulation system, above it all. These vast labyrinths gradually have been removing millions of shoppers from the street and into what are called "protected environments." Their developers—mostly large, corporate, and international—knew a good thing when they got it, and in their advertisements they reinforced the public's fear of places not yet citadelized and still exposed to everyday street life.

Thus the citadel-builders reinforced the run on the street, either by getting legal control of streets and air rights from complaisant city officials, or by making it easier and more profitable to do business off the street or above the street. Minneapolis, Minnesota, (not merely because it is an intensely cold city in winter) now has a dozen downtown blocks of stores and offices interconnected, thus removing a large population from the street scene. Here and elsewhere, developers seek to create yet more mixed-use enclaves under private control.

Yet one still finds an occasional best-of-both-worlds, as in the District of Columbia's historic Georgetown, where then-resident

John Fitzgerald Kennedy was only one of hundreds of powerful figures whose eyes helped patrol and protect those streets. Georgetown has become its own low-rise form of citadel, one of America's most profitable places to do business along the streets, alleys, C&O Canal, and courtyards.

The old Chesapeake and Ohio Canal has become the successful spine of off-street development. Here in Georgetown Park (actually an enclosed mall), Garfinkels Department Store, Rizzoli's smart bookstore, and other famed retailers were jostling for customers along the crowded concourse. Conran's from London was competing just across the canal. These high-return business blocks were chock-a-block with packed and intently cared-for townhouses and restored mansions a short walk away, and the whole of it was overseen by several aggressively protective associations. Having all these guardians-cum-customers as resident kibitzers right next door, Georgetown would do very well indeed. And it became an exemplar for other, less-prosperous places to copy.

Shortly after examining the new inner life at Georgetown, I was treated (and, as it turned out, subjected) to one of those fashionable slide-and-sound shows ("son et flash"?) called "Street Smart," designed for parents of grade-school children and teachers of grades six through 10. It was an expert stitchery of current cliches, with a black boy and blond white girl, aged 12, chasing, dancing, skipping, and jaunting their way, against a soundtrack of upbeat jazz, from one remodeled city block to the next. It was the very picture of biracial gentrification. My own reaction (voiced impolitely at one of those national conferences for Environmental Education Programmers) was to give it my own title: "Okey, Dokey, Hokey, Phoney." There are more like this one in the new catalogs, part of a backlash of promotional media trying to assert that downtown really hasn't changed; it's still [the same old] Wonderful Place to Be.

## FROM COLIN BUCHANAN TO JANE JACOBS

Not every book or slideshow in the new revisionist literature paints a uniform picture, nor is every author so disaffected as to offer an attack. But most of these, taken together, represent the continuation of a massive critique that was set in motion by that remarkable British civil servant and planner, Colin Buchanan, back in the 1950s. His analysis of the Pimlico Site controversy, revolving around the redesign of Piccadilly Circus, was published in the British *Town*

*Planning Review* and remains a classic today; it also propelled him into high levels of authority.

Buchanan, who became Sir Colin and famous in Great Britain, was the leader of a government task force that in 1963 produced *Traffic in Towns*, which by the mid-sixties had become a well-selling paperback. His detailed and tightly argued critique of modern traffic concluded with a then-daring recipe for defending neighborhoods *Against* traffic. In 1961, Jane Jacobs had brought out her own book, *The Death and Life of Great American Cities*, which had much the same antidevelopment effect in the United States as Buchanan's Traffic in Towns had in Britain and Europe. They set in motion both a popular and a scholarly revisionism to the formerly accepted wisdom of the American Society of State Highway Officials, one that has become widespread in Europe and North America.

Donald Appleyard, whom I mentioned earlier, in the early 1980s brought out a significant book in the early 1980s called *Livable Streets*. He traced the efforts of the 1950s to control traffic via urban renewal, by rerouting streets, adding expressway loops around the city center, and by diverting through-traffic. But "renewal" often resulted in concentrating more traffic on wider streets which, as Appleyard's trenchant studies in San Francisco showed, were more difficult to cross—especially in slums where suburban commuters tended to speedup, with lethal results for the residents of those streets. Protests grew.

And so it now appears inevitable that the full expansion of the Interstate Highway System provided fuel for the antidevelopment forces. It stirred up neighborhood groups against expressways; it spawned lawsuits; and it provided training ground for that large populist movement that continues to be reflected in publications of the New Left Turn.

With some exceptions, these books share common attitudes. There is a general tone of optimism: "You can *do* something about this problem!" They are also assertive and declaratory. No indecision here, though plenty of scholarly on-the-other-handedness. Most of them are quite environmentally deterministic, that is, their authors see streets as causative factors: A society gets the streets it deserves. But it can change itself by changing its streets. However, only one of the many authors we are concerned with here, Michael Corbett, links his analysis of streets to a larger critique of a high-tech and energy-reckless society. No Marxist analysis appears here, although the writings of Richard Sennett convey a dark, if not conspiratorial, view of city planning as an elitist control technique.

## RADICALIZED ACCEPTED WISDOM

Taken together, however, the books and authors I am considering represent a radicalizing of the former view that physical development of new roads and free geographic access from one place to another are unchallengeable goods. That view is well down the drain. We have become a society of canny, if not suspicious count-the-costers.

In *A Better Place to Live*, Michael Corbett comes closest to nineteenth-century utopian-populist traditions with his critique of our energy-wasting economy and its city streets, especially in single-family subdivisions: "Unless we restructure our urban form and our centralized system of production, energy conservation will provide only temporary relief." A large part of this hoped-for conversion away from high-tech, high-energy form of life will arise, he thinks, from local communities. Here again is the old populist-uplift refrain: Each community must do its own thing, invent its own new forms of life and production. And Corbett, who is reinforced by highly liberal and innovative clients (they buy his houses, practice his ideas), and the City of Davis, California, have done just that. From 1972 into the 1980s, Corbett has designed and built a neighborhood community called Village Homes that is a living exhibition of his ideas. Were his examples not located off-center in a college town, remote from the media centers, Village Homes would have long since become an oft-visited source of inspiration and imitation—as were the earlier Radburn, New Jersey; Reston, Virginia; Columbia, Maryland; and Welyn, Vallingby; and Cumbernauld overseas.

Corbett's "appropriate planning area" is a small town, with its rain-absorbing greenways, its bikepaths, and stream valleys. All its houses turn their long axes (and their solar roof collectors) to the sun. All trees bear fruit and enshadow the narrow streets. Any schemes other than these hark backwards to the age of notorious energy waste.

Surely the best of its recent kind—and light years ahead of those dull Citizens Guides to Zoning that appeared in the 1950s—is a book by Raquel Ramati called *How to Save Your Own Street*. This one is oriented to New York City, which needs all the saviors it can get. The "you" in Ramati's book is an activist middle-to-upperclass New York. Her case studies are taken at Mulberry Street, Little Italy; at Newkirk Place, Brooklyn; and at Beach 20th Street, Queens. Drawings and plans are high-quality stuff, many of them in full color.

Ramati's street-saving lessons sound conservative. Think of your own street as a room: Yours! Learn your neighborhood, organize your neighbors, co-opt the official planners, outflank the highway special interests, get your own plan built. It's your street, ergo your responsibility. This is old-fashioned citizen activism, even given its optimistic assumption that any neighborhood residents can bootstrap themselves into political power. In practice, the notion—implied in this and other books of this sort—that the street actually and politically belongs to its residents will strike mayors, aldermen, and administrators as the most dangerous and obstructive radicalism.

Appleyard turns out to be the most detailed and thoughtful of all these observers. His *Livable Streets* tells us more than most of us want to know about individual street dynamics in San Francisco, but I suspect it will offer precise ammunition to both planners and activists for years to come. For some years, British-trained Appleyard explored street dynamics, first as coauthor with Boris Pushkarev of the pioneering *View from the Road*, and later in the most lifelike of studies using video-scanned scale models in his environmental laboratory at University of California, Berkeley. And his view was consistently international, as when he criticized Buchanan for looking at the traffic/town equation as a design issue, without coping with questions of equity or political process. Appleyard's work stints neither of these and will remain a benchmark against which successors should be measured.

Also, Appleyard worked hard to introduce American readers to "woonerft," the Dutch neighborhood experiments in limiting auto traffic that achieved international prominence through his efforts. These experiments were largely successful, especially in Delft, Holland, where they began. The woonerft concept "legally changes the rules of traffic behavior within the protected area," not merely in having frequent stop signs, which have spread like pox over U.S. neighborhoods—to the despair of most drivers. Not merely one-waying or narrowing residential streets, either. But rather the redesign of street, sidewalk, signs, plus motorists' behavior. Pedestrians and vehicles *share* street space, where vehicle drivers are legally placed on their good behavior. The gestalt here is: "This street belongs to its residents. All users must take care of each other"— surely a most agreeable concept compared with the angry confrontation politics run rampant in the United States.

Appleyard's conclusions are in his details. In a propaganda sense, his last book fell somewhat short of becoming The Grand Tract on the Buchanan or Jane Jacobs model. Appleyard remained a superb collaborator and memorable teacher to the end,[2] and not a polemicist. But as a resource for the future, his last book is a classic.

Knowing that another of these books, *Streets Ahead*, was produced by Great Britan's Design Council and its Royal Town Planning Institute tells most of its story. Its signed essays seem to aim at the "you" represented chiefly by British readers of design magazines: planners, architects, landscape architects, well-placed officials, and developers. It is clean, crisp, well-illustrated in color, highly artifactual; lots of close-ups of street facades and street furniture, plenty of the old cobble-and-bollard scenes made memorable by Gordon Cullen's *Townscape*. For American skimmers and scavengers scooping up tested examples, this is a lovely grab-bag, but one should not expect to be radicalized by these veddy proper pages.

In another American book, *Main Street*, Carole Rivkin carefully tackles the reality of a single North American street type, with overtones of flag-waving patriotism. Along with Home, Mother, and Apple Pie, Main Street comes through Rivkin's text as a candidate for world export, "a vital force in the nation's history. " Rivkin does pick up a touch of vinegar in her direct critique of what urban renewal of the 1950s ("a woefully inadequate . . . palliative") did to Main Streets all over the country—a critique similar to that raised by visiting nineteenth-century Europeans who first confronted the American gridiron street layouts and haven't recovered yet from the shock.

In contrast with most books, where captions seem to have been written off-stage, perhaps on the moon, Rivkin's captions for her 255 clear photos and plans were written with care and content. Her appendix on "Photographing Main Street" recounts the strategic meeting in 1936 between photographer Paul Stryker and Robert Lynd, coauthor of *Middletown*. As a result, Stryker's instructions to his New Deal photographers became insistently sociological, and the ensuing photos intently penetrating, in ways not seen again until the 1960s, and unfortunately, not in this book.

Being organized as a kind of Good Taste Catalog, *Streetscape Equipment Sourcebook* turns out to be one of the most useful of a new breed arising out of the last decade. This one was well-edited by Harold Malt, even though it assumed the impossible: that all those poles, pipes, wires, crossarms, signs, directions, guides, and benches that litter our streets can be taken in hand by one all-powerful agency and reconstituted into Coherent Street Furniture. This is surely one of the most difficult of all municipal enterprises— to induce unity among all that multitude who jealously guard their poles, their underground networks, their signs, their signals. Many a design consultant has found his advice scorned after a dismal failure to coordinate street furniture. More power to Malt and his clients, but if I read the signs aright, street furniture is still stuck in the holdout zone for local chaos. If there's any place a determined neighborhood group can have some impact, it is most likely here.

Among the most influential on this scene is William H. Whyte, who has been involved in analysis of prescriptions for street life ever since *The Exploding Metropolis* (1958), having whetted his appetite for environmental determinism by examining friendship-formation among suburbanites for his earlier book, *The Organization Man*. His most recent book, The *Social Life of Small Urban Spaces,* is an outgrowth of studies that helped (as did Whyte in other contexts) to reshape New York City's zoning rules, so as now to require sitting places in Manhattan's stark new street-level plazas. Whyte's is also a delightfully popular analysis of who-does-what-to-whom on Manhattan streets and sidewalks. Just that. No global solutions (although audiences of businessmen all over the U.S. seem to delight in applying Whyte's observations and advice to their own downtown haunts). People need comfortable places to sit: in the sun, out of the wind, with high visibility so as to seen and be seen without embarrassment. Big plazas are no damn good if you cannot sit or stand-and-talk with comfort. The fun is in the showing-and-telling. Whyte's movies are a popular sideshow, if not the main story, to his public appearances.

Meanwhile, the ferment of local activities continues to bubble; Save Downtowners caught their second wind in the 1980s, even as many a federal subsidy disappeared under the hatchet of the Reagan Administration. Local television stations picked up the initiative abandoned by many city newspapers, doing "exposes" that often amounted to warming over old Whyte or Jane Jacobs cliches.

"Neighborhood Watch" signs blossomed from thousands of light poles, and the inward-looking focus on My Place, My Street, My Neighborhood showed no signs of diminishing. It will not be surprising if continued unrest over inflation, over threats of war, and over regional and class disparities will continue to show themselves in one form or another out in the street.

---

# Ultimate Flood Weapon: Indian Bend Wash

You are driving along the desert, Rocky Mountains off in the distance. Real desert: rocks, cactus, sand, dust, and windblown plastic and tumbleweed. Occasionally the road dips down through a wash, gully, arroyo, wadi: a dry watercourse.

This time, however, you hear a rumble, somewhat like a distant oncoming train. Just in time, out of the corner of the eye, you glimpse a confused tangle of tumbling trash and muddy water moving down on you. You speed up, cross the wadi barely in time to escape an incredibly swift runoff from heavy rain in those mountains a few miles away. That dry streambed becomes a floodway.

Such floodways, multiplied by the thousands, are familiar to long-time residents along 3,000 miles of the American Rockies and their adjacent regions. When rainfall breaks records, when that "500-year-flood" arrives, all forms of settlements are endangered, especially in the more southern parts of the Rockies.

In early 1980 the Phoenix, Arizona, metropolitan area came under the impact of the same rainstorm patterns that severely damaged California. Flooding of the Verde and Salt Rivers split Phoenix; only two bridges stayed open, traffic snarled for miles, and a new Department of Transportation train was dragooned to carry commuters.

I happened to be in Phoenix just after such destructive high waters had come and gone, leaving a flood line of broken trees, stranded lumber, and trash blocks away from the now-tiny stream of the Salt River. Close-up, the river looked rather shrunken and mundane—just another braided stream of sandbars, little sandy islands, and beat-up willows along the fringes. But there, far out in

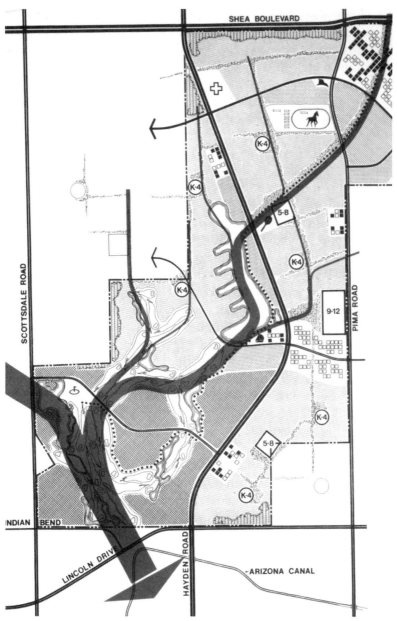

4–7. Once flowing in a shallow arroyo or swale through the desert east of Denver, the episodic waters in Indian Bend Wash were labeled "floods" by local whites, and "threat" after the subdivision of Scottsdale began. When the Kaiser–Aetna–McCormick Ranch was turned into a subdivision, Victor Gruen's firm redesigned the Wash as a community greenway with golf course laid out to accommodate occasional flooding.

the flats, was a yellow auto, buried halfway up the doors in sand, its top bent and partly crushed. "Oh, those were people thought they could make it," said my guide. What they didn't make was the low-lying stretch of Scottsdale Road as it crossed the Salt River.

At nearby Scottsdale, one of the more inventive landscape architectural projects of the 1970s at Indian Bend Wash proved itself by readily handling the floodwaters cascading through this suburb of Phoenix.

"Hallelujah, It Works!" was the headline for a picture in the February 20, 1980, issue of the *Phoenix Gazette*.

"It" is the Indian Bend Wash improvements, a flood control and community open-space project.

Indian Bend Wash—with a history of 15 floods between 1921 and 1975—is now a predominantly greened floodway six miles long, redesigned jointly by the city of Scottsdale, Maricopa County Flood Control District, and the U.S. Army Corps of Engineers. Master plans for major parts of the development were done by landscape architects Royston, Hanamoto, Beck and Abey; and by the firms of Arthur Barton, and Ribera and Sue.

Scottsdale came through flooding far better than its neighbors, Phoenix and Tempe, partly because it does not abut the rampaging Salt and Verde Rivers, but also because of what city officials call their "ultimate flood weapon"—Indian Bend Wash. Scottsdale's Dick Bowers, director of flood field services, said the Wash had passed its "greatest test" to date.

(PS: For visitors' information, Indian Bend Wash today winds through a series of parks, subdivision greenways and golf courses, all designed as part of the floodway, to be overflowed occasionally with little or no damage to structures. The hundreds of acres of open land absorb floodwaters, replenish underground acquifers, and reduce the cost of floods.)

---

# The Olmsted Code

All great religions require a code of conduct, a catechism, a set of commandments about how one must act—not only among one's fellow creatures, but also how one must act in Holy Places. By any such yardstick, the New Olmsted Movement lacks only an official code of conduct.

We were prompted to such musings while attending the movement's conference in Boston and Cambridge—officially the annual convention of the National Association of Olmsted Parks. From small beginnings a decade ago, amongst a few disciples, this effort to identify and to restore places made and made memorable by Frederick Law Olmsted has grown mightily.

Contrary to what one might then have expected, the movement has mushroomed beyond the tiny, scholarly, and rather elitist New England crowd among whom it exercised its first spell. The Boston/ Cambridge meetings in 1981 attracted several hundred disciples and aspirants from around the country—students, politicians, citizen organizers, garden lovers. They heard excellent and other papers by scholars and adherents, and followed in the footsteps of Master Designer Olmsted through many of the 40 Boston parks and parkways that he and his trainees had designed.

It was all quite inspiring. I felt I was present at the moment the whole thing had finally achieved critical mass and soon would become a Movement. But the Great Code of Conduct was missing, and as I sat through bus tours and listened to cries of alarm about Olmsted scenery in danger from assault by yet another pagan roadbuilder, I found myself filling gaps in my journal with a personal version of an Olmsted Code. It might go something like this:

Go ye among the multitudes and preach this, the Way of the Great Designer, so that all may come and share his handiwork forevermore.

Impose not thy foreign will upon this place. Seek ye its Spirit and all else will follow.

Look thou to the earth and the trees for thy sustenance, and bring them no harm.

Know ye that the earth it is good, and that he who treats it well, he shall gain his own reward. And from him who bringeth damage and great harm, all shall be taken away.

Make no undue noises unto the high heavens. Nor shall ye push and shove thy neighbor between a rock and a hard place. Carry thyself gently and there shall be space for all.

Bring not into this place any arms of war. Nor shall ye form yourselves into phalanxes or warlike groups. For this is a place of peace and peaceful shall ye remain.

Do this in remembrance of the great place-maker, whose firm hand can make us free to enjoy his places forever.

But if this is all too theological for your taste, how about:

Keep off the Grass
Stay on the Paths
Don't Litter
Talk to Strangers
No Weapons
Bike Paths for Bikers Only
Leave the Place Cleaner than When You Came
Enjoy the Views
No Artificial Noise-makers
Treat This as Your Home.

---

# Making It
# in the
# Scruburbs

Like a shimmering mirage that reveals to desert travelers the distant oasis over the horizon, those conical stacks in our industrial suburbs suggest a growing trend in land development, which is the manufacture of new topsoil.

We saw the first of these cones years ago, cast out upon the semi-desert floor south of Denver, Colorado, appearing from the distance like a giant's Tent City. Its main features were low-rise conical mounds of cow manure, sheep manure, sand, silt, loam, rotted sawdust, new sawdust, and other piles of ingredients to be mixed. As I came closer I could see them rising as high as two-story buildings. Great machines were gulping down gobs of this and that. With long, maneuverable conveyor belts, like some giant insect's ovipositor, they dribbled out new piles of custom-made topsoil that would provide front-yard seedbeds for new suburbanites and their lawns.

This was my first enounter with mass-produced "topsoil," a commodity that subsequently entered the marketplace under many trade-names and descriptions all over North America—where one would think there's already plenty of natural topsoil readily available.

Not so. In waves of migration throughout the history of this country, settlers—foolhardy and brave—have gambled their families and lives on their ability to "make the desert bloom." But not all deserts come alive with the application of irrigation water, which is only a part of fertility.

Furthermore, even in some fertile parts of the country, good, rich, and naturally occurring topsoil has become a scarce resource as well as an expensive commodity. So much so that many towns and cities have begun to prohibit the stripping of topsoil for sale. A landowner is prohibited from selling off his topsoil, for such sales could ultimately convert a lovely town into a pockmarked and unproductive wasteland. This is especially true in New England, according to Carol Johnson, a landscape architect of Cambridge, Massachusetts, whose firm does work all over the region. She has discovered that town boards have begun to guard their patrimony of good soil with zeal and gusto. As a result, the best way to get good topsoil is to make your own—to specify it in bid proposals, as Johnson's firm did when it redesigned Bostons Mystic River Reservation and had to provide grassed meadows over old city dumps. All this may not be nature's mixture as before, but in many soil-poor locations, it is getting to be the only alternative to having local man-made deserts around you.

All this came vividly to my mind during a series of commuting trips into Rio de Janiero. I was visiting for several weeks with an American friend near the village of Ilha de Guaratiba some 30 miles west of Rio. On trips into Rio, our bus took us over a steep mountain and straight down the coast, past hundreds of small homesteads, tropical plant nurseries strung along the road, and miles of new houses and skyscraper condominiums near the Atlantic Ocean beaches.

Wherever I traveled in Brazil, I was never far from the ravages of 200 years or more of slash-and-burn tactics, hillsides and sandy flatlands burned deliberately or accidentally ever since the first settlers arrived in the early sixteenth century. And along this scrub-urban highway outside Rio, there seemed to be no such thing as naturally friable and fertile soil. It was either swampy, and had to be windrowed into long ridges to raise the plants' roots above the groundwater, or else it was white sand with only the scrubbiest grasses and trees finding a roothold. In the new subdivisions homeowners had dug pits into the sand or hardpan, filled them with compost hauled in at undoubted expense, and only then could they manage to get trees take hold and grow.

Is it no accident that I began this account with evidence from a semi-desert south of Denver, where shortages dominate everyday life? And that the last account comes from a Brazilian landscape that has been ill-used and burned over for as long as the history of human settlements can unravel the story?

Perhaps it is always to the deserts, the mountain fastnesses, the have-not and despoiled regions that we should look, both for the dangers to come (as in the Mongol hordes of history), for shortages that may someday strike us all, and for solutions we may soon be desperate to find.

---

# Marketing Arousal: The Arena Effect

The long-distance voice wanted me to comment, for publication, on "the future of golf course design," the sort of inquiry that occasionally drops into my lap when things are dull in New York City. It came from one of those slick Manhattan magazines competing for the $150,000-a-year-and-upscale readers. But, much preferring to share such thoughts with more than one audience, the next time I found myself on a golf course—it turned out to be near Grandfather Mountain, North Carolina—I was moved to these further observations:

Definition. Golf course: a ballistic-missile site designed as a pleasure ground. Designer: a specialist in optical illusions, in the deceptive organization of distances, in the sly concealment of obstacles. To become such a designer requires a high level of skills, single-mindedness of purpose, and the inspiration of true artistry.

Djinns and evil spirits come to inhabit golf courses, just as do the more benign sort of genii. Golf course designers profess to interpret both in their effort to be all things to all golfers.

As for players, some play the ball, others play the landscape with the ball being merely a means to an end. The latter requires the greater skill.

The putting green is the ultimate outdoor artifact—the prototypical American lawn. A homeowner looks longingly at the green. Homeowner asks,"Why doesn't my lawn look like that?"—forgetting that the Course Committee of that particular club has just budgeted some $10,000 just to redo one recalcitrant green. And from that homeowner's question springs sweat, hard labor, much expense, and possibly an early heart attack. Suburbanites of the last 50 years saw greens as Model Lawns. It takes years of frustration to relieved of that impossible vision.

Golf courses are also handy devices for jacking up neighborhood values. The value of a house that can be marketed with a "fairway view" is the key to many high-priced land development profits. The process works as follows: One 450-yard hole (or in laymen's terms, a fairway plus green and tee) can add up to $180,000 to real estate values by providing lots having fairway views. As it works out, 450 yards equals 1,350 feet, which, when divided into lots with 150 feet of frontage, gives nine lots for each side of the fairway, or 18 lots. If you can get $10,000 more per lot because of fairway proximity, and can tuck 324 lots alongside the entire golf course, that comes to a neat $3,240,000 potential added value to a golf-course oriented subdivision.

It's not all gravy. There's lots of risk. But in good times and bad, the opportunity to watch grown men and women hitting little white balls across expensive scenery will continue to entice developers— through hook and slice and beyond the rough. Fore!

But in concentrating on the new look that's taken hold of the golf course, it is easy to overlook the effect of big-purse, telecast golfing competitions. Something new has been added beyond the crowds and the gallery that cheer good shots and mourn when their hero gets off in the rough.

The whole golf course has been redesigned for television. "This club saw the big PGA competitions going to other clubs with courses designed for spectator crowds," explained my guide as we drove past the Birmingham Country Club, which was undergoing a massive earth-moving surgery in 1985. "If you want to compete, you've got to measure up to PGA standards with the latest design."

Which means, among other things, regrading the terrain to create a new "natural" amphitheater around the greens, especially on the final holes, so that thousands of fans can watch the current champions and challengers during that "sudden death" playoff. What began on the Scottish moors with their natural hazards—sand dunes and rocky outcrops—has been transformed into a formal stage setting so that the visible climax penetrates unto the farthest livingroom via television. [Golf pro Jack Nicklaus became a specialist in designing "spectator mounds," which accommodated the huge new galleries as well as television crews.]

Or consider the racetrack, and especially the end of the race. Remember that bygone day when two subalterns, dragooned from the ranks of bystanders, held a white string across the track at breast height to show who won the footrace? Today the finish line has expanded into a complex zone of electronic interaction. The finish of the race—whether human, horse, or automotive—must provide space and unobstructed views for cameras, their crews and stands and gear, and for a host of officials and influential kibitzers—not to mention local police and National Guardsmen. The actual finish is recorded on tape, sound, and for many audiences. The finish zone must be clearly visible to tens of thousands of on-site spectators so that, after watching the finish, they can carry something home beside frustration.

In football, there's this stretch of end zone once called "pay dirt" and extending beyond the goal line. Once upon a time, in the pre-television dark ages, players crossed the goal line fighting, squirming, struggling, entangled, and possibly in great pain. Just getting the ball across was enough. But no longer. With a million fans watching on television, the goal line has become just another dramatic prop. Plays are designed with the dramatic finish in mind—preferably plays that put the ball-carrier or pass-receiver across the line standing up. He is immediately engulfed by his buddies, hoisted to their shoulders, and carried off, waving enthusiastically at the crowds. No longer is the end zone mere grass. For television it may well be a pastel plastic grass, part of the new stage setting. No longer does such sport show its origin in play.[3]

Nowhere is this form of mutation better seen than at Indianapolis, Indiana. The instrument of this transition has been The Brickyard, as the Indianapolis 500 racetrack is called. This great ritual has been co-opted by both the auto industry and the Indianapolis civic boosters, who have capitalized on the race's nickname to advertise the entire city as INDY. Once known as "Indi-aNOPLACE," the city has added a dozen major sports facilities— track, swimming, field sports—and now flourishes on its new image as a great sports center.

This enlargement of play to sport, of action to performance, of

4–8. Flowing from faraway factories, prefab components of future surburban houses wait at a Knoxville, Tennessee, parking lot for their next over-the-road hauler. Such flows of building parts, mortgage money, and settlers converge at urban fringes, especially where large chunks of open land can be assembled in a hurry.

playing field to dramatic stage, of direct vision to televised imagery is all around us. No big marina developer would dream of investing his millions without considering "how it'll look on television" when he launches his first regatta. The design of race tracks, stadiums, arenas—as was dramatically evident at the Los Angeles Olympics—has been radically overhauled for the projection of visual imagery once removed. Sport for the fun of it—lonely, unobserved, casual, and happenstantial—has taken a back seat. If it cannot be observed by large crowds, preferably on television, it does not exist.

---

# Cruising
# The Urban
# Fronts

Let's not all jump madly for joy and encourage those city haters amongst us to proclaim with loud hooray that the countryside populace has risen at last against the Evil City.

For the figures from the 1980 Census, as they come to be analyzed across the land, do indeed reveal that there has been a mighty slowdown in what loosely is called "the rate of urbanization" in the U.S. There indeed has been a statistical diminution in the rate at which cities, large and midsize, have increased their population. There indeed has been a slight (though possibly significant) rise during 1970-80 in the "rural non-farm population" of the land. And—to make the picture more tightly drawn—the overall population density of urban regions has been dropping.

But there's little that is startling or new in this picture. For more than 200 years now, the American public has been using space as a social lubricant, inserting bits and pieces or whole sections of it between settlers, houses, farmsteads, between families and individuals—as much as the budget would allow. And that has produced Suburbia, Spread City, Sprawl, and all those other words used to describe the way most Americans either live or appear to wish to live—on their own quarter-acre lot or some reasonable facsimile.

So if you've been reading papers and magazines lately, you know all about "the rush to populate the countryside." As *Scientific American* headlined it, "The rural population is growing as fast as the urban population for the first time."

But hold on there, just one minute now. If you look at really long-term trends and don't get caught up in over-emphasizing minor changes from one census to the next, we're merely getting more of the same. The citizens of the U.S. are still using what dollars they can spare to live spread-out, to put more space between themselves and the folks next door. And they're doing it with every strategem available—taking new risks, using any trick not yet in the book—down-shifting from eight to six to four cylinders, cheapening their houses, narrowing their lots, extending their commutes, translating bus and train schedules, and enduring all such pioneering difficulties to enjoy some continuing version of The Country Life.

This extensive form of living for millions of families in North America, as well as in many other countries, continues to put pressure on newly urbanizing landscapes.

"Urbanizing?" you ask. What's urban about a country place 10 miles from the nearest town, with kids catching country school buses, Dad car-pooling to an industrial job 40 minutes away, and Mom working part-time at the shopping center down at the interchange?

You can choose your label. Call it "The Good Life in the Country" or "Making the Best of Sprawl." No matter what you call it, the new pattern is distinctly urban connected. For the most part, the "move to the Blacktop," as geographer John Fraser Hart has termed it, is intimately linked with the surplus energies available from big and smaller cities that enable families to live in a scattered pattern well outside the older, high-density cities. Not much self-sufficiency here. Such "country life" would be short-lived indeed were it not for the urbanization of the countryside—the location of new factory jobs well outside the old industrial districts, at the outer reaches of urban/suburban water supplies, along the outer edges of the 60-minute commuting zones.

## ON THE DUNE-BOG FRONTIER

From the window of his log house nestled atop a forested dune, the noted geographer Chauncey Harris looks out from his study and sees a bare dune's sandy top a quarter-mile away. From his dining room, there's a southern view across forested dunes to the Valparaiso Moraine. And from his living room, he can peer westward into what he affectionately calls, with geographic license, "a remnant prairie." Turning another 90 degrees, he looks into thick evergreen forest. On quiet nights, the roar of Lake Michigan's surface penetrates his bedroom.

When not enjoying weekend quietude at this end-of-the-road hideaway, Harris can be found most weekdays capping a long and distinguished career at the University of Chicago some 50 miles to the west. Harris's part of The Dunes is the weekend or year-round retreat of several hundred families, chiefly from the Chicago metro region. From a few choice dunetops, one can see Chicago's skyscrapers on the western horizon. Looking east, the giant plume of a utility company's cooling tower rises at Michigan City.

"It's a quiet place. We don't like to brag about it. Too many people would crowd in on us," observed a lithe and tanned white woman sunning on the nearby beach. "This is unspoiled, nothing like Gary. You don't want to go there. . . . "

On summer weekends, the supermarket at nearby Chesterton and the produce markets along the highways crowd with summer people and tourists; kids, pets, and surfing gear overflow their station wagons. Nothing looks sacred along the highways, these bleak and semi-wooded zones of high turnover, bearing the chain-saw gashes and bulldozer leavings of hundreds of forays by speculators, vacationers, drive-in operators—all depositing their visible spoor along the margins.

The Dunes are beloved for many reasons, not the least for having been "the birthplace of ecology." Cowles Bog, not far from Chauncey Harris, was named for the indefatigable Prof. Henry Chandler Cowles, whose papers on vegetative cycles and plant succession from 1898 helped establish the infant science of ecology.

Two tides, one composed of water and sand, continue their work upon the dune landscape, a process that Cowles called "a variable approaching a variable, rather than a constant." The other tide is human: tourists and Chicago commuters conversing on this fragile stretch of 30 miles at the foot of Lake Michigan.

Old dunes, new dunes, rolling dunes, dunes in repose, aggressive dunes—all lie across the marked paths through the natural zones as evidence of the restless forces of wind, seed, rain, and time.

The National Park Service and Indiana State Parks have stabilized huge tracts by buying dunes, bogs, forests, and large colonies of summer houses. Cowles would enjoy applying his diagrams to the incessant waves of newcomers sorting themselves out upon this strange and oddly shifting frontier.

4–9. Where a suburban highway divides one municipality from another north of Toronto, differing zoning and land-protection policies produce this rare, sharp urban edge. This view from a bus shows skyscrapers on one side, open farmland on the other.

4–10. The harsh Nevada desert maintains its hold on land outside Las Vegas, as suburban homeowners stoutly fence their irrigated yards against roving dogs, blowing plastic, tumbleweed, and desert winds: another rare sharp-edged city.

## FLYING THE GREEN CIRCLE ROUTE

Shuddering slightly in the wind, the high-wing Cessna banks and brings us in line with the north-south section lines, and then northwest over the Platte River valley, 500 feet below our flight path.

Soon the CPI rigs appear below, those quarter-mile-long contraptions of four-inch aluminum pipe mounted on auto-tired wheels and anchored to a central point. Under them, deep wells penetrate hundreds of feet into water-bearing sands and ancient gravels. We look hard to find these center-pivot irrigation rigs, thin silver lines against the snow-covered ground.

Not nearly so dramatic is this wintertime view, but in summer (as we know from satellite photos and other flights), the Platte River valley is transformed into a high-technology scene. Center-pivot irrigation brought prosperity and land speculators to the Platte. By 1976 the invasion of speculative money was reaching its peak. Each CPI rig brings water to all the corn growing in a prescribed circle. Some of the new rigs have special pipe extenders, which splay out automatically to spray water on the gores, those hard-to-reach corners of the mile-square fields.

Fewer farmers out here, says my guide; CPI is so efficient one farmer can live in town and manage several sections of irrigated corn. Brings in contract crews to harvest the crops. During the heavy cultivation and harvest, he works day and night, sleeps in his truck. Maybe spends the winter in Florida or Mexico. Hard life, lots of money, lots of risk.

Reporters come and go, writing gee-whiz or learned articles about the draw-down of the great aquifer, the danger of future drought. In scenes such as this, the 1973 oil embargo and high fuel prices drove many farmers into bankruptcies, unable to pay the soaring pumpage costs. But the overwhelming presence here is invisible—the pressure of speculative capital from all over the world, pushing the CPI rigs further out on marginal soils, long since abandoned by local and undercapitalized farmers.

From the University of Nebraska, Prof. Richard Sutton likes to journey out among the abandoned farms, recording a fading pattern of homestead, barn, shelterbelt. Even the old shelterbelts are being grubbed out of the path of these long, new aluminum arms reaching out for new ground, new owners.

## WILD DOGS AND NEW FASHIONS

Where the old Hightower Trail crosses the right-of-way for two giant underground pipelines (Louisiana to New York), we pause in the landowner's station-wagon. A long 30/30 rifle lies in the back seat. The driver peers intently across the fields and pastures. "Wild dogs," he complains. "A bad pack and a bunch of pups. They got some sheep awhile back. The minute you stop to get a shot, they take off. But I'll get a shot soon. It's these new people. They move out into the country with city dogs and turn them loose."

This old cotton farm, once deeply gullied and eroded, now well-grassed and tended, has come within the commuting fringe of three county seats, as well as the new belt of industries around Atlanta, 45 miles away.

Of 2,400 acres that stayed in one-family ownership through the Civil War into the 1960s, 400 remain. The rest, sold in 1968 to land developers and partitioned into 2.5-acre "baby ranches," is now occupied mostly by younger families, some still in mobile homes. The town is incorporated; its beer license taxes paid for a new fire station. Up in the village, a few old-settlers' houses remain in early-family hands, but for the most part, church, school, and stores are occupied by new people. Water comes in pipelines from the Chattahoochee River nearly 50 miles north, food that once grew in large, mule-tended gardens now arrives from distant warehouses to the local supermarket.

Old habits, new forms—one black farm manager runs a "truck route," carrying homegrown vegetables to city market. Kudzu vine, enthusiastically planted in the 1930s to slow down soil erosion, is now seen as a rampageous pest, hard to control, expensive to eliminate. The tidy, cream-brick Methodist Church, built by local volunteers a half-century back, now can attract Emory University graduates doing their obligatory mission-preaching at several country churches. No more do the old, unlearned and fiery evangelistic fundamentalists shout their hosannahs.

Landscape design from the University of Georgia's College of Environmental Design at Athens, 40 miles away, has penetrated these parts. Red brick houses are festooned with the standard shrub baseplanting of the 1950s, as newer fashions slowly penetrate— fewer water oak, more flowering mimosa and crepe myrtle; fewer bare and swept sandy yards, more grassy lawns. The dominant landscape feature of the Depression Thirties—those wiggling, winding terraces through the cotton fields—are now buried amid the ubiquitous pine plantations. The road from Walnut Grove to Stone Mountain, once treeless, with miles of open cotton-field visibility, now bores through dense pinewoods.

One county away, the Georgia Pacific Company, with new headquarters on Peachtree Street in Atlanta, has converted hundreds of old cotton farms to new pine plantations, many already being machine-harvested and replanted. My guide points to an abandoned rail siding near Madison, Georgia, once a cotton-shipping depot and now a ruin. Across the road—and this is open country now—suburban-looking women in new cars drive from all points of the compass to the beauty parlor run by the farmer's wife. We're a long way from the old cotton-chopping routines and an easy drive to a dozen shopping centers.

### GROUND TRUTH BEYOND O'HARE

Flying out of O'Hare International Airport the other day, we bent our gaze earthward for the latest signs of Chicago's appetite for farmland, only to discover something quite different—Chicago's impact on suburban waters. As we looked down, we could see a clear line of demarcation between city and country—one we'd never found in the textbooks. The new rule goes like this: Country has green ponds; city has clear ponds.

Check it out for yourself. The bright-green, algae-covered pond almost invariably is old and perhaps silted-up, either natural or fabricated, on a farm not yet subdivided. Most likely, it is doused with farmland runoff containing huge amounts of fertilizer and manure. ("Didn't you know that 40 percent of all fertilizer put on the ground in the Midwest runs off into streams?" observed an ecological planner. No, we didn't.) On the other hand, "city ponds" are rather new, some with still-raw edges. No scum, no algae, and plenty of depth so that algae is less likely to form.

Is this a sign that new suburbanites who dig ponds understand a ground truth that old farmers have forgotten? Is it the hopeful sign of new thinking about suburban development? Until recently, the verb "to suburbanize" meant also "to dry up, to desiccate." Developers went to great pains to conduct surface waters quickly away into manufactured swales, ditches, and/or stormwater sewers. Even rainwater that fell on house roofs was guttered and downspouted into sewers.

But down below, in Outer Chicagoland, many of these new ponds now are required by subdivision regulations. Legally, they're stormwater retention basins, built to hold that fast runoff from the new suburbs, designed to keep streamflows near normal, and, at least those I could see, stand bright, clear and sparkling in the noonday sun. Evidence that the ecological teachings of the past decade are beginning to take hold?

---

## Caution: Future Under Construction

It would be a mistake to assume that the places explored here can stand alone in space, that they are self-contained, and that they

4-11. Long-term phenomena, such as the drainage of North America, leave odd and rare reminders of the event. These are advertising cut-outs of pipemen whose work speeded up the century-long process of ditching, diking, pumping, and draining the great Kankakee River swamps in northern Indiana. Their end-products stretch off to the horizons: flat fields of corn and soybeans.

work as neatly and as self-sufficiently as the planners' land-use diagrams might suggest. The truth of the matter lies in the vast interplay of forces, not the least of which are the sun and gravity, exerting themselves upon each and every place. It is true that by naming these places, we attach to them our own meanings and limits. That is inevitable when we indulge our civilized form of place-claiming by place-naming. But we should accept the fact that to name a place is merely to put a loose kimono around it in hopes that its flutterings will distinguish it from its surroundings and give us another chance to examine it more closely.

Only by looking at places with the assumption that they are parts of a living, emerging whole can we grasp at least some of their meanings and potentials. If we think of the world as an embryo, as Dr. Lewis Thomas[4] has suggested, then every part of that vast changeling is merely in transition. Looking at a croquet court or roadside dump may not require of us more than some bits of technical knowledge—unless we consider how it relates to its surroundings and what new forces are available to impinge upon, to restrict, or to reconstruct what we see today.

Anyone who has examined a particular place with more than casual attention will, sooner rather than later, stagger back at the awesome array of unknowns, at the unanswered and possibly unanswerable questions about any particular place. Merely to ask, "How did it come to be?" is to lift the lid from the unfathomable. If one merely dares to wonder what this may look like 25 years hence, one is quickly locked into the prospects of erosion, the possibilites of newcomers, the likelihood of a change in energy flows, the inevitable workings of the Second Law of Thermodynamics, a whole universe of prospects. And to discover "how-it-came-to-be," one must unravel not only local histories, folk memories, and badly filed documents, but also linkages with surroundings that have changed beyond recognition. Even that newest of historical fields of specialty, "local history," is filled with disappointed newcomers whose diggings through local records uncover gaps that seem impossible to close.

No place is what it seems on first sighting. All places are ambiguous and refuse to follow rigid rules. No place "knows its place," for such knowledge is human and imposed by people upon the spaces they may fancy they "own." Look at a playground deserted by its players, neglected by its neighbors, shortchanged by its owners distant at city hall. Consider a baseball diamond between seasons, a drive-in theater at dawn, an abandoned farm, a prematurely subdivided field, each of them a place now bereft of a host of hints and meanings that came from being occupied, busy.

And yet how places are used, misused, or not used tells only a fragment of the truth about them. Their very materials can speak volumes. I have in mind a richly colored brownstone wall along a property line in Limestone Country. For miles around, every old wall is of limestone, gleaming grey-to-white in the sunshine. Yet here is this brown aberration, its stones brought from distant hills— by what struggling? at what expense? prompted by what aesthetic dreams?

Every place offers its own warped and clouded window on the world. Manufactured concepts such as ownership, zoning, inheritance, and deeds of title may surround properties, sometimes with a rosy glow of anticipation. But it is our own exploration of places that alone can expose us to the magic beyond deeds, and to visual revelations beyond history.

## NOTES

1. Completion of the 54,000-mile system is envisioned by the $87 billion transportation bill introduced into Congress in March 1987.

2. Donald Appleyard, whose books form a scholarly analysis of speed's effects, was killed September 23, 1982, by a speeding (100 m.p.h.) motorist in Athens, Greece.

3. Michael Ellis, then of the Children's Research Center, University of Illinois, defined "play behavior" as a form of "arousal," something we learn unconsciously that is exhibited in what he called "arousal situations." I find the word "arousal" useful in separating play from sport. (From author's *Journal*, Vol 34, page 66, while attending sessions of the Envornmental Design Research Association, Los Angeles, January 24, 1972.)

4. "Things Unflattened by Science,"—address to the Cosmos Club, Washington, D.C., May 10, 1982.

# Index